Beyond Grief and Nothing

Beyond Grief
and Nothing

A READING OF **DON DELILLO**

Joseph Dewey

The University of South Carolina Press

Published by the University of South Carolina Press
Columbia, South Carolina 29208

www.sc.edu/uscpress

Manufactured in the United States of America

15 14 13 12 11 10 09 08 07 06   10 9 8 7 6 5 4 3 2 1

Library of Congress Cataloging-in-Publication Data

Dewey, Joseph, 1957–
   Beyond grief and nothing : a reading of Don DeLillo / Joseph Dewey.
     p. cm.
   Includes bibliographical references and index.
   ISBN-13: 978-1-57003-644-6 (alk. paper)
   ISBN-10: 1-57003-644-6 (alk. paper)
   1. DeLillo, Don—Criticism and interpretation. I. Title.
   PS3554.E4425Z63 2006
   813'.54—dc22

                    2006010654

This book was printed on a Glatfelter recycled paper wth 20 percent postconsumer
waste content

Contents

Acknowledgments

I would like to thank the staff at the University of South Carolina Press, particularly Barry Blose, for his enthusiastic endorsement of this project, and Karen Beidel, who had the wisdom to send the manuscript to Daniel Simon for copyediting. The press has provided consistent professionalism and help throughout the preparation of this manuscript. I would like to recognize the helpful direction provided by the press's outside readers.

I would also like to acknowledge and thank Jay Parini (Middlebury College) who, as the editor of the 2004 *Oxford Encyclopedia of American Literature,* first gave me the opportunity to engage DeLillo and his work. A very early draft of the present introduction appeared in that volume. I would like to acknowledge the critical support of those who during the evolution of this study directly or indirectly kept the project focused and progressing: Robert McLaughlin (Illinois State University), Richard Powers (University of Illinois), Irving Malin, Tom LeClair (University of Cincinnati), Steven Kellman (University of Texas–San Antonio), Phillip Maciak (University of Virginia), and, most profoundly, Jeff Pruchnic (Penn State). In addition, I owe a debt of gratitude to Sara Herr of the University of Pittsburgh at Johnstown interlibrary library loan system, who for more than a year and a half cheerfully and efficiently tracked down the most obscure pieces on DeLillo. I would also like to thank Matthew Bruccoli for his encouragement and advice. Finally, all my love and thanks to Julie, Carolyn, and Mark—and, of course, to Penny.

Introduction
The Writer

Yes, he thought, *between grief and nothing I will take grief.*

—Harry Wilbourne, in William Faulkner's
The Wild Palms, 1939

I'd choose nothingness . . . grief is a compromise. You've got to have all or nothing.

—Michel, in Jean-Luc Godard's
Breathless, 1959

There's a drive and a daring that is beyond technical invention. I think it's right to call it a life-drive even though these books deal at times very directly with death. No optimism, no pessimism. No homesickness for lost values or for the way fiction used to be written. These books open out onto some larger mystery.

—Don DeLillo, in an interview
with Tom LeClair, 1982

There has always appeared to be something inaccessible about the fiction—and even the person—of Don DeLillo. By any measure—productivity, longevity, influence, scope, gravitas—the dominant, even defining novelist of fin de millennium America, DeLillo nevertheless has long resisted the expectations of celebrity writers in the media age: the orchestrated public appearances, the slick promotional Web sites, the prestigious university appointments, the saturation strategy of talk-show blitzes, the glitzy conference readings, the performance-art spectacle of book signings, the garish hoopla of film deals; even his interviews (frequent despite an early reputation for reclusiveness) can prove dense and forbidding. In an era of tell-all glamour and inquiring minds, what little DeLillo has offered of his autobiography has rarely figured in his fiction: his first-generation immigrant family background, both parents born in the Abruzzi region of central Italy; his birth (November 20, 1936) in the midst of his adopted nation's decade-long struggle with economic devastation; his modest childhood, his father a payroll clerk for Metropolitan Life Insurance; his early love for the neighborhood life in the Bronx and particularly for the boisterous street games along Arthur Avenue; his childhood fascination with comic books; his indifference to formal education (he "slept through" his years at Cardinal Hayes High School and "didn't study much of anything" while earning a 1958 communication arts degree from Fordham University, although the Jesuit curriculum introduced DeLillo to both theology and philosophy);[1] his initial experience of serious literature—first Faulkner, then gloriously Joyce—at eighteen while killing time as a summer playground parking-lot attendant; his five-year stint as a copywriter for the prestigious Manhattan advertising firm of Ogilvie and Mather (working on campaigns for Sears tires and Zippo lighters, among others); his quirky decision in 1964 to quit advertising, not necessarily to write (although he had published two stories in *Epoch,* a small, reputable academic journal) but rather to leave a deadening career he found unfulfilling in order to "smoke cigarettes, drink coffee and look at the world";[2] and his four-year effort in a spartan, unheated Murray Hill apartment to write his first novel.

Since the publication of that novel when DeLillo was in his mid-thirties, he has maintained a singularly low-key life: he married (in 1975, to bank executive–turned–landscape designer Barbara Bennett) and has traveled a bit (most notably throughout the Mediterranean and Middle East on a Guggenheim grant in the late 1970s), but mainly he has worked: in a little over thirty years, fourteen novels—as well as a gathering of provocative essays, finely crafted stories, and experimental plays—a steady rate of production that defies the template for so many contemporary writers of serious fiction whose works can often be defined by the decade in which they appear. Apart from the Guggenheim years, DeLillo has lived within the environs of Manhattan, save for a year in the mid-1970s in Toronto while his wife worked for Citibank. "I became a writer by living in New York," DeLillo said in 1997, "and seeing and hearing and feeling all the great, amazing and dangerous things the city endlessly assembles."[3] At seventy, he now lives in the elegant suburbs of Westchester County, which describes itself as America's most expensive residential neighborhood, a scant ten miles from the Bronx neighborhoods where he grew up. The rest of what we know about DeLillo barely rises to the level of factoids. Despite a career-long fascination with the metaphoric possibilities of the child figure, he and his wife never had children. He is a lifelong runner. He is a Yankees fan known to go to the stadium with a glove for the chance errant ball. In short, his has been a life spent writing. Indeed, as late as 2003, DeLillo described himself as a "struggling writer trying to get through another book."[4]

Similarly, the novels themselves resist inviting intimacy: no gripping plotlines compelled by the steady pressure of suspense; no convenient symbols to interpret along the way to a tidy closing; no handy theme or two; and no sympathetic characters who, in the familiar pound of colloquial chat, fret over the usual: love and death, family and work. DeLillo even resists a defining genre: novel to novel, he has experimented with (and at times skewed) the western, sci-fi, the murder mystery, the bildungsroman, the sex farce, the political thriller, the spy novel, metafiction, the nonfiction novel, the disaster novel, the college novel, the sport story, the ghost story, Menippean satire, even the visionary parable. Loosely, his are novels of ideas, less narratives than speculations, unsettling and provocative, with characters who do not so much talk as think aloud, their conversations polished and accomplished. Indeed, DeLillo has long disdained other sorts of fiction for their modest scope and their narrowed reach—"around-the-house-and-in-the-yard" realism, as he has termed it. From the beginning, DeLillo has challenged his readers: "Making things difficult for the reader is less an attack on the reader than it is on the age and its facile knowledge-market. . . . The writer is working against the age and so he feels some satisfaction at not being widely read. He is diminished by an audience."[5] Given such a challenge, it is not entirely surprising that, unlike other novelists of his generation, DeLillo has never produced a character embraced by the American imagination—no Billy Pilgrim or Holden Caulfield, no Moses Herzog or Harry Angstrom, no Alexander Portnoy or Yossarian, no Celie or Randle Patrick McMurphy. His characters are decidedly uncharismatic, aloof, and distant, even from the action within their own narrative.

Moreover, despite the apparent intimacy of his shortened first name (only his first three stories were published under the name Donald), DeLillo himself has never been an embraced novelist, although his works have sustained accomplished critical dissection (including a half-dozen book-length single-author studies, Web sites that analyze his works, scores of dissertations, and an academic society entirely devoted to his oeuvre). That ascent into academic canonization began earnestly in the mid-1980s with the publication of *White Noise* and was ultimately secured by the 1997 publication of *Underworld*. During that time, DeLillo garnered significant accolades: the 1985 National Book Award for *White Noise*; the 1991 PEN/Faulkner Award for *Mao II*; the 2000 William Dean Howells Medal for *Underworld* (presented every five years by the American Academy of Arts and Letters for the "most distinguished work in American fiction"); and, most notably, in 1999 the prestigious Jerusalem Prize, presented biennially during the Jerusalem International Book Fair to a writer of international stature whose work celebrates the dignity and freedom of the individual. DeLillo was the first American to win the award, which had previously been given to, among others, Octavio Paz, Bertrand Russell, V. S. Naipaul, and J. M. Coetzee, all Nobel laureates. Certainly, a generation of younger novelists enthusiastically cite DeLillo's influence, notably Richard Powers, William Vollmann, Paul Auster, David Foster Wallace, Rick Moody, Jeffrey Eugenides, Jonathan Franzen. But save for *Libra,* a best-seller largely because of its creative reworking of the Kennedy assassination and the predictable attendant public outrage/fascination over such appropriation; *White*

Noise, a syllabus-staple welcomed as a "teachable" postmodern text—that is, one that forsakes tedious self-reflexivity for actual characters, trenchant humor, and a sustaining plot; and *Underworld,* whose sheer heft made it one of that year's books to buy (if not read), the novels have generated only modest sales. And despite DeLillo's advertising background, his provocative take on the hip culture of images, and his unaffected love for 1950s European New Wave filmmakers such as Jean-Luc Godard, and despite exploring potentially attractive cinematic subjects—including environmental disasters, sports heroics, unscrupulous financial speculators, the bang and shock of terrorism, the fanaticism of celebrity worship, and the shadowy behavior of government operatives gone bad—no DeLillo novel has ever been transcribed for the screen; although film rights for *Underworld* and *White Noise* were acquired, both have eluded interpretation. Indeed, DeLillo is famously indifferent to the pressure of having an audience—he is a consummate stylist ("I write for the page" [LeClair 87]), engaged, by his own admission, in mastering the technology of language itself, experimenting with the sonic dimension of his sentences, testing their harmonies, tracking their rhythms, syllable to syllable. "What writing means to me is trying to make interesting, clear, beautiful language" (LeClair 82).

This has created a peculiar dilemma—out of place among the most-loved or most-read novelists of his era, DeLillo has become rather one of the most dissected, entirely sustained within the tending hothouse of academia. Since *White Noise,* "Don DeLillo" has become an elegantly engineered construct of that resilient if ever-diminishing elite corps: professional readers of serious fiction, literature professors, and postdocs. With the exception of Pynchon, surely no living American writer has generated such an accumulation of explication. The result, after twenty years or so, is problematic: DeLillo has been enmoated within academia, paid forward to a fortunate posterity that will certainly appreciate what DeLillo's own low-octane culture could not, the author a sterling example of exactly why lay readers cannot be trusted to define a national literature. DeLillo explicators have preserved his works by dint of their own privileged efforts, speaking largely one to another.

Even within such protective custody, however, the DeLillo canon has been unevenly treated. After twenty-five years, we have an impressive accumulation of takes on several designated DeLillo novels—evidenced by even a casual examination of online bibliographies—but such targeted analysis necessarily lacks a satisfying arc, a helpful trajectory that reads DeLillo from his earliest stories to his most recent work. DeLillo has occasioned such full-dressed single-author critical studies. There is Douglas Keesey's invaluable introduction—but it is now more than fifteen years old, problematic given a writer whose productivity over the last decade redefined his sensibility. And authors of other single-book studies—Tom LeClair,

David Cowart, Mark Osteen—address DeLillo at a rarified level of theoretical argument that can intimidate a reader first approaching DeLillo. What is left for such readers? Introductory readings confined by the narrowed parameters of journal articles or fanzine profiles given to broad generalities and generous plot summaries. It is not to suggest that, at seventy, DeLillo has reached the quietus of his career or that it is time for final assessments of a writer who has written himself out (the evidence of the urban parable *Cosmopolis* decidedly dismisses such a notion); rather, at present DeLillo is beginning to reach a new generation of serious readers of fiction, intrigued but unfamiliar with a body of work so often mentioned among the signature literary achievements of his era.

It is that audience, intrigued by DeLillo, ready for the work of approaching DeLillo's texts, that this study addresses. My analysis charts a workable trajectory, a viable arc of evolution that involves DeLillo's short stories, plays, and novels. The present study does not favor select DeLillo novels at the expense of "lesser" productions but, rather, maintains a rigorous egalitarianism. Given his unparalleled attention to craft and his relatively late entry into the field, DeLillo is that rare literary figure, massively productive yet without requiring critical apology: he never endured an embarrassing apprenticeship; never produced a shoddy text; never mailed in a manuscript to satisfy a contractual obligation; never, novel to novel, resorted to formula, to repetition; never pandered to public interests in the hope of a best-seller or a film contract. In turning to these texts, in foregrounding the texts themselves, this study is informed but not defined by the considerable theoretical analyses DeLillo has occasioned (such material is surveyed in the notes). Theoretical analyses surely await the reader who here may be intrigued by the sweep and audacity of this era-defining novelist. This study thus presents an introduction to DeLillo, a way into the writer, a reading that accepts, indeed invites, eventual amendment and evolution.

We begin perforce with DeLillo's particular sensibility. Finding pedestrian, even shopworn, the anxieties of the heart and the attendant excavations into the hidden poetry of small lives that so compelled the serious fiction of the 1940s and 1950s, DeLillo does not bind his characters to suburbs and bedrooms. Rather, DeLillo is compelled by American culture itself. By virtue of his status as a first-generation American, the son of immigrants, DeLillo approaches American culture from a position once removed from its suasive energy; an outsider whose fascination is necessarily tempered by a cautious disdain, compelled as much by its beauty as by its mayhem. It is telling that in the earliest stages of drafting his first novel (*Americana*, its title defiantly announcing the sweep of its cultural analysis), DeLillo recalls two events in the summer of 1966 that would mark that novel's inception: on a sailing vacation at Maine's Mt. Desert Island, he was momentarily captivated by the small defining charms of the remote town's beautiful tree-lined streets and picturesque old houses, the stillness and wistfulness so typical of the American cultural landscape—and then within days he joined a shocked nation struggling to understand the implications of the ninety-six-minute shooting spree, televised live, of Charles Whitman bunkered atop the University of Texas clocktower. Given America's contradictory matrix of innocence and mayhem, DeLillo tests the viability, indeed the very relevancy of the self. What has been the effect, DeLillo speculates, of the unprecedented reach of electronic media in late-twentieth-century America? The problem, as DeLillo has articulated now across five decades of fiction, is the loss of the authentic self after a half-century assault of images from film, television, tabloids, and advertising that have produced a shallow culture too enamored of simulations, unable to respond to authentic emotional moments without recourse to media models and the blather of processed dialogue, thus content to live like voyeurs to their own reality shows, staring at a complex of domestic screens and thus dislocated from the unfolding momentum of history, enthralled rather by the sound bites of the evening news, taught by an onslaught of commercials not to dream—that, after all, is a complex expression of the individual—but rather to want, part of the potato-collective that mass media inevitably fashions. Whatever poignancy DeLillo's characters manage comes when they demand the privilege of a self to explore, fearing in clearer moments that it simply is not there.

Given such a provocative focus, DeLillo has emerged as one of the most articulate anatomists of fin de millennium America—but not a particularly comforting one. As cultural anatomist, DeLillo confronts his age with an unblinking eye and an intimidating intelligence; he has tackled the difficult implications of popular culture, high and low—his topics have ranged from nuclear apocalypse to rock music, the Kennedy assassination to the porn industry, high-risk Wall Street speculations to astrophysics, college football to religious cults, sports-memorabilia mania to religious fanaticism. In conducting this wide-ranging cultural dissection, DeLillo maintained early on two thermal settings virtually simultaneously: the caustic cool of a satirist, full of insult and indictment, and the white-hot fury of a latter-day prophet, full of discontent and desperation. As authorial postures, both are necessarily aloof, unforgiving, and predisposed to seeing a culture in permanent crisis, thus resisting easy intimacy with a reader living—happily unaware, of course—within the same troubling culture. It is only with his work in the new century, as he approached the age of seventy, that DeLillo tapped a most difficult transcendence, a slender if radiant confirmation of a spirituality that has moved his authorial voice beyond rage, beyond satire, to affirmation. In that sense, DeLillo has come full circle: in his first published work, the 1960 black-comic story "The River Jordan," a tireless street preacher, himself seventy, burns to bring the message of salvation to the subways and sidewalks of New York, to the complacent lost souls who would prefer a convenient parking space, cheap air conditioning, and butter on their movie popcorn to salvation, a man who embraces the vicissitudes of being a voice crying in a concrete-and-steel wilderness.

If DeLillo's career has focused on the heroic struggle to confirm the validity and value of the self in the late twentieth century, what has so threatened the individual? Because he casts a wide eye on his cultural moment, any listing would diminish that reach. But DeLillo has centered on three specific cultural pressures that, since midcentury, have been particularly telling, their toll particularly heavy on the individual: the intoxicating (melo)drama of the cold war; the 1963 street shooting of John F. Kennedy; and, supremely, the steady, irresistible pressures of electronic media.

Born too late to have relished the triumph of the Greatest Generation, DeLillo came of age during the killing frost of the early cold war, his generation wrestling with an unshakeable helplessness against the imminence of a nuclear exchange. The paper war may have provided the appeal of coherence, squaring a fractious world into a manageable clarity by the imposition of a conjured order, but its iron logic imposed on its culture a choking paranoia. Its embracing schema could (and did) account for nearly every traumatic news event; there was no surprise, only the disquieting certainty of cultivated suspicion, the enticing spell of manageable intricacy, the perfect rendering into plot of all the free-floating post-Hiroshima anxieties. The chilling logic of such tidiness is everywhere evident in DeLillo's characters: terrorists and religious cultists; FBI agents and corporate wheeler-dealers; fascists and Catholics; spies and college professors; mathematicians and football coaches. How greedily, DeLillo cautions, we accepted the elegant simplicity of explanations that insulated the individual from the anxiety over a free-fall pitch into pure contingency, in short, from engaging the larger plane of raw experience.

That free fall was perhaps best defined by the ambush of John Kennedy on the sun-washed intersections of Dealey Plaza, a shooting DeLillo has often defined as a generational trauma, the crude intrusion of mortality that left a generation suspended—permanently, as it turned out—between explanation and mystery, between design and accident, between conspiracy and happenstance. Despite two hillsides of eyewitnesses, the perfect illumination of a noontime sun, and the unblinking testimony of dozens of cameras, the Dallas shooting has never approached an absolute reading. But more than invalidating a culture's governing presumptions concerning the ultimate availability of solutions, the assassination engaged DeLillo not as a political act or a domestic terrorist assault but as a media event, indeed the first—therefore defining—television event. The vertiginous handheld camera work along the emergency backramps at Parkland Hospital, the shocking live feed of Oswald's shooting, the somber coverage of the funeral cortege up Pennsylvania Avenue, that November weekend engendered the video age—created television news and licensed the rush to pitch catastrophe into living rooms and kitchens. Here, DeLillo sees a culture begin its disturbing addiction to spectacle violence in a way that has deadened, inevitably, the ability to react with traditional sensitivity to suddenly quaint notions concerning the sacramental dimension of individual life and the private privilege of individual death. The chaos and gore of the Vietnam back-jungles, the sidewalk shootings of both Pope John Paul II and Ronald Reagan, the trailing bone-white clouds of the exploded *Challenger*, the street beating of Rodney King, the fragile shadow standing absurdly alone before the rolling tank in Tiananmen Square, the joystick warfare in Kuwait and later Iraq, the terrified students scrambling through the cafeteria windows of Columbine, the lone United Airlines jet flying eerily, unerringly into the south tower of the World Trade Center: a culture has come to crave the image. Amid faddish reality-television programming, grinding hours of talk-show psychobabbling, predatory paparazzi, omnipresent surveillance cameras, home-video cameras deployed for every tornado and house fire, platoons of news crews in a frenzy to entertain us with disaster, high-definition catastrophe has become as routine, as available, as mouthwash commercials. DeLillo, whose only career other than novel-writing was in advertising, examines the implications of the sheer reach of electronic media: not merely the evening news but commercials, films, television, tabloids, the faux intimacy of pornography, the measureless parallel universe of the World Wide Web. These relentless forces have created an oppressive virtual reality, an electronic media-scape of composed images and enhanced simulations that simply did not exist a mere fifty years ago. Such invasive technologies, DeLillo argues, have created an addiction for the larger-than-life and have thus anesthetized the unsuspecting consumers, film-fed and image-fat, to the apparently unspectacular life immediately about them. Ironically, the real becomes distant, the familiar estranged, the everyday irrelevant.

The three strategies for restoring the self to authenticity that DeLillo has tested during a forty-year career are strikingly traditional but appear provocative largely because they have been asserted in an era—and often within narratives—in which they can appear ironic: initially, he embraced the street, specifically an unabashed love for the reach of the alert senses; then, he tested his own deep fascination with the word as our species' defining and empowering gesture and, in turn, tested the aspirations (and limitations) of both the artist-writer and the participatory reader; and most recently, he has turned to the implications of the soul, the difficult confirmation of a viable spiritual dimension. Such a schema, of course, is far too tidy, far too seductive for a writer as deliberately elusive as DeLillo; systematizing his narratives is at best a tentative configuration—book to book, DeLillo moves restlessly about each solution, testing, speculating, recasting. But each strategy for reconnecting the contemporary individual with authenticity and identity—the street, the word, and the soul—can provide an enticing touchstone for approaching DeLillo.

Early on, DeLillo counseled his reluctant characters to relax into wonder, to relish the thrust and lift of the immediate, to accept its unpredictability and their vulnerability, to step away from the protective bunker of depthless images and prefabricated media realities and to approach each moment for what it is, an imperfect respite from what the human creature alone understands is inevitable: mortality. Those characters able to do so would be strikingly rare in the early fiction. But those few who do embrace the horizontal plane accept the body as a living organism measured in time, subject to the persuasive itch of passion and inevitably succumbing to deterioration. They turn to the immediate—most often for DeLillo an urban—geography, that, once carefully detailed, is suddenly shot through with unsuspected radiance; the grace and heft of an unremarkable city block becomes jarringly vivid—the colors, the jazzy welter of voices, the unexpected mayhem, the effortless collisions of line and shape. Not surprisingly, DeLillo has acknowledged the revelatory experience as a teenager of reading the *Studs Lonigan* trilogy, its gritty poetic realism awakening in this kid from the Bronx the potential of city streets scrutinized by the generous eye of a careful writer. Thus, early on, DeLillo offered reconnection—joy, terror, and wonder—as remedy for the stifling ennui of the late century, lyrical passages of Whitmanesque brio that reflect the sensual satisfactions of his early love of the Bronx neighborhoods: the buzz and rush of the ordinary dazzled into immediacy, its turmoil and commotion, the improv jive of conversation (reflecting DeLillo's early passion for the kinetic hard bebop of Charles Mingus, Thelonious Monk, and John Coltrane), the casual chiaroscuro of sunlight and streetlights. Two of his early stories—"Take the 'A' Train" (1962) and "Spaghetti and Meatballs" (1965)—evoke Bronx street chatter as working-class characters struggle with sidewalk crises ranging from the unceremonious eviction from an apartment to an estranged marriage, from unsympathetic loan sharks to the taste of a meatball hoagie.

But it would not be enough to tap such immediacy. Under the potent influence of his Guggenheim years abroad, when he relearned the extraordinary power of language, DeLillo would come to valorize the sublime exertion of articulation that encodes such awareness into the stunning (im)precision of words, the act of writing itself that confers a kind of permanence to such moments and in the process creates the comforting solace of the writer-reader community. Much like the modernists who initially stirred his love for the enterprise of serious literature, DeLillo would investigate language. Indeed, he has often spoken of the sensuous feel of pressing ink onto paper, of creating words by striking each letter—long after computer technologies were available, he continued to write on a manual typewriter,

relishing the sculptural immediacy of the stately hammer strokes—and of accumulating scrawled-on discarded pages during the drafting stages.

Clearly, although elevating the writer and the writing act recalls modernists
such as Joyce and Faulkner, whom DeLillo came to love in his twenties, DeLillo's
fascination with the mystery and limits of language could be traced much earlier.
Although DeLillo has often acknowledged that, except for comics, books were not
part of his early home life, he did relish the radio, the sonic and aural force of
broadcast language, the harmonic ad-lib of words and pauses, the drama of inflec-
tion, the dense syncopation of accents and syllables. In one of DeLillo's most affective stories, 1983's "Human Moments in World War III," three astronauts hovering
in orbit, gathering intelligence data on troop deployment high above an Earth
engaged in the full-tilt insanity of precipitating a nuclear war, are enthralled when
they inexplicably begin to receive signal transmissions of classic radio shows—they
delight to the sweet spell of the well-timed bantering, the eloquence, yearning, and
vigor of those original broadcasts. An announcer, after all, is a conjurer (as a child,
DeLillo himself would "broadcast" imaginary baseball games until his cousins tired
of his ceaseless inventions), an artist involved with an unnameable but real audience—the two of them in accidental intimacy creating a viable, if fragile reality, a
dazzling construction, a shape entirely of words, an aesthetic thing constructed,
a sanctuary of order and execution. Similarly, the writer, engaged in observation,
constructs a massively subjective system of representation—called a novel—that
(unlike paintings or music or films, DeLillo's other passions) contains rather than
freezes the contradictory impulses of experience. In the act of recording, in the
precise engineering of prose, the transient becomes stable; the inconsequential,
significant; the neglected, the examined. In the defining works of the 1980s and
1990s, then, DeLillo would interrogate the reader-writer contract and immodestly
affirm the writer—the observer/recorder, the architect/musician—as the precious
vestige of individuality in the electronic age, the instrument of engaged resistance
to the larger cultural drift toward conformity and indifference. In part because
his investigations appeared at a time when American graduate schools tangled
with seminal European speculations about language theory, DeLillo's books gained
immediate cachet within the academic community as his novels appeared to interrogate these very theories—although DeLillo has carefully avoided acknowledging
any direct line of influence. Thus, DeLillo's famously inaccessible texts succeed by
provoking the deepest sort of intimacy: diligent writer and committed reader who
meet apart, two lonely figures in separate lonely rooms who manage, nevertheless,
to engage each other in the sustained imaginative give-and-take of narrative itself
—a process necessarily flawed, however, because it can only be undertaken by
those aware of its fragility.

Because of this fragility, DeLillo could not endorse the aesthetic expression without qualifying its evident fallibility. Indeed, there has always lurked within his vision the ennobling assumption of a plane of experience that is unironically vertical rather than horizontal. In one of DeLillo's earliest stories, "In the Men's Room of the Sixteenth Century" (1971), a New York City undercover detective, dressed in elaborate drag-queen disguise (he is known on the streets as Lady Madonna), moves among the whores, addicts, and assorted grotesques of the midtown nightlife in a garish neon-washed apocalyptic that transcribes such decadence into the religious vocabulary of sorrows and afflictions, corruption and salvation, and concludes without irony that amid such casual amorality the "greatest sorrow is simply to be" (243). Schooled in Roman Catholicism, drawn by the deep rituals of the Mass and by the drama of the sacraments, raised within the absolute logic of the *Baltimore Catechism* and therefore trained to conceive of an apparently pedestrian universe that necessarily hovers about the edges of extraordinary revelation, DeLillo has recalled even as a child being comfortable with big questions about the cosmic implication of human events, necessarily aware of the imminence of death and the intriguing presence of a soul. If DeLillo relishes the satisfactions of the immediate and respects the reach and audacity of language, he understands as well the nature of yearning for something beyond both of these: a hunger for confirmation of what is by definition impossible to confirm, a radiance that is neither sense-bound nor the conjurings of an inspired artist. Catholicism gives DeLillo's work an essential vocabulary of spirituality (later channeled into his evident fascination with the vision and metaphors of Eastern traditions), it endows his vision with a gravitas, a sense of a complexity to existence, of expectation/apprehension that lends value to doubt, confers on the struggle with confusion the dignity of self-definition—the individual coming to grasp the implications of itself as an intended rather than accidental entity—and grants dignity and grand drama to mortality (interestingly, the earliest novel DeLillo recalls reading was Bram Stoker's morbid, gothic classic *Dracula*). From the beginning, DeLillo's characters have struggled for some evidence of a transcendent realm—what DeLillo has called the "things that keep the planet warm"—some validation of an essential entity that would defy the otherwise iron parameters of dust and lust, that would elude the carnivorous recording appetites of the media age: call it a soul, a life-drive, at once intensely individual yet grandly universal, an elemental something that privileges purpose, order, dignity, and direction within a universe that only appears damaged into shapelessness by chaos and roiling unpredictability. His characters fear most keenly abandonment to the horizontal, the loss of the spiritual dimension entirely. Certainly in the works that have defined his movement into the new millennium—the two-act play *Valparaiso*, the slender companion parables of *The Body Artist* and

Cosmopolis, and supremely the drama *Love-Lies-Bleeding*—DeLillo investigates this elusive certainty, his most recent fictions opening out into a bracing confidence that the material world cannot bear to be simply what it is.

Amid the manic criminal excess of Jean-Luc Godard's *Breathless,* that relentlessly metatextual film from a midcentury auteur whose experimental sensibility so compelled a young DeLillo, Michel, the endlessly self-ironic gangster intent not so much on breaking the law as "being" Bogart, revisits an obscure quote from William Faulkner's *The Wild Palms.* We recall that Harry Wilbourne, Faulkner's innocent twenty-something intern, engages in a passionate escapade with the bored (and very married) Charlotte that ends with Harry facing fifty years in a grim Mississippi prison farm after botching her abortion. Gazing out his cell window, he decides that, resisting the easy surrender to suicide (Charlotte's cuckolded husband, in a gesture of complex friendship, had secreted him a cyanide capsule), he will accept grief, the palpable heaviness of sorrow and memory, as sustenance. Between grief and nothing, Harry heroically affirms, I will take grief.

A mere generation later, Godard cannot access such unaffected nobility, such romantic affirmation, much less such epiphanic insight—his Michel, who has pointlessly shot a policeman during a routine traffic stop and has subsequently found himself playing out his favorite Hollywood gangster clichés with Patricia, an American girl who ultimately turns him into the police, lacks the grandeur, the poignant nuance that doomed passion had given Faulkner's Harry. Pounded into spiritual thinness by the suffocating impress of pop culture and consumerism (hence the title), Michel, unambitious, untalented, immoral, cannot approach the redemptive grace of tragedy. Asked by his "moll" to choose between grief and nothing, Michel, his face ever obscured by the hanging fog from the Gauloises he perpetually smokes, glibly chooses nothingness. "Grief is a compromise. You've got to have all or nothing." It is a telling measure of the impact of post-Hiroshima realities, how meaningless the premise of nobility and heroism had become in a scant twenty years, how easy nothingness had become.

DeLillo—uniquely positioned by virtue of being influenced first by Faulkner and then by Godard—comes ultimately to resist the disturbing dilemma premised by Harry's initial choice: either the heart-sinking epiphany of grief, that within the hard lock of the immediate, life frustrates those who struggle to assert the grace of nobility and sustains only the slow-motion crush of disappointment, or the flip, smirking embrace of nothingness, a deep and desperate cynicism amid an accumulation of indecencies, a shrill nihilism that endorses pointlessness with a show of self-conscious (and manifestly shallow) toughness. Schooled by Faulkner but engaged by Godard, DeLillo tests both—sorrow and irony—and ultimately embraces what

Harry could not and what Michel would not: affirmation of something beyond dust and lust, beyond grief and nothing.

DeLillo's has been by any definition an impressive evolution, from hip, urban existentialist cooling in the streets, to passionate interrogator of the writer-reader dynamic, to, ultimately, gnomic revelator of an essential spirituality. What has compelled such an evolution, what has unified its trajectory, is DeLillo's restless curiosity about the implications of human complexity, his refusal to accept the easy discontent of living in an age so impressed by surfaces and imitations, his refusal to abdicate the responsibility of wonder. To a media-spawned generation, dead-eyed, thin-souled, and uncomplicated by emotional involvement in its own moment, DeLillo, like other defining American religious writers of the twentieth century such as Nathanael West, Flannery O'Connor, and Walker Percy, challenges his own time to accept its stunning possibility. His work has zealously guarded the notion of a self and the persistence of dignity, despite the outrage and assault of a culture diminished by its own drift from authenticity, passion, and commitment. It is that struggle which forms the defining conflict of DeLillo's works.

Part One

The Street

On a spring evening some years ago, during the time when my wife was
very ill, when she was nearing the very end, I walked up a street in the
upper Thirties and turned right onto Park Avenue and there was the Pan Am
Building, a mile high and half-a-mile wide, every light blazing, an impossible
slab of squared-off rock hulking above me and crowding everything else out
of the way, even the sky. It looked like God. I had never seen the Pan Am
Building from that particular spot and I wasn't prepared for the colossal surprise of it, the way it crowded out the sky, that overwhelming tier of lights.
I swear to you it looked like God the Father.

—*Americana*

But when he opened his eyes again and looked above, he saw clouds moving
across the sky like fields of black lava, and below, on the street, a treeless
expanse of cars, people, neon lights. Jazz blared in epileptic fits; smoke
seeped from manhole covers. And a few feet away, beneath a subway grat-
ing, charged the distant enveloping suddenness of a train. It roared beneath
the sidewalk, its sound so sustained, and so contained within his ears, that
he could not separate it from silence; its sound so sustained, in its pounding
rhythm, that this rhythm was transmuted to the quick-quickening pulse of
his heart.

—"The River Jordan"

1

Narratives of Retreat

Americana (1971)

It is Christmas in Manhattan, and television executive David Bell is on his way, like Eliot's J. Alfred Prufrock, to endure yet another soiree among the insufferably shallow. Glibly, he notes the contradictory impulses of the city at holiday time: the tidal roar of predatory shopping set against the martial call of Salvation Army corner bands and their clanging kettle bells that attempt to bother the thin conscience of that mercenary shopforce with intrusive thoughts of compassion and altruism. How effortlessly, DeLillo argues, American culture accepts its own hypocrisy, spins the cutting need of its own materialism by unironically masquerading it as something spiritual. When Bell arrives at the party, however, there amid the boredom, chain-smokers, and stale ethnic jokes, he overhears a fragmentary conversation about, of all things, India. In rapid succession, two other guests introduce decidedly Eastern topics into this Christmas setting: an ex-lover of Bell's mentions a brother fighting in Vietnam, and later a sculptor, whose exotic Native American features haunt Bell, chats with a Pakistani who cradles a drink (although he will not drink) and an ashtray (although he will not smoke) even as he confesses that his Muslim upbringing has been sorely tested by his adopted Western environment. Not entirely surprising, neither incident registers much with Bell—unable to serve in the military because of a trick knee, he thinks of Vietnam as a low-rated television program and dismisses the dull Muslim as an "ashtray."[1] But these opening pages introduce what will become a telling tension, East versus West, a strategy of problem and solution that frames DeLillo's first novel and in many ways defines an agenda DeLillo will pursue over the next thirty years.

David Bell, network wunderkind, functions less as a character—that would require depth and nuance and definition—and more as a premise. He is that staple of postwar American fiction, the empty form shaped by a gray-flannel suit, the Corporate Every-WASP. Tanned, athletic, blue-eyed, handsome, wealthy, David Bell has only to board a plane and someone, certain that Bell must be famous, will approach him for an autograph. That indicates his problem. Bell is not specific—he is generic; he is not somebody—he looks like somebody, a convincing simulation of an authentic person. He finds professional success tedious, interminable rounds of petty realpolitik among indistinguishable colleagues, a routine spiced only by the empty fury of bored adulteries, his own included. More problematic, he has lost any notion of an authentic self. He is a performance piece: a collage culled both from film personae (particularly those of Burt Lancaster and Kirk Douglas, whose big-screen images long ago "spliced" [13] into Bell's molecular make-up in a fusion he describes as religious in intensity) and from commercials (his father, an advertising giant, subjected him as a child to hours of test commercials in the basement). Not surprisingly, then, Bell is terminally superficial. His consuming concerns are dandruff flakes, bad breath, and unsightly nose hair, surface anxieties encouraged by the paranoia implicit in the innocuous assault of commercial advertising. Thus, when, at the Christmas party (in the very season for epiphanies), Bell announces to Sullivan his plans to undertake a documentary assignment out west to capture the primitive culture of the vestigial tribes of Navaho in Arizona, it is tellingly shallow. He is compelled, he confides to Sullivan, to get out of New York—buying into the trendy Beat cliché that geography, like, stifles who you are, man. He flippantly terms the film assignment a pilgrimage, a religious journey into the heart of the American soul, heading out, he glibly says, to recover the "yin and yang in Kansas. That scene." (10).

What is clearly a casual cliché to this shallow television executive is manifestly not to DeLillo. A product of the same High '50s embrace of Eastern traditions that defined the freeing energy of the emerging counterculture in the works of contemporaries from Kerouac to Salinger, from Kesey to Pynchon,[2] DeLillo introduces the disquieting argument that Western traditions have uncomplicated the self into a commodity, have substituted a surfeit of carnal itches for the soul, and have encouraged faux-interior explorations via clichéd escapes, specifically alcohol and drugs, bad poetry and sports cars. Here the only solace Judeo-Christian religion can promise the harried Western self, so obsessed with immediate gain and competitive success, is St. Dymphna, the patron saint of nervous breakdowns, for whom Bell's ivy-shrouded Episcopalian boarding school is named. A far more appealing solution, however, lurks eastward, for DeLillo, suggesting a mindset, primitive and powerful, tied to the ancient argument of the Earth itself and thus innocent of the mediation of capitalism, technology, and media. It will provide the first evidence of DeLillo's fascination with the vertical plane of experience.

Of course, DeLillo does not endorse a specific Eastern religion; rather, like his contemporaries, DeLillo introduces the Eastern mindset to open the possibility of liberating the self from the strictures of the Western assumption that the self is to be defined rather than explored. In addition to Eastern religions and exotic Eastern locales mentioned by name, DeLillo regularly introduces the Eastern mindset: it is in the frenetic freedom of bebop jazz artists, among them John Coltrane, Charles Mingus, and Ornette Coleman; the primitive magic of Native Americans, their desert meditation exercises, and their considerable body of telluric wisdom literature; the "orgasmic frenzy" (93) of the open-mike monologues by the first-generation prophet-menaces of talk radio; and even in the Zen-like complex simplicity of base-ball. Of course, Bell's toney Manhattan in-crowd flirts with things Eastern: they drink in chic Eastern-themed bars; they arrange pricey package safaris to Africa to "touch" the primitive life; a network executive tries to titillate his secretary by read-ing from the *Kama Sutra*; Bell's friends decorate their apartments in trendy East-ern motifs, take copious notes on primitive religions in night-school seminars, and even exchange Eastern gimcracks as gifts. But clearly the depth and passion of such non-Western thinking is not part of the fast track's mindset (Bell notices that the bathroom in an ex-lover's apartment, decorated with a tasteless mélange of Mao revolution posters, carved Buddhas, and ashtrays shaped like samurai swords, is alive with roaches).

Bell feels the pull of Eastern sensibility, however. He recalls his tectonic reac-tion to first hearing Coltrane; inexplicably, impulsively, during an interminable executive meeting, he waves to agile construction workers, all members of the dwindling Mohawk nation, balancing on girders on a emerging high-rise across from his office; he is compelled by Sullivan's dark features, which he describes as "pre-Columbian" (9); in college, amid friends who nodded off, Bell struggled to achieve the interior calm promised in the instructional lectures of his fragile Japan-ese professor of Zen; in an effort to impress an old college buddy, he claims to be living with a beautiful Vietnamese woman; he is enthralled by the verbal weave of the late-night radio rants of another college buddy, Warren Beasley; a film major, Bell has lovingly dissected Kurosawa; drunk, he gets involved in an improbable bar fight with a Chinese patron over their conflicting ideas about an afterlife; later, he is fascinated by the evident sunniness of counterculture kids living commune-style on government land in Texas. Much like the American military machine itself at the time, Bell is caught in a tension that pits East against West. Recall a curious memory offered by Bell's father. It centers on filming a mouthwash ad set in the winner's circle at a racetrack where a hunky driver is to accept the buttery adula-tion of a beauty queen—until she gets a whiff of his stale breath. Only a quick swish of the sponsor's handy product saves the day. When the rushes were pre-viewed for the corporate bigwigs, however, they were disturbed to see an ancient, sickly Oriental figure hovering at the fringe of the surging crowd. That slender, sobering Eastern presence—no one can identify the man or explain his presence—ruins the shoot; he is a tonic force of uncorrupted honesty, which upsets the slick superficiality of the Madison Avenue mindset that self-improvement is an enter-prise best addressed by personal hygiene. What can save America? DeLillo asks. As Sullivan argues, "America can be saved only by what it's trying to destroy" (256). What has so threatened it? A century earlier, it was the Native American presence (Sullivan tells of a Sioux holy man who cautioned that the continent's only hope was that white people would grow weary of the cities they were so relentlessly erecting on the ruins of the garden they stole, so tired of right angles and straight lines and cookie-cutter buildings that they would choose, finally, not to die of suffocating sameness); but within Bell's own era, in a narrative set during the jungle war in Vietnam, it is defiantly the Eastern sensibility.

If an Eastern sensibility is Bell's solution, what is Bell's problem? He is discontented, angry, desperate. He is an office terrorist: at the Christmas party he spits into the ice-cube trays; he leaves a soiled handkerchief in the desk drawer of a colleague whose criticism irked him. He deals with intense headaches and inexplicable bouts of sadness. He reveals an unnerving tendency to knee-jerk violence, most disturbingly against women. He lacks drive and cannot embrace the satisfactions of success. He is the deathless dead, to borrow the unforgiving imagery of an Augustine quote sent around the office in an anonymous memo Bell suspects comes from a colleague named Warburton, whose advanced years and uncompromising honesty give him the credibility to act as company conscience (not surprisingly, he is dead by novel's end). Bell is a child of television, advertising, and movies (when he passes his television set, he feels the blue-staccato flickering actually draw him in and hold him, his "molecules mating with those million dots" [43]). DeLillo's dead-on (and howlingly funny) recreation of the network corporate world in part 1 reveals its stunning emptiness: the ennui, the contrived crises, the pretense of executives whose office-speak is strung clichés. Bell wants only to touch the real—but he is stubbornly literal.[3] During a long afternoon in his office, Bell actually unzips his pants and cradles his penis.

Believing he can escape that world literally—simply by driving away from it—Bell recruits three buddies to accompany him on his road trip west: a sixty-year-old eccentric named Pike who repairs small electrical appliances and is fascinated by the compelling reality of animals (a tonic change from the network executives so centered on the pseudoreality of their contrived media-scape); Bobby Brand, a burned-out Air Force bomber pilot shattered by his engagement with the Vietnam War and his life in strategic retreat ever since, now a pharmaceutical connoisseur at work on a bizarre (and apparently unfinishable) novel about an American president who gradually turns into a woman; and the mysterious Sullivan herself. In filming the Navaho, they will set out to touch the real, the authentic America. However, Bell's odyssey takes an unexpected turn when he glimpses a neighbor steadily reclaiming a bush from a heavy accumulation of overgrowth. It becomes for him an ignition image for an epiphanic decision that closes part 1: to abandon the Navaho assignment entirely and to risk his standing at the network by pursuing a conceptual autobiographical film—he will recover his "self" much as the woman "found" the hedge.

DeLillo commences that narrative in part 2. This section, the book's most poetic, marks Bell's pursuit of self-reclamation via the clumsiest sort of Western literalness:

the confessional autobiography. We recall that Bell's only notable contribution to the network lineup had been a short-lived hour-long program called *Soliloquy* (a network executive lambasted it as a "crashing bore" [70]), in which guests talked their life into narrative form for the benefit of a single camera. The novel's second part is clearly Bell's version of *Soliloquy*: a language assault in the form of memory vignettes drawn from Bell's "unassembled past" (129), recollections of his upbringing amid the privilege and pretense of Eisenhower prosperity. It is a strategy that strikingly violates the governing premise of Bell's life to that point, best summarized by his discovery, after being married, that his wife's need for confidences was best satisfied by simply making things up, an exercise in invention he compares to "godlike creativity" (58) that livens up the dreariness of real life. From a childhood in the swanky Westchester suburbs outside Manhattan, Bell recalls, at twelve, shoveling snow in a rare moment of intimacy with his often distant father; and he recalls his mother, a displaced southerner, the daughter of a minister, who struggled with depression (she was apparently molested during a routine pelvic examination by a doctor who lived in the neighborhood) and with poor health, succumbing to a particularly virulent sort of cervical cancer. Bell also recounts studying film at an obscure southern California college hedged by the alluring openness of the desert. He details one sister's conventional marriage and another's decision to leave school to pursue an eccentric romance with a married syndicate hit man. And he recalls his own quirky courtship and formula marriage. The recollections, however, move toward the evening of a long summer party when Bell's inebriated mother stopped him in the darkened threshold of their pantry and touched him lingeringly on the shoulder, apparently suggesting the dark possibility of an incestuous entanglement (although only sixteen, he feels the "promise of fantastic release" [196]), the awkward tension dispelled only by the chance interruption of Bell's father.

    That moment summarizes the unfathomable complexity that will come to define the everyday in DeLillo's early fiction.[4] Such a raw event demands confrontation—but cannot sustain explanation. It embodies the very sort of untidy reality (Faulkner's grief-world) that exists just beyond the frame of the television screen, the muddled everyday that commercial advertising claims can be magically resolved with appropriate hygiene and the right car in the driveway. As the section closes, Bell recalls his father in the basement showing him and his sister two radically different test commercials for beauty products: one the conventional distanced-from-reality parable of a homely girl who needs only to bring a small bottle of the nameless product into a room where her parents are arguing and peace reigns; the other a gruesome slice-of-life toothpaste ad in which a hapless boy trips down steps and ends up unconscious and bloody. After watching that disturbing film clip with its grim suggestion of indeterminacy and the terrifying vulnerability of real life, the young Bell, predictably, disappears into the protective sanctuary and virtual escape of his imagination: he imagines "old men playing violins" and "women in white convertibles" driving him to Mexico (200). Like network programming itself, however, the narrative fragments that Bell offers in part 2 stay stubbornly episodic, suggestive rather than definitive, individually enthralling but collectively conjuring no clearer sense of how Bell ends up, at twenty-eight, confronting the manifest meaninglessness of his existence. The more Bell reveals, the less we/he understand.

When Bell's attempted soliloquy fails, we return in part 3 to the narrative westward. Now, Bell will deploy film instead of words. He scripts critical memories of his life into lengthy, mesmerizing monologues and then films ordinary people from a small Midwestern town named Fort Curtis reading those recollections in his hotel room. Not surprisingly, the film project also fails—these fragmentary ruminations cannot cohere, Bell cannot compose himself into meaning. It is, finally, a stubbornly Western notion that the self can be reclaimed from experience (like the woman's de-shagged hedge); captured, frame by frame or word by word; it becomes a convincing simulation, a form that appears to be real but is finally a conjuring, a convincing patterning of motive and explanation, all machined by an interfering imagineer. As Bell comes to argue, the camera implies meaning rather than locates it, creates it rather than discovers it. Point the camera, Bell discovers, and people will be drawn toward it, certain that the camera's presence makes important what is otherwise the trivial or the ephemeral. The captured image inevitably becomes a substitute system, a place apart.

The film Bell himself produces, not surprisingly, becomes a massive, unmanageable absurdity (its final, unfinished form is a week long) because, as DeLillo underscores, the lived life is too fluid, too defiantly open to be rendered within the freeze-frame logic of the camera with its fleeting series of thinned images. Bell's determined efforts to capture his life are ultimately strategies of retreat and insulation, not engagement. The film project itself aborts after his consummation with the haunting Sullivan. The encounter turns out to be something less than we (and Bell) expect. The sexual positions are graphically rendered; thus, the scene never touches the transcendent or even the erotic (it is all about biting and licking and holes and fingers) but stays unappealingly fleshy, described in graceless metaphors of military occupation. Afterward, Sullivan shatters Bell, first by admitting she acted more out of pity than love, and then by casually admitting to regular assignations with the druggie Brand all during the trip. As with his creepy confrontation long ago with his needful mother, Bell is ambushed by a grief-world that refuses to conform to predictable patternings (even before they make love, Bell had asked Sullivan to tell him a bedtime story—and she uncorks a lurid confession that her uncle was actually her father). In a gesture that parodies clichéd Hollywood gallantry, Bell immediately sallies forth to a nearby bar to challenge a befuddled Brand to a fight (the confrontation fizzles and ends with a limp handshake). Then Bell opts for what Bell does best: he runs. He packs his camera and cans of film and heads into the southwestern desert wastes, into the very "wilderness dream of all poets and scoutmasters" (341), for what he assumes will be the ultimate self-confrontation, where, quite alone, he will enjoy an environment that he controls.

What he discovers, however, is more evidence of the shock and surprise of the sensual animal. After he accepts a ride from a stranger, a supervisor of a Texas test track for car and truck tires, Bell visits the hippie commune in New Mexico, a precious collective of bright-eyed misfits. He is enthralled by their retreat into apparent bliss—they have rejected outright American culture ("the festival of death out there" [355]) to work the land; they cooperate for food and housing; they sustain a gentle calmness in a cosmos they see as sheer love. But DeLillo is not so sure. With their uniform outfits, their lives eerily resistant to surprise (they accept without issue the imminent "return" of squadrons of UFOs), their world too carefully controlled (to avoid the inevitable complications for carnal urges, they redirect whatever sexual attractions they might feel by masturbating), their islandlike refuge is the ultimate secured retreat—safe, antiseptic, self-sustaining. They invite Bell to stay, and only reluctantly does he return to his ride.

Quickly, he is again jolted by the unpredictable. First, he finds himself in the middle of a violent Boschian orgy at the Texas test track, and then, when he escapes that, he is threatened with sodomy by a one-armed man wearing Navy blues who picks him up on the road. Disgusted, Bell, upon returning to Manhattan, apparently decides on his preferred strategy of adjustment: flight, specifically, some twenty years of self-imposed silence (foreshadowed by the last ride he accepts in Texas from a deaf-mute couple), a life of elected exile to an unnamed deserted island somewhere off Africa, there to contemplate the implications of his own narrow past, watching in endless loop the unfinished film he made and composing the manuscript that we have been reading. But is this quasi-Buddhist retreat a generous gesture of self-preservation? Has Bell achieve release from the relentless press of the Western mindset? Has he achieved authenticity?

In a strategy that will come to define DeLillo's first four central characters, David Bell's is a most problematic retreat from the implications of himself and his own cultural moment. The more David Bell engages the enterprise of discovering his self, the more furiously he films and writes, the more absurd he becomes. He is convinced there must be a core self buried in him, there to locate, a deeply flawed premise (a childhood favorite is the hokey *Treasure Island*). With the nervy confidence of a first-time novelist, DeLillo dismisses his own character in a satire of the dead end of self-involvement inevitable in an American culture in which advertising, film, and television have fostered a nearly irresistible rationale for distancing the self from the immediate. A first-time novelist, schooled in 1950s avant-garde irreverence, DeLillo dismisses the very assumptions of his own medium: the self cannot be talked into shape, will not abide the oppression of explanation. Much as a Jackson Pollack canvas renders representation itself irrelevant or an Ornette Coleman riff detonates the premise of melody or a Godard film abuses the audience's need for character and plot, DeLillo's novel rejects its very assumption of authority, that assumption inherited from the grand modernist tomes that enthralled the young Bell in college (and a young DeLillo), among them *Ulysses,* Joyce's masterwork that unironically set out to shape all human history within the pedestrian events of a single day.

If DeLillo finds arrogant and untenable Western assumptions that the self is definable and that as life unfolds it confirms patterns, he finds the Eastern sensibility far more appealing. Within its logic, the self is not a hedge to be trimmed into shape—rather, it is the hedge itself, beautifully unruly and intriguingly chaotic, whatever shape it appears to possess merely temporary. The self is not a commodity but rather a vital force, like the weather. Manic radio jock Warren Beasley, in what turned out to be his final broadcast as a Los Angeles meteorologist, ranted to a no doubt puzzled audience that weather was actually internal.[5] It is surely the cornerstone assumption of Eastern thought that the self is a dynamic system, not some static core but rather a fluid and open matrix, part of an ever-shifting universe of wildly conflicting energies (a network documentary on China runs afoul when, after months of taping and files of factoids, the network crew concedes that China itself remained stubbornly unreadable). Bell suspects as much. As the filming of his autobiography expands beyond his control, as he listens to the irregular whirrings of the night insects, he considers abandoning the project entirely, in effect smashing his own assembled likeness, that "prism of . . . images," to live simply by his own "power and smell" (236). But film and language are finally too seductive, they appeal to Bell's fetishistic love of the object: in exile, he finds comfort bunkered behind the canisters of shot film, and he relishes the boxy sturdiness of his accumulating manuscript. That comfort—along with his self-imposed island retreat—marks Bell's failure to engage the real without the insulating protection of aesthetic shapes.

DeLillo skewers his own character by revealing the staggering waste of Bell's defeat. Where is Bell? He claims to be on a nameless Atlantic island on the fringes of the African continent; he claims to have been there for more than twenty years (the trip westward occurs sometime in the late 1960s; in the narrative present, Bell anticipates the approaching clickover to the new century). It is unlikely that the exile is intended to be real—what desert island has electricity?[6] The premise is more likely Bell's hokey—and misanthropic—conjuring, a fantastic (and improbable) storyboard premise drawn from his childhood fascination with Robert Louis Stevenson as well as from a hodgepodge of hackneyed television and film clichés about island maroonings. Exile is more likely a self-ennobling metaphor for Bell's elected isolation, his soured antilife of strategic retreat that disdains the glorious jazz of the streets of Manhattan Island (occasional passages capture this street kinesis, ironic given the first-person narration; Bell's own father confesses to a moment in the spring during his wife's slow slide toward death when, amid the rush of his executive's day, he was blown away by the "colossal surprise" of a chance glimpse upward at the Pan Am Building at night—"It looked like God" [274]).

Fearful of experience, Bell-in-exile suggests, strolling there in his cuffed white trousers along the edge of his virtual ocean on his made-up island retreat, Eliot's Prufrock straining to hear the mermaids singing each to each but terrified of the implication of actual passion and engagement. Bell closes the narrative distanced from our perception (and our sympathy), securely buried within the heavy cocooning of his own words and pictures—indeed, one motif here is premature burial: the former tenant of Sullivan's Manhattan loft, an eccentric inventor and self-described "Cocoonist," hung the apartment walls and ceilings with heavy insulating wrap; Bell's film thesis in college was an experimental short in which a man in the desert buries himself up to his neck; his father's most searing war memories concern being compelled in the Philippines to bury a man alive (the story is appropriated by Bell, the memory itself a metaphor for the insulation of words: when the actor hired to play Bell's father comes to deliver the Bataan monologue, Bell has written its thousands of words on the walls and ceiling of the hotel room where the sequence will be filmed). It is such an entombed figure that Bell suggests as this narrative closes, delivered from the chaos that alone, the young DeLillo argues, can give existence the nuance and depth for which Bell so clearly searched. Despite Bell's massive efforts, again and again experience beggars the cozy tidiness of explanation. Indeed, the final locale Bell visits before returning to Manhattan is the haunted intersection of Dealey Plaza, where America itself ran headlong into the unsearchable black of surprise.

Bell is a tempting figure. Find the self, take its fullest measure by removing it from its contaminating cultural context, protect it from the gash and rip of surprise, safeguard it from the toxic itch of the unreliable heart (every gesture at love here sours into base sexual exercise, collapses into banality, or settles into unbridgeable distances). But DeLillo is too much a cultural anatomist to endorse such strategy of deliberate entombment. Like Swift's Gulliver, Bell is compelled by too easy disgust and too clean distrust. Attempting to understand the self into a convenient form by simply removing it from its wider context—either cultural or relational— is akin to lopping off a low branch of some magnificent tree (itself testimony to the imperfect energies of the living world) and then studying it in some sterile lab—the branch becomes not an animated, infinitely complex being but rather a dead thing with no function, save to be observed.

Ironically the Kurosawa film to which Bell actually alludes is not one of Kurosawa's signature samurai epics but rather the poignant 1952 character study *Ikiru,* in which a low-level civil-service drone in Tokyo's city hall struggles with the revelation that stomach cancer has given him only months to live. Confronted by the waste of his life, distanced from family and friends, he determines to give his closing months meaning by personally maneuvering through the cumbersome government bureaucracy the paperwork for converting a vacant city lot into a small park for disadvantaged kids. He succeeds, and the old clerk spends his last hours on a swing in that park, snow lightly falling on his thin shoulders, as he sings "Life Is Short." Kurosawa's parable argues that life, absurdly compelled by blind chance, can touch heroic purpose only through compassionate engagement with others. Its title translates into the command: "live." It is a lesson ultimately lost on the dead man's associates—the film's ending shows the government office after the funeral returning to its inefficient indifference.

It is clearly lost on Bell as well. Despite a last name that recalls the massive communications giant, Bell's constant late-night phoning to friends distant and close serves merely to reinforce his isolation. He comes to sever (whether literally or metaphorically) all ties with others (as a prep-school basketball star, he was first in scoring, last in assists). He comes to reject the rich unpredictability of the immediate for an empty bunker of words and images. He claims no tie even to an audience—both his film and his manuscript are closed loops of communication, self-sustaining and self-generated exercises. In what will become a defining position in DeLillo's early fiction, Bell, exposed but not educated, unwilling to accept vulnerability, abandons the imperative to live, dismisses its evident complexities. He opts rather to relive, locking himself into permanent rewind, relentlessly reviewing his life's critical moments in a ghastly parody of network syndication, hoping that, as with advertising and television itself, repetition will conjure comfort, description will provide meaning, and form will offer consolation.

End Zone (1972)

Gary Harkness, the promising college halfback in DeLillo's sophomore effort, begins essentially where David Bell ends—metaphorically (and voluntarily) buried alive, determined to make sense of the grief in the world by withdrawing from it. Unlike Bell, however, Harkness refuses even the closed loop of self-narration. Harkness takes only a scant handful of pages to recount a troubled adolescence that included, while passing through four prestigious college football programs, numerous brushes with mental collapse, retreating each time to his family home in the Adirondacks in upstate New York. His grief has been significant. At Syracuse, he barricaded himself in a dorm with a troubled friend, ate Oreos, and read from an economics textbook; at Penn State, he became deeply bothered by the sheer sameness of each day; at Miami, he became enthralled by nuclear holocaust; and at Michigan State, he took part in a vicious tackle from which an opposing player eventually died. Despite the implied intimacy of a first-person narration, Harkness resists Bell's autobiographical urge to deploy language to give such raw event, such evident grief, the audacious presumption of form. Estranged from his go-getter father, a vitamin entrepreneur who advises his son to gut out the tough times, Harkness is terrified by the evident vulnerability of the puny self in an absurd world prone to the sudden, harsh thump of surprise. Unlike David Bell, Harkness does not want to define the self—he simply wants to dispense with it.

He thus retreats to obscure Logos College in the desert wastes of west Texas— there, by his own admission, to disappear. He plays for an enigmatic, Ahab-like coach, a control freak who conducts practices atop an imposing tower, motivates through power-clichés, admires the fanatic discipline of Teresa of Ávila, and demands that his players adhere to a conservative code of behavior (dress neatly, be courteous, write home often). The tight control of this gameworld will provide Harkness what film and language offered David Bell: a protective, seductive shelter.[7] During a hotly contested late-season showdown with a cross-state rival, a battered Harkness, preparing to return to the field after halftime, loses himself momentarily in a vivid dream-fantasy: a woman in a garden awash in the precise elegance of a Bach cantata, a tempting assertion of order, a welcoming, safe environment.

Deploying a wide matrix of metaphoric systems that each suggests such control (tarot cards, crash diets, football plays, war games, vitamin supplements, science fiction, prayer, marijuana), DeLillo plays on the tension between the need for order and the fear of chaos. After all, the end zone is the sole *un*contested zone within the field of football, a sort of sanctuary within a sanctuary. Characters take comfort in retreat, terrified by the implications of engaging the larger world of accident and mayhem. Anatole Bloomberg, Harkness's roommate, is an East Coast transplant who has come to the Texas desert in an absurd effort to "unjew" himself (tired of the guilt, determined to change everything from his weight to his speech patterns, he will eventually succeed simply by renaming himself "Ek-seventeen"). Bloomberg recounts a phone call in which he is told that his mother had been shot dead by an unidentified "lunatic."[8] Reeling within the shock waves of his exposed vulnerability, he retreats to the desert and paints a single stone black, that desperate gesture of control measuring his struggle against the cutting intervention of surprise, the ache of grief.

Barely twenty, Harkness has similarly lost his taste for chaos. He begins the narrative in grateful retreat at a college whose founder believed the world could be explained into a manageable order through the clean exercise of reason. When Bloomberg first meets Harkness, he asks who is the greater figure: Archimedes, the ur-scientist who conjured from the evident violence of the natural world a harmonic cosmos and called it science, or Edward Gibbon, the ur-historian who shaped from the manifest mess of unfolding event a linear narrative and called it history. It is, of course, a loaded question—both figures accepted the premise of explanation. Ironically, the college is run now by the founder's imposing widow ("Lincolnesque" as Harkness describes her [6]) who herself collides with the world that cannot be contained by explanation—she will be killed in a freakish plane accident (much as Lincoln himself collided with surprise at Ford's Theater).

But Harkness finds comfort, even pleasure in the merciless discipline of long scrimmages in the undulating Texas heat. He finds security and direction in Coach Creed's playbook that structures an ironclad gameworld where accident and chance are excluded. He relishes the barrenness of options available to him in the backfield, the thrill of being automatic, of surrendering his self to the unit. He thrives within the riskless model-world of virtual violence licensed by rules, directed by logic, and confined within chalk lines. Off-field, he indulges similar artificial exercises in discipline: he mimics the postures of meditation; he adds a new vocabulary word each day; he memorizes the names of the presidents; he walks in a carefully plotted circle in the desert around the college. When his teammates play Bang You're Dead along the deserted campus walkways, Harkness relishes the "dark joys" (32) of hamming up his "death" when "shot" by his friends' pointed fingers. Once the semester begins, he is enthralled by the tidiness of nuclear war as mapped out by an ROTC professor of military strategy. Unbothered by the evident insanity of imminent self-inflicted species extermination, he loves the clean vocabulary of nuclear strategy, enticed by the erotics of virtual apocalypse. Like football, such projections charm violence into an uncomplicated exercise in control, a perfect closed system in which the individual is denied both responsibility and initiative. Recall the odd letter Harkness receives from his father at Christmastime, the lengthy contents of which detail, step by tedious step, precisely how Harkness is to arrange a flight home, leaving Harkness no room for independent thought or range of reaction.

Language for DeLillo, however, is perhaps the most seductive strategy of control, largely because it would seem the best available way to engage the immediate.[9] Like football, like nuclear war scenarios, language creates distance and, in turn, a strong addiction to the protective fusillade of its environment. Language is continually foregrounded in *End Zone* (the name of the college itself means "the word," although the founder, ironically, was mute). We are exposed to a range of language technologies, the reader shuttled from one register to the next, among them the heavy miasma of military jargon and nukespeak; the enticing pornography of

motivational clichés; the sculpted eloquence of classroom lectures; the slick gob-
bledygook of public relations; and the harsh, quasimilitary rhetoric of the locker
room. Even the characters do not talk as much as they expound in stylized monologues, often witty and epigrammatic, that demand to be read as written, not spoken communications. Language here creates distance, offers only a translation
of the press and feel of the immediate at the expense of engagement itself. Consider terms such as "suicide," "car accident," "nuclear devastation," "concentration
camps," "murder" (each of which figures in the plot). The quotation marks themselves expose each as an artificial unit, a tidy, comforting environment of prefabricated control that is in fact an entirely arbitrary conglomeration of lines, squiggles,
and random spaces intended to make accessible the unfathomable realities they
merely pretend to encode.

Seduced by form, terrorized by the implications of the real, comfortably centripetal, Harkness thus handles awkwardly the intrusion of reality. He simply ignores
the unnerving press of a dense silence he senses hanging about the campus,
metaphorically the larger world decidedly unaffected by the sound and fury of his
adopted football regimen. That world continually intrudes. When a player is killed
in a particularly gruesome car accident, Harkness witnesses the desperate rescue
efforts and is intrigued by the shattered car and its bloodied occupants. But too
long desensitized by artifice, he responds inappropriately, salaciously: trying to
sleep later that night, he has a morbid fantasy recalling the open bloody legs of
the dead girl in the front seat. Then, days later, again trying to fall asleep, Harkness
thinks absently about one of the assistant coaches. Because he had never actually
talked to the coach and knows only superficial factoids—that he smokes a pipe and
never swears—Harkness retreats to the virtual reality of his imagination to gamely
fill in the coach's form—where he came from, what he does off-field. Of course,
the game fails. The coach remains elusive—indeed, Harkness is stunned only
weeks later when he is told the same coach, who had apparently struggled with
health problems Harkness never suspected, takes his own life with a single shot to
the head.

Such is the consequence, DeLillo cautions, if the world is too casually dismissed by a culture grown apprehensive by the implications of chaos, the vulnerabilities of grief, grown too fond of retreat into virtual realities. Myna Corbett,
Harkness's girlfriend, an aficionado of an obscure Mongolian science-fiction writer,
recounts one of the writer's eccentric tales in which a giant mollusk on a forbidding oceanic planet is irradiated with a strange black light that divides its brain, one
section bound to the real world, the other observing that connection and busily
striking words that over millennia dominate at the expense of the things themselves. The mild-mannered mollusk becomes an evolutionary monstrosity, ironically, beyond words, defying even its creator/author's ability to describe it exactly.

Then one day, inexplicably, one of the words erases itself. What then becomes of the thing the word once represented?

Consider the narrative set piece in part 2, the account of the Big Game with West Centrex Biotechnical Institute. Here DeLillo plays ironically with the expectations of old-school sportswriting, specifically its traditional manipulation of language to create the cozy illusion of riveting immediacy. Here, by contrast, we experience the game secondhand, filtered through a deliberately impenetrable scrim of language. DeLillo himself steps into the narrative in a stern parenthetical opening that cautions us against expecting yet another you-are-there account of a game. The narrative's generous illusion brusquely shattered by the intrusive presence of the author himself, we are subjected to pages of playbook-ese, inaccessible x's and o's, jersey numbers and play codes, that drain the game of any emotional texture, spontaneity, or passion. Even the score, the defining dramatic element in any game, is difficult to track. We are in effect denied the experience of the football game. We must be content with the rendered artifice, the clean form—until, after thirty pages of such a smothering verbal assault, we hunger for the simplest unmediated reality, a position DeLillo surely encourages. Within this narrative, however, we are not sure where to turn. After all, when Harkness spends a long afternoon with his professor of modern warfare dissecting all the terrifying angles of nuclear war, including the massive stockpiles of weapons available, the inevitability of their deployment, and, most horrifically, the long-term effects of radiation, Harkness stumbles back to campus panicked, figuratively nuked by language, desperate simply to touch something real, something without ambiguity, without levels of interpretation. His witty proseline is momentarily blasted to bits, detonated to a spare recitation of nouns: "The sun. The desert. The sky. The silence. The flat stones. The insects. The wind and the clouds. The moon. The stars. The west and east. The song, the color, the smell of the earth" (87). Nothing calms him. The world is too overwhelmingly layered. Eventually he happens upon a low mound of fresh dog shit—and even that sends him into a panicked catalog of the vast presence of shit in the world.

This, then, would appear to be our decidedly bleak options: either restructure the evident chaos of the everyday into fragile forms, which in turn foster an addiction to insulation and an illusory sense of control, or accept a vast and terrifying world that is shabby, feral, shitty, and uncontainable. Insuperable arrogance or unendurable chaos. DeLillo knows it is not so simple. Consider the elaborate evasions his characters indulge: a Bach cantata, a crash diet, tarot cards, a marijuana joint, science fiction, college itself, a football playbook, Defense Department policy papers, nutritional supplements and power vitamins, even prayer—what is missing? Embracing the complexity of the imperfect everyday, the forbidding magic of the immediate, the street world simply as it is, its every moment shot through with unsuspected implication, the rich vulnerability of surprise, the visceral jolt of inelegant rawness, the very medium of the world that lurks beyond the reach of our need for form—indeed, Logos College offers a course in the Untellable.

Appropriately, then, the novel does not end with the Big Game Showdown—part 3 records the difficult adjustments to postseason realities, the return to engagement that must follow the football season. Quickly, Harkness collides with absurdity, surprise, and violence. In the meaningless last game of the season, Harkness, at Myna's suggestion, decides to smoke a joint and finds himself so distanced from the action on-field that he simply walks off. He is surprised, however, when not only is he not disciplined but the coach actually promotes him to co-captain for next season. Then when teammates play a pickup game during a heavy snowstorm, Harkness, amid the forbidding cold and the thick confusion of falling snow, engages football without the elegance of form—no pads, no huddles, no time-space coordinates to control the action, no fancy reverses, no clever pass patterns, no rehearsed fakes—just straight-ahead runs with uncontrollable skidding, jarring collisions, and the inevitable blood and pain of unchoreographed violence. Then after the "game," the team is shaken by reports that one of the players, Nix, had gone berserk the night before and had "started throwing ash cans through windows" until six people finally restrained him (203).

Feeling the enclosing pressure of the absurd world and the vulnerability of surprise, Harkness opts for a series of problematic gestures of control and retreat. After visiting a dorm room where an entomology major had assembled an insect collection, dozens of desert bugs trapped in large sealed jars, Harkness, jolted by such appealing evidence of control and containment, writes a rambling six-page letter (addressed to no one in particular) on space-time, an attractive subject given its pretense to contain infinity itself within measurable axes (although Harkness admits he knows nothing about it). He then visits Taft Robinson, the team's blue-chip African American running back, who has elected not to return next season, indeed, to pass on what Harkness sees as inevitable celebrity in the pros, motivated largely by bitterness over racism.[10] In nonviolent protest, Robinson has shaved his head and has withdrawn to his bare dorm room, where Harkness finds him cross-legged on his bed, wearing sunglasses, a newspaper carelessly strewn about him. Like David Bell, Robinson has retreated to a static and drab environment over which he exercises total control—creating a self-sustaining and entirely self-justifying order from the choreographed play of random shapes. He has embunkered himself amid books (as a disturbing measure of his shallowness, he is enthralled by books on the Holocaust, particularly descriptions of atrocities committed against Jewish children). Time here is relentlessly tracked by the room's redundant clocks, Robinson certain that accuracy can be achieved by averaging

their times. The larger world is diminished to irrelevancy—he listens a few minutes each day to a small portable radio. The rest of his time he exists (like the
desert bugs in the jars) in a protected silence. Once known for his dazzling on-field
speed and ad-lib moves, he is content now to idle in a creepy neutral, using as
rationale for this absurd fanaticism and joyless retreat his decision (based on his
own superficial study) to pursue Islam.

After this visit, as the novel ends, Harkness himself will execute a similarly misguided strategy of control with similarly ironic religious dimensions—a ruinous
fast, a disturbing strategy of self-annihilation, the inevitable endgame of a confused
young man desperate to disappear. The strategy leaves him so weak that he must
be taken to the university infirmary, and we leave him there, helpless, attached to
plastic feeding tubes. Both Robinson and Harkness have drained the moment of
its depth and nuance, its shattering energy and complication; both have lost their
appetite for surprise and absurdity; both have dispensed with any sacramental
sense of the body—and both are left at risk, the cost of control, finally, too dear.

As in *Americana,* to counter the characters' movement toward retreat, DeLillo
affirms grief: the terror and wonder, mayhem and splendor of the unmediated now.
Yet unlike *Americana,* there is little counterforce to the characters' collective movement toward isolation and disengagement. There is only the minor reclamation of
Myna Corbett, who begins the narrative defiantly rejecting a world she sees as
hypocritical and shallow, hiding her own vulnerabilities too comfortably behind
an excess of weight, an unkempt appearance, and over-the-top outfits.[11] But she
returns from Christmas break (as in *Americana,* the season of promising epiphanies) compelled by humility and curiosity, determined not only to lose the weight
and tone down her outfits but to learn who she is by reengaging a world she had so
contemptibly dismissed (she had before worn a T-shirt with a mushroom cloud
appliqué; previously her answer to every complicated situation was her dream to
run away, like David Bell, to Mexico). Not surprisingly, Harkness rejects this new
Myna outright. How then can DeLillo distance himself from the narrative's larger
concession to the deadening strategy of control-by-retreat?

The only way he can: he shatters form itself, exposes narrative for the preposterous arrogance that it embodies.[12] After all, the critical moments—the spiritual
anxieties that bring Harkness to west Texas, the suicide of the young coach, the
death of the player in the terrible car accident, the shooting death of Bloomberg's
mother, the plane wreck that kills the college's president—are rendered in a depthless deadpan, a starved proseline that ignores the implications of the evident mystery of such events and pretends to contain them within the clean logic of tight,
tidy sentences. The closing paragraph itself is shockingly abrupt—without explanation, with barely four lines left in the novel, Harkness begins the fast, and we
are left with only the image of a recovering Harkness in the infirmary bound to a

network of feeding tubes. We are denied even the barest explanation, we are abruptly cut off from the minimum accommodations of any narrative artifice. In short, we are left like Myna: vulnerable, fending for ourselves outside the insulating shape of a contrived order. Of course, DeLillo is not rejecting outright the solace of aesthetic forms, the splendid retreat we all find within the well-structured tidiness of a narrative (or, for that matter, within a carefully executed cantata, a well-made film, a labyrinthine theme park, or even the designed plays of an athletic contest). As artist, DeLillo recognizes the tonic relief afforded by temporary retreat into such symbolic landscapes where cause and effect work, where actions follow linear logic, where absurdity is leashed and accident suspended, where time/space cooperate, where surprise is ultimately a controlled, dramatic effect. DeLillo sympathizes with our need for form—Bloomberg confesses that as a child, terrified by the black rush of nightfall and the irrefutable implication of his own insignificance, vulnerability, and solitude, he would tap steadily on the shadowy wall of his bedroom, hoping for some return acknowledgment and then celebrating one night what he knew were only the meaningless scratches of a rat trapped in the walls of an adjoining warehouse. But if we retreat within symbolic landscapes, it is ultimately to reengage the unfashioned immediate, revitalized. Our lives, DeLillo cautions, cannot expect tidiness, cannot demand control. Indeed, the richest (and most terrifying) experiences—love and death—exist at exactly those arch-moments in which control fails. In addition to his evident difficulty accepting death, Harkness's odd romance with Myna never touches the sheer incandescence that love can ignite (a professor of exobiology describes that energy by saying love actually denies gravity, permits generous ascent). In love, Harkness is compelled only by superficialities (Myna's odd clothing, her sloppy weight, her eccentric habits), and when they make love, it is a quick-stab (appropriately) in the library stacks (as foreplay they read dictionary definitions and pronounce words slowly syllable by syllable). Thus, given a narrative of those unwilling to engage full throttle the chaos of the immediate, those too content with refuge, the reader alone is left to relish DeLillo's irreverent undercutting of his own narrative, to enjoy the setting-free implicit in the narrative's nonclosure. We must provide the centrifugal counterforce to the characters' settling-in to form; in short, we must relish our rude ouster from the narrative itself and the implied return to the consequence, danger, and surprise of the grief-world, the unmediated now.

Great Jones Street (1973)

It is fitting, given his evident interest in the struggle to engage the immediate and to define an authentic self amid the garish distractions of the media age, that DeLillo would explore the wonderland logic of celebrity itself, that media-age exercise in sustained self-conjuring undertaken by those dubbed "public figures" who carefully construct a self solely for wide consumption, authenticity being, finally, irrelevant. Bucky Wunderlick is a celebrity, a rock star / singer-songwriter whose three albums have propelled him in three quick years into the public arena as the temperamental front man of a raucous band, known for overloaded decibels and explosive concerts that often degenerate into directionless violence. If David Bell struggles to recover a self and Gary Harkness struggles to dispense with it, Bucky, just shy of his twenty-sixth birthday, has no self at all—he is pure confection. When Bucky retreats to Manhattan (as the novel opens, he has abruptly left the band in midtour), hysterical fans report dozens of sightings of him around the world, suggesting the tenuousness of anything like a "real" Bucky. Not surprisingly, despite the implied intimacy of Bucky's first-person narration and the generous narration of his retreat, we will learn nothing else about him: his childhood, his family, his evolution into music, his response to fame, not even his real name (could that wonderfully preposterous name be anything but a stage coinage?). He comes to us ready-made and remains (as all celebrities must) stubbornly two-dimensional and relentlessly present-tense. Indeed, if the reader identifies at all with Bucky, it is only because we are part of the late-twentieth-century celebrity age in which such divas are regularly fashioned by corporate promoters and then sustained by predatory paparazzi. But Bucky's sudden departure from his band after a concert in Houston (and his withdrawal to his girlfriend's seedy apartment in a forlorn neighborhood of Manhattan) marks his resistance to this fame and his determination to separate from that created self.[13] To do so, however, Bucky has retreated—a self-entombment strategy that DeLillo satirizes in his first two novels as unworkable because it creates insuperable silences and inviolable isolation.

Unlike David Bell or Gary Harkness, however, Bucky Wunderlick is an artist—and for the first time DeLillo confronts the dilemma of the viability and relevancy of an artist of language (we are given samplings of Bucky's lyrics without, of course, the accompanying music) in a media-saturated era that threatens to make quaintly nostalgic the very notion of language's workability.[14] What sort of artist is Bucky Wunderlick? With each of his three albums, Bucky has struck a different linguistic pose with chameleon ease. Album to album, literally from one year to the next, Bucky's sensibility has been radically different, revealing a telling lack of any core self, any consistent vision. His first record, for example, is rife with trendy change-the-world late-1960s countercultural political activism, faux-angry denunciations and anti-establishment posturings that call (predictably) for an end to hypocrisy, social injustice, and violence (the thinness of his conviction is revealed by a newspaper clipping DeLillo offers along with the lyric sampling in which an airsick Bucky uses his cigarette lighter to singe a stewardess trying to calm him before takeoff). Bucky's second album mimics the dreary posturings of the sensitive singer-songwriter, the indulgence of private aches and emotional intensities; but again it is a confected persona (one "confessional" lyric, for instance, deals with the oppressive angst of a suburbanite on the way to another day in the office, another tells of a kinky affair with a New Orleans hooker). Bucky's third's album is a contrived experiment in avant-garde guerrilla shock treatment: it deconstructs the premise of language itself with lyrics that imitate the babblings of a newborn (the album is titled *Pee-Pee-Maw-Maw*), content to play self-consciously with language—Bucky's fans sport the nonsensical lyrics on T-shirts. So which voice —political activist, sensitive songwriter, campy shock-experimenter—is Bucky's authentic/artistic one?

There is a fourth project, unreleased reel-to-reel tapes of twenty-three songs that Bucky recorded alone fourteen months earlier during a sleepless three-day stay in a mountain retreat. These so-called mountain tapes would appear to promise a substantive artistic departure for Bucky.[15] Unlike his studio releases, each of which casually assumed a hip posture and thus refuted the assumed premise of artistic expression (that is, authenticity), these tapes testify to a Bucky unmediated and unpackaged. With rambling lyrics concocted spontaneously and rife with elusive imagery (months later, Bucky still does not know what the lyrics "mean"), with often desolate melodies ad-libbed on an acoustic guitar and with Bucky's voice scoured to a rasp from the grind of touring, the tapes embody the very mystery and compelling magic of the authentic, Faulkner's grief-world. Ultimately, however, despite their raw expressiveness, the mountain tapes are form-bound. They are, after all, confined to recording tape, real/reel objects, and they perforce exist within the stubborn paradox unavoidable (as DeLillo concedes) in any artistic enterprise, from novels to paintings to film: as form, they are finally/finely contained spontaneity, hot emotions and spontaneous confessions inevitably cooled into the static and the defined and therefore vulnerable to exploitation as a commodity. Indeed, the tapes become contested property: they are crassly targeted for acquisition by Bucky's own record label. His own manager, the reptilian Globke, whose soulless pursuit of financial success is uncomplicated by ethics—we first meet him as he retrieves a dime he dropped in Bucky's toilet—actually has the tapes stolen in order to process them into a vinyl release.

Within DeLillo's deliberately excessive plotlines (how better to expose the contrivance of form than to overburden his own slender novel with crisscrossing lines of conspiracies and intrigues that eventually involve sinister narcotics interests), the mountain tapes eventually become involved in an international drug-running scheme and are ultimately destroyed by a shadowy, extremist urban-guerrilla organization known ironically as the Happy Valley Farm Commune, leftover hippies fanatically committed to the American tradition of self-reliance and privacy. When Bucky abruptly departs from his band, the commune embraces him (and decides to use his apartment to stash stolen drugs) because Bucky's ballyhooed departure from the glitzy world of celebrity appears to endorse their own aggressive belief in the right to isolation. Determined to stop Bucky from abandoning his elective seclusion and using the mountain tapes to jump-start his career, commune agents blow up the studio in Cincinnati where the tapes are being processed by Bucky's record company.

Thus, with the tapes irredeemably lost, the narrative appears to move toward rejecting the aesthetic enterprise entirely: after all, the superstar Bucky is exposed early on as a sham artist devoid of authentic center, his pseudo-art untouched by even the sparest interest in authenticity, a Warholic, measured by his fifteen minutes, intrigued by spectacle, eccentricity, and contrived experimentation, bound finally by the form of aesthetic expression in ways that recall David Bell's misplaced confidence in words and film and Gary Harkness's anxious faith in the coach's massive playbook. And even when Bucky does manage to tap honestly into his ambiguous interior life and attempts to deploy aesthetic strategies to commit those conflicting passions to form, that form, the mountain tapes, is ultimately, pointlessly destroyed. At his own birthday party, which Bucky reluctantly hosts at the Great Jones Street apartment, among the pretentious Manhattan artistes (the "neon creepies"[16]), a performance artist tells of his grandiose plans to stage an earthquake in Mexico by deploying tons of TNT along a fault line just to be able to take "live" photos of the disaster. Such, in DeLillo's delicious satire, is the contemporary artist: dismissing the available everyday to pursue mock authenticity, too fascinated by form—an exercise ultimately in empty self-absorption (one of the guests is fond of stroking her own navel).

What, then, is an artist to do?

As in his first two novels, DeLillo's satire here works by offering reclamation to a character unwilling to accept its implications or its responsibilities. From the start, Bucky Wunderlick retreats to the wasteland backstreets of the Bowery, determined, like both David Bell and Gary Harkness, to recover a self by simplifying its context (it backfires, of course, as his "disappearance" merely increases his celebrity appeal). It is as if the apocalyptic ruin that so enthralled Gary Harkness did not have to wait for the hot rain of nuclear fire—Bucky looks out from his cracked tenement window onto a desolate urban emptiness, a post-catastrophic cityscape that seems in its gray, wintry desolation and with its unrelenting obscenities the perfect environment for self-realization, the urban equivalent of the desert wastes that Harkness and Bell both find so seductive. A telling anecdote will suffice: Opel Hampson, Bucky's lover, recalls at Christmastime a corner Santa fleeing a suspect derelict who, after Opel offered him money, exposes himself. Bucky initially is distanced from such a squalid neighborhood, unimpressed by its unpromising drab ("the ugliness of every inch" [18]), uninterested in its considerable voice. He stays to his closed room and gets no closer to the world than the window, his phone disconnected, the clock unwound and on the closet floor, unread newspapers and magazines drifting in heaps.

Bucky's dilemma as artist is underscored by his apartment's positioning literally between two extremes of the aesthetic enterprise: the artist as crass public commodity and the artist as tormented private entity. Above him lives an unknown underground writer named Eddie Fenig, a professional scribbler with a gargantuan appetite for text-production, who willingly tests any genre he deems potentially profitable, from science fiction, poetry, and mysteries to a particularly repellent genre he invents: kiddie pornography—that is, sexually explicit stories written for children. Jagged by massive dosages of caffeine, endlessly pacing his tiny apartment to coax inspiration, Fenig furiously cranks out pages of material with minimum emotional investment or integrity, millions of words specifically targeted for a marketplace whose fickleness haunts him—as the novel closes, Fenig toys with fictions of apocalyptic violence. Below Bucky, however, lives an autistic man-child whose parents never even bothered to name him. The Micklewhite child, at twenty, cannot speak at all, a genetic mishap damaged by a soft skull (his father once considered placing the freakish boy in a carnival). Now, as Bucky observes when he visits the apartment, the helpless child must be secured to chairs for his own protection, and his verbal production is limited to moans while he sleeps, distressing cries that Bucky hears overhead but which are, finally, fragile and ephemeral. Clearly, both neighbors represent extreme positions for the language artist: form without emotion or emotion without form. As extremis figures within a satire, neither of course entirely satisfies DeLillo, although Bucky is momentarily impressed by Fenig's industrial output and later is touched by the haunting figure of the retarded man-child. As suggested by his positioning between the apartments, Bucky will eventually tap a saving via media—only to reject it, much like David Bell and Gary Harkness.

When Bucky's exile is violated by menacing strangers who will involve a reluctant Bucky in an intrigue centering on a powerful new mind-altering drug, DeLillo ushers his character toward reclamation. The synthetic drug has been stolen from a Long Island government testing facility by agents of the Happy Valley Farm Commune and is being hotly pursued by a number of underground interests. Bucky later finds out the drug temporarily destroys speech skills—initially tested during the Vietnam War by sinister branches of the federal intelligence community to brainwash North Vietnamese guerrillas—but now is being proposed to silence (literally) domestic political dissenters in the aftermath of the turbulent 1960s. The commune, however, wants to analyze the drug for possible distribution as a potent street-downer. A commune courier, a long-faced woman named Skippy, shows up at Bucky's door unannounced and simply leaves the stolen package, she says, until arrangements can be made to get the sample to the cartel's mysterious Dr. Pepper for chemical analysis. In an effort to secure the contested drug package before the commune can acquire its chemical makeup, however, a snaky record-company courier named Hanes (DeLillo plays broadly with brand names to underscore the commodifying of the powerful narcotic) actually switches the package with a similarly taped-up package that in fact contains Bucky's pirated mountain tapes, which the record company had obtained from Opel. DeLillo thus draws discomforting parallels between the tapes, and the aesthetic impulse they more generally suggest, and powerful narcotics: both, finally, offer insulating zones of retreat, pleasure prisons—fragile enclaves, attractive and addictive.[17]

Like David Bell and Gary Harkness, then, Bucky must be enticed to engage the unstructured immediate. It begins with the compelling (if brief) return of Bucky's lover, Opel, a lapsed musician and former groupie and currently a drug runner overtired of her lonely globe-trotting lifestyle and physically worn out by its demands. Although she has returned to Bucky ostensibly to make an offer for the drug package for the unnamed interests she represents, Opel offers Bucky far more, indeed what neither David Bell with his flavor-of-the-week appetite for secretaries nor Gary Harkness with his mocking infatuation for Myna ever approach: an impulse toward intimacy—not only through the spontaneous sexual frictions that momentarily heat Bucky's cold apartment (much of Opel's stay is spent in the apartment's huge bed) but, more significantly, in generous conversations they undertake in bed that tap into language's ancient privilege to conjure community.[18] Opel is frank, candid, and expansive—she hides nothing—indeed, she is most often naked. After what became a lifelong flight from the considerable pull of her wealthy Texas family and her conservative Christian upbringing (she recalls her river baptism at age six), Opel, although weak from developing pneumonia, has returned to Manhattan in the dead of winter not merely to negotiate another drug deal but rather to tell the self-exiled Bucky that flight, finally, is no answer. It is Opel, not Bucky, who recognizes the promise of the mountain tapes—she originally takes the tapes from the mountain hideaway after Bucky dismisses their import, and in New York she will give the tapes to the record company with specific instructions to return them to Bucky as a birthday gift, a gesture of attempted salvation. Opel will not survive the narrative: after she confesses how trafficking in the drug market has left her less a person than a commodity, she dies quietly in the apartment's massive bed, her thin body conceding to her "thinging," exhausted from a lifetime of flight without direction, motion without purpose, acquisition without wealth.

For DeLillo, the tension that defines the contemporary artist is not so much between types of expression—or the forms of expression that so define Bucky's career—but rather the tension between the suasive lure of isolation and silence against the responsibility to engage the accessible and imperfect world, to accept membership within its (extra)ordinary legions. Unlike David Bell or Gary Hark-ness, Bucky sees his retreat as temporary—he plans to return to his career. But how, without, as the outrageously mercenary British rock recluse Watley counsels him, committing suicide as a beneficial career move? After record-company thugs break into Bucky's apartment and steal the mountain tapes, Bucky finds himself nabbed by extremist elements of the commune and taken to their Lower East Side headquarters where, to help ensure his commitment to isolation, he is actually injected with a sample of the experimental drug stolen from Hanes, who is himself nearly catatonic from experimenting with the superdrug. Bucky feels its impact immediately: for weeks, his speech center is completely blown. It is a telling igni-tion moment for the reclamation of the artist: a character actually separated from expression, articulation impossible, spoken words reduced to mushy, droolly sounds.

What, then, is left to define the artist? What Bucky still has intact, DeLillo sug-gests: the ability to respond. Impulsively, on a most unpromising day, amid the chilling sleet of an early spring afternoon, the stricken Bucky takes a looping walk from the Bowery through Chinatown and then down to the Battery and back again via the subway, the very streets he disdained in earlier chapters.[19] In an expansive closing chapter of Whitmanesque largesse, Bucky finds the most common street scenes uncommonly endowed with unsuspected urgency, pedestrian objects sud-denly vivid with symbolic resonance, the accidental collision of shape, shadow, line, color stunning in its unchoreographed symmetry, like the colored stones in a kaleidoscope effortlessly finding their way to design: a toothless vendor bellows out his fruits; two deaf men circle each other menacingly with boards; a wheelchair-bound woman feeds pigeons and watches longingly as they sail off into the gray city skies; a vagrant neatly retches into his tattered scarf; steam shovels tear into the earth to clear lots for the new housing projects; a gaggle of briefcase-toting lawyers mill about the courthouse; down by the river, amid the harbor's thick chemical stench, fishermen gut silvery trout on flaked ice in bloody pans.

This eight-page closing chapter is unprecedented in DeLillo's early fiction. Language here, syllables lovingly pitched sound against sound, recreates the chiaroscuro texture of the city landscape, its beat and rip. Forsaking the formulaic epiphany that extends only the private horizon of a single character by offering the hard reward of earned insight, here DeLillo generously offers to the reader the far more dramatic opportunity for an ongoing, unending, and unearned epiphany of the open eye turned suddenly to the stubborn urgency of the now. Unlike the mountain tapes, in which such immediacy stales within form, here we get Bucky, alert and receiving, denied the busyness of communication and the distraction of articulation. Language boldly, dramatically summons the ongoing rush of the immediate—"NEWSPAPERS VOMIT SHIT GLASS CARDBOARD BOTTLE" (260). Bucky lucks into ascent, the sheer richness of the authentic, discovering what David Bell so glibly set out to find among the Navahos: the yin and yang, or as Bucky observes, the "Pigeons and meningitis. Chocolate and mouse droppings. Licorice and roach hairs" of the unmediated city (262). In this slender chapter, there is no distracting narrative action (indeed, it is a welcome respite from DeLillo's rococo plotline tracking the two identical packages, the drugs and the tapes); there is no insistent theme, no such intrusive authorial contrivances: it is language recreating the stunning weave of the immediate, a turning outward, a loving jazzy riff that relishes language's privileged power to renew the world by embracing it, to note what goes unnoted, to recover without irony the difficult beauty that sparkles unsuspected in the meanest intersections of the most accessible neighborhoods. It is, DeLillo concedes, art not as form but as experience, not as record (literally or metaphorically), static and fabricated, but rather as response, vibrant and changing, alert and sensuous. Art does not leave a mark—art is the mark. DeLillo, schooled in the audacious premise of '50s avant-garde jazz and abstract expressionism and thus profoundly uneasy over the pretense of form and the inevitable distraction of the form-maker, defines the artistic impulse by separating the impulse (available to anyone with a pulse and alert senses) from its confinement into form (the familiar, wide-ranging catalog of contrived aesthetic shapes, most obviously words and images). In a novel that ultimately parallels drugs and art, here is breathtaking liberation.

It is a celebratory message that DeLillo shares with the reader (read aloud, the closing eight pages soar and invite) but that Bucky himself will not endorse. With soured misanthropy, Bucky disdains any community larger than his reclaimed self, his is a private restoration that is finally yet another disturbing variation on exile (on his walk, Bucky is drawn momentarily to a tiny island he glimpses obscured in the fog-bound harbor). He obviously commits his revelations to paper but disdains the idea of sharing. Even as he feels the effects of the injection begin to wear off and his language skills slowly return (the first word he shapes, ironically, is "mouth"), he returns to his apartment's massive bed, resists the idea of sharing his recovered sensibility, rejects the sympathy implicit in deploying language for binding. Even as he tours Manhattan, he wears an insulating wrap of four sweaters and actually walks alongside a forlorn looking Skippy, now wracked by a wet cough and hacking up blood, without even acknowledging her or evincing interest in her obvious health distress. He is content, as the narrative closes, to allow the world to assume he is a mute, a deliberate rejection of community that violates DeLillo's own embracing urgency in presenting the reader a closing chapter that so resonates with the texture of the immediate. As we leave Bucky, accepting isolation in a churlish strategy that recalls David Bell and Gary Harkness, he mocks the urban legend circulating that has him ministering among the beggars and syphilitics in

New York's blighted neighborhoods, dismissing the notion thereby implied of self-less sympathy; gifted with a moment's authenticity that neither Bell nor Harkness approach, Bucky feels no compulsion to share such stunning affirmation, his epiphany more autistic than artistic. Thus he is unable to complete the process of his evolution as an artist—he rejects his place within the community of the generic and will not bring to that community the stunning message of its own unsuspected magic.

Ratner's Star (1976)

In what might stand as a kind of cumulative text for DeLillo's early career, *Ratner's Star* functions as both a satire on exile and an exercise in it, a massive, impudently self-indulgent work that tempts the reader to accept the position of retreat that has defined the centering characters in DeLillo's first three novels, a work that encourages our withdrawal into the self-sustaining delight of a forbidding enclosure that within its four-hundred-plus pages of extravagant architecture invokes and skews an accumulation of genres—including science fiction, autobiography, hip parable, Menippean satire, bildungsroman, and cautionary allegory. With its encyclopedic command of arcane mathematics; its impenetrable dialogue among scientific whizzes; its Alice-in-Wonderland cast of oddball scientists who, without irony, pursue eccentric projects radically disconnected from any practical application as part of a government think tank somewhere (absurdly enough) in the central Asian wastes; its studied avoidance of linear plot, recognizable setting, and sympathetic characters; and its careful emulation of esoteric mathematical architectures as the basis for its narrative structure, *Ratner's Star* (itself three years in the making) represents both the triumph—and the sabotage—of form.[20] Like David Bell's island-refuge, like Gary Harkness's football field, like Bucky Wunderlick's Bowery hideaway, the text itself offers sanctuary—willingly accommodating the curious (albeit patient) reader. But like a terrorist in the works, DeLillo constructs this labyrinth-narrative only to implode its legitimacy by arguing ultimately that exile within such a fetching form, within such a clever construction, denies the reader the experience of that ill-wrought, splendidly messy world that so terrifies characters in his first four novels.

Like a master-maze or vast theme park or, for that matter, any number of labyrinthine postmodern excess-texts such as Thomas Pynchon's *Gravity's Rainbow* or William Gaddis's *The Recognitions* (both narrative audacities that DeLillo has publicly admired), *Ratner's Star* inevitably generates one of two reactions: the hunger to explore it or the desire to leave it. Like the tantalizing sequence of 101 pulsations picked up from deep space near Ratner's star that Billy Twillig, a brilliant fourteen-year-old Nobel laureate in mathematics, has been asked to decode, *Ratner's Star* has proven a charismatic text, enticing an exile-into-form by a generation of professional readers who have cleverly and persuasively "decoded" its myriad historical references, its eccentric applications of mathematical theories, its subtly contrived two-part mirrored narrative-as-boomerang structure, its clever homage to (among other texts) *Rasselas, Candide, Alice's Adventures in Wonderland,* and *Gulliver's Travels.* Less practiced readers, however, quickly fatigue within such a massively allusive/elusive text that thwarts even the modest goal of plot summary; the promise of a sci-fi narrative about a cryptic message from outer space is quickly lost as the loony scientists come and go, declaiming tediously on obscure theoretical speculations that range from intriguing to absurd. It becomes, for such lay readers, a claustrophobic text-space (which DeLillo encourages: save for the closing pages, the action takes place in enclosed laboratories, individually assigned work canisters within the vast cycloid-shaped think tank itself, or in underground chambers). Thus the book can invite being set aside, the frustrated lay reader gratefully returning to the world of experience that DeLillo himself in the closing pages ultimately sanctions. Like pure mathematics itself—which offers a reassuring, if contrived, sense of order and form by rendering a tightly squared model-world with intriguing, if demanding, clarity—the narrative here testifies to the ingenuity of its contriver; reveals, ultimately, the remarkable engine of DeLillo's mind at full tilt.

The difficult irony that DeLillo exploits here is that nature has contrived to sink the mind capable of such stunning architecture—whether performing mathematics or conjuring narratives—within a body that clumsily deforms without predictable process; that must be subject to whims and itches that cannot be explained; that sweats, exerts, bleeds, defecates, copulates, ages, sickens, dies, and ultimately rots in a maddeningly freestyle exercise that, despite science's efforts to mold into predictability, stays stubbornly free of such coercion and taps, rather, authentic mystery and magic, the "screech and claw of the inexpressible."[21] *Ratner's Star* thus tests the counterpulls of mind and body and, by extension, of retreat and engagement. Although any explication of such a dense, eccentric text is necessarily provisional and reductive, we can approach the text as a binary construction, its two parts functioning in a boomerang configuration, a movement first away (part 1 begins as Billy soars into the horizon on a plane bound for the Far East) and then back toward (part 2) the untidiness of the material world.[22] As Billy Twillig comes to question both his naive faith in order and his adolescent fear of disorder, his evolution/reclamation becomes the dramatic question of DeLillo's subtle bildungs-roman.

Initially, the body hardly intrigues Billy. The obvious imperfections of his maturing body disgust him; he feels uneasy confusion over the curious itch of sexuality and a persistent fascination about his own privates, about women's bodies, and about the physical exercise of sex itself; and, most distressingly, he broods at length on his own death, including his own funeral and the gruesome cellular holocaust of decomposition. Early on, Billy, in flight to the think tank, resists visiting the plane's bathroom following an elderly woman, certain that the enclosed facility will reek of her "old people's shitpiss" (7). What he happily finds, however, is a pristine stainless steel compartment that has efficiently whisked away any evidence of the woman's visit. The cost of such "stingy purity"? The price of all DeLillo's sanctuaries to date: isolation, artificiality, and sterility. Long uneasy over his own body (born premature, he spent his first days, appropriately, within the protective capsule of a hospital incubator), Billy has found in the mind, specifically in mathematics, access to a satisfying model-universe that is a closed exercise in predictability. He long ago abandoned words as clumsy and unreliable—conversations he overheard as a child proved again and again sinister in their ability to mislead, to threaten; his mother even changed his name, deciding "Terwillinger" was too cumbersome for a budding prodigy. Anxiety and fear of vulnerability, thus, compelled Billy into mathematics (impressed upon the young Billy when he accompanied his father, a subway engineer, on a harrowing walk through the system's forbidding tunnels); the precision and contrived symmetry of mathematics promised clean solution and reliable manageability, engrossing patterns that dismiss as irrelevant larger questions of purpose or meaning (exactly why *does* 1 + 1 = 2?), relying rather on the seduction of order and artifice. But as Billy's name suggests (*twi:* two; *lig:* binding), he will be challenged to do what no DeLillo character to this point has achieved: balance the cool/urgent creativity of the mind with the sweet/messy exertions of the body.

As with traditional Menippean satires that use characters to mock pretentious erudition (*Gulliver's Travels* and *Huckleberry Finn* are helpful examples), part 1 celebrates (and simultaneously skews) the towering achievement of the mind. Not surprisingly, part 1 is all about solutions—the ultimate expression of the mind engaged. There are Billy's ongoing efforts to decode the baffling deep-space transmission. As he meets his eccentric colleagues, he is given detailed overviews of their impenetrable projects that collectively assume a knowable universe rife with solvable problems. As Billy meets one by one these scientists with their goofy names and their equally goofy hypotheses, DeLillo deploys each as a mouthpiece for a movement in the history of mathematics since Mesopotamia, a movement from an ancient faith in the mystical spirituality of numbers, to a post-Enlightenment conviction in the reliability of numbers and science to parse the world into an inevitable clarity, to, finally, an anxious struggle in a post-Einstein cosmos deformed by the unsettling imprecision of uncertainty and relativity.[23] DeLillo's readers recognize this dilemma. It has haunted DeLillo's novels to date. Because, over the centuries, mathematics lost its ability to manage inexactness, it can now offer (like advertising, film, sports, and nuclear war games) only a theoretical environment radically divorced from the ongoing operations of the immediate, consoling our deepest fears by projecting a privileged model-universe in harmony with reason despite the evidence of mayhem and indeterminacy we experience firsthand every day. Part 1 also introduces Billy's pioneering work in theoretical mathematics, his creation of two entities—the twillig nilpotent and the stellated twilligon—whose severe beauty and deft form are by his own admission useless. Rather, they reveal the power of Billy's intellect to impose design on the free-flowing chaos around him. Contemporary science, as DeLillo satirizes here, drains the natural world of its spontaneity, its contradictions, and dismisses mystery as a glitch in the works, a temporary loss of signal. Science, DeLillo cautions, exploits the fragile mystery of the immediate into a commodity, a product to possess, neatly defined and tamed—to underscore the parallels between science and market economics, DeLillo introduces an absurd subplot in which the shadowy cartel that owns the think tank attempts to corner the world market of bat guano.

These bizarre scientific projects, however, are interspersed with recollections of Billy's decidedly unspectacular childhood spent (like DeLillo's) in an ordinary Bronx neighborhood, a paradoxical grief-world at once defined by the stunning intrusion of random violence (street shootings and bar brawls) yet oppressed by numbing banality, compelled by the harsh unpredictability of contingency yet sustained by dreary predictability (his mother regularly defrosting the refrigerator with pots of boiling water; his father, puffing an ever-present Camel and nursing a Champale, watching baseball and forever adjusting the television; ritual summer trips to Long Island beaches and endless dreary bus rides to school). Billy recalls a neighbor who, after undergoing a hysterectomy, spends long nights screaming in her darkened apartment, its walls scribbled with her anguished thoughts in black wax, but he recalls as well the giddy urgency he felt when he glimpsed rapid stunning bolts of summer lightning. What do we do, DeLillo queries, when science cannot provide solution, when it must confront the yin-yang world it pretends to measure?

In part 1, DeLillo offers two dead-end responses: anxious frustration and fuzzy mysticism. Henrik Endor, the master mathematician initially brought in to decode the message from Ratner's star, could not crack the coded sequence. His faith in science badly shaken, he retreats to a twelve-foot hole that he digs himself where he drinks rainwater and eats grubs and roots (a grossly literal return to the earth). He cautions Billy that science is, finally, not fact at all but rather faith in its own suasive argument. Its neatness leads the uninformed to reject the evidence of their own senses, a measure of the depth of the need for the universe to answer to order ("There is *want* at the center of the earth" [87]). He warns Billy darkly (and correctly, as it turns out) that the message from Ratner's star, once decoded from deep space, will—like all science—only reveal ourselves to us. The other response is far more mystical. When Billy is given the opportunity to meet Shazar Lazarus Ratner himself, an ancient desiccated wreck of a man kept alive within a protective bio-membrane by a battery of specialists, he offers Billy a cosmic vision that preserves the magic of an unknowable universe, a vision that recalls the writings of Pythagoras himself. Numbers, he whispers to Billy, possess ultimately unfathomable spiritual harmonics (he tells Billy of his own mystical illumination while scoping the stars one night in Pittsburgh); although study of them can surely offer limited illumination of reassuring order within the physical universe, numbers ultimately promise a decidedly metaphysical vision of a unity far in excess of our puny abilities to comprehend. In short, numbers give to the cosmos what the Judeo-Christian God does: manifest form independent of our clear understanding of it. As post-Newtonian mathematics lost such spiritual sensibility, indeed dismissed it as embarrassing mumbo jumbo, it willingly narrowed itself to the dead-end thinking that smugly redefined mystery, with its implication of vulnerability and uncertainty, as merely the first stage of inevitable solution, and that has led inevitably to the grand silliness of the think tank. The universe is solvable? To quote Billy's mother, "K.b.i.s.f.b." ("Keep believing it, shit-for-brains"). Yet its compelling logic and attractive tidiness have made disappointing, inevitably, any turn to the world simply as it is.

To compel Billy back to the mystery of the immediate is the work of part 2. As part 2 opens, Billy is escorted through an emergency exit by his project mentor, Robert Softly, and is taken below ground, into a secret antrum where he is introduced to the larger (and grandly mad) covert mission of the think tank: a hand-picked team of specialists at work around the clock to create a pure language system, code-named Logicon, based on mathematical symbols and radio pulses, a self-referential language system purified of content that would factor out the clumsy imprecision of words and would permit clean communication via radio signals with rational beings anywhere in the universe. Clearly DeLillo, as the text's authority, would have a vested interest in undercutting a project so elaborately determined to purify language of its nuance and thus its ability to record the splendid chaos and intoxicating ambiguities of experience—and, not surprisingly, much of part 2 reveals the absurdity of the Logicon project.[24] Its coordinator, the decidedly seedy Softly, despite his massive intelligence, maintains an uneasy rapprochement with the body: he is a genetic mishap (a dwarf), ingests fists of pharmaceuticals to maintain his energy level, struggles with bouts of depression, and relishes the sexual encounters with Jean Venable, a writer in residence gathering materials for a book on the secret project. One by one, the Nobel laureates Softly has summoned to serve on this dream team confront indeterminacy, tap the difficult lure of mystery, the grief-world, and along the way (as suggested by the section's underground setting) reveal probing psychologies (unlike the cartoons of part 1). Furthermore, each in turn comes to be impressed by the nuances of animated matter, an appreciation that patently rejects Logicon's premise of tidy solution. For instance, Jean Venable, suffering writer's block, abandons the premise of objectivity implied by nonfiction and opts to pursue her history of Logicon by deploying the more pliable realities of fiction; communication theorist Edna Lown ponders the levels of nuance implicit in the simplest words, and further, using children and their gradual discovery of language as a model, hypothesizes on words as bridges to realize the rich pull of others; Maurice Wu, archaeologist-spelunker who, digging in caves for artifacts of ancient civilizations, discovers, in a significant reversal of accepted historical understanding, that the deeper he digs the more sophisticated the artifacts become, is momentarily trapped in the absolute dark of a cave, but he stays calm and even laughs amid the structureless dark and the wild chaotic flight of exiting bats; Billy himself is fascinated by the voyeuristic opportunities to observe Softly and Venable make love, the torrid pitch of their physical friction, itself structureless and spontaneous, ultimately short-circuiting their speech into hot babbling. Clearly, each scientist feels the compelling pull of disorder and mystery, not the reach but rather the limits of the mind.

More to the point, part 2 celebrates chaos and, indeed, reveals apparent chaos is more an unsuspected cooperative, its subtle organization perhaps more difficult to access but nevertheless authentic and active. For instance, within the narrative cool of part 1, the omniscient narrator-authority moves discreetly and without comment from one absurd project to another. Such tidiness is wildly violated in part 2. The reader shuffles without evident patterning among the consciousnesses of the Logicon's members, at times shifting characters paragraph to paragraph, a collective narration, a choral consciousness as apparent chaos coheres into reasonable plot. Part 2 is even divided into episodes, each fragment sectioned off by an intrusive boldfaced heading—again, fragments that nevertheless cohere. Those headings further introduce a first-person intimacy, coaxing the reader to accept Billy as a sympathetic narrative center. DeLillo here is about the business of joining, making the connection (Billy even receives a chain letter). Indeed, the team must cooperate to decode the message from Ratner's star. Unlike part 1, in which DeLillo underscores the isolation of each scientist-projector furiously at work within the dubious logic of individual crackpot theories, here the team works together, each contributing toward the eventual translation of the cryptic message from Ratner's star: a message, it turns out, from an ancient and hitherto unknown advanced civilization on Earth itself, a message that was trapped within the closed corridors of curved, relative space (termed Moholean relativity) and that has boomeranged back to its home planet thousands of years later, a message that, as Billy comes to decipher it, is actually a time (28 minutes and 57 seconds after 2 P.M.) that coincides with a spectacular—but unscheduled—solar eclipse (a "noncognate celestial anomaly" [434]), which panics the smug think-tank eggheads as they must accept the obvious limits of their ability to understand the universe into predictability. Although there is no danger from the eclipse (save from the implications of its unpredictability), Softly literally flees in the face of such terrifying vulnerability (suggested by the approaching swatch of darkness cast by the eclipse) and, miles from the think tank, wedges himself into Henrik Endor's hole, digging past Endor's worm-infested corpse.

In the five dramatic pages that recount the slow sweep of the eclipse across the belly of central Asia, DeLillo at last opens the claustrophobic text to the very material world that mathematics so casually dismisses. The set piece boldly deploys a second-person "you," defying the artificial parameters of time and space by addressing the Ratnerians themselves. It is, in short, a message sent back. With the stunning lyrical florescence, this magisterial account of the furious busyness of the quarter-slice of the planet shadowed by the eclipse's moving arc reveals in random images a world of plenitude and scale and a species as much soul as body, a grief-world both oppressively physical (the impoverished struggle for sustenance in the streets; children die of cholera in the gutter; bowed women slush across rice fields) and defiantly spiritual (children cavort in the exhilarating suddenness of night-in-day; couples romance in spontaneous intimacy; holy men in ashrams and students in the cities struggle with the implications of the cosmic surprise). Defying the hare-brained premise of the Logicon project, here language stirs with a tonic, incantatory suggestiveness that manipulates nuance and detail, the prose line suddenly shaken up with sinewy catalogs, sensual and vivid, in sentences suddenly alert with color and sound, heat and depth, with images paradoxically both precise and evocative. It is an exuberant sort of ad-lib, a single, unbroken five-page paragraph bursting with animation. As in the peroration of *Great Jones Street,* Bucky's looping Manhattan walk, DeLillo here recovers the street-real: the evident chaos of the passage defies easy patternings but recovers a sense, nevertheless, of loose and unforced structure, delights in its grasping reach, its pulsing appetite, and the paradox of its shattering sense of ordered chaos—particle bits ultimately resolving into a grand system, much like the natural world that has always thrived just beyond the frame of scientific inquiry and the fragile play-models of human structures.

Into such rich uncertainty and excessive mystery rides young Billy, identified now only as the boy (rendered generic, always a promising position for DeLillo— the trick, of course, being to elevate rather than denigrate such a position). Billy has been exposed, but has he been educated? Robbed of his dispassionate scientific demeanor and privileged intellect, Billy is in flight from the think tank and furiously pedaling a tricycle (a mode of transportation suggesting his awkward in-betweenness) just ahead of the band of approaching daytime darkness, thus poised uneasily between threatening light and approaching dark. He is trying to ring the bike's tinny bell, a gesture that suggests both childlike exuberance and apocalyptic panic. But, as he pedals, whatever sound the bell makes is lost in the noise Billy himself makes, which, unlike his polished in-field discourse with his think-tank colleagues and his bitingly witty conversations in part 1, is unformed, unstructured, and spontaneous, suspended between joy and terror. DeLillo coins a term for Billy's reaction—a "zorgasm," entwining mind and body, the abstract mathematical symbol (the zorg) with the rinsing (and sweetly terrifying) vulnerability of the orgasm. Billy thus closes the narrative uncertainly, chooses grief, compelled to live in the very randomness that mathematics has so long kept at bay, a man-child reclaiming, with mixed emotions, the middest, that promising geography which has offered characters in DeLillo's first novels the difficult consolation of engagement, the fear and awe of a world whose beauty is as much fact as mystery.

In these first novels, then, DeLillo renders, indeed embraces a world that without an intrusive deity manages a grace entangled with violence, a world whose every vibrant form is ringed in death and whose exuberance and renewal, mystery and struggle resist the rigid translation implied by science. In the face of sheer irrationality, stunned by the intervention of surprise, Billy on the tricycle flees—much like the three centering characters of DeLillo's other early narratives, who each in turn concede to the attractive stillness of emotional paralysis, each committing a sort of suicide in self-defense, in gestures of flight that promise only dead-end isolation and anxiety. With characters thus unable to handle the manifest mystery of the immediate, unwilling to choose grief, the participatory reader, then, is ultimately sent the message from *Ratner's Star*, to defy the suasive frame-worlds of what DeLillo's first fictions have cataloged—be it television, commercials, film, athletic contests, political propaganda, science, religion, or even narrative itself—and to engage the difficult implications of unpredictability. In short, to choose grief.

2

Narratives of Failed Engagement

Players (1977)

Appropriately DeLillo's next novel begins literally in flight—specifically, in a piano lounge on some generic airplane. Seven nameless characters, without emotional coloring and only the barest physical detailing, gather about the piano to watch, without headphones, the in-flight movie. One passenger, settled at the piano, provides an impromptu accompaniment using familiar quotations from silent-movie comedy scores. In the film, a nondescript suburban golf outing on a bucolic morning is shockingly—and inexplicably—interrupted by gun-toting hippie-styled terrorists who shoot the helpless golfers and then hack them to death with machetes. Such gore, filmed in stylized slow motion, is considerably lightened, however, by the incongruous ad-lib piano accompaniment. The passengers find themselves laughing and even cheering the attackers, evidence, the narrative voice-over intones, of the "glamour of revolutionary violence,"[1] that is, violence observed from a safe distance. As the plane descends, the passengers drift from the film and prepare to resume their everyday lives, the very movement toward engagement that DeLillo characters have, to date, avoided.

Thus the prologue to *Players* ends. It is a set piece (indeed, a version of it first appeared back in 1970 as the short story "The Uniforms"), a pure act of fiction absent of logical plot, enticing suspense, character motivation, reader sympathy, theme, or moral dimension.[2] It takes place in a contrived aesthetic vacuum, separated from the narrative proper; it is unavoidably an artifice. We are insulated from the movie's graphic and senseless violence—we simply watch people watching. Indeed, only after a second read do we suspect (assume?) that these seven nameless passengers might, in fact, be the seven principal characters in the novel that follows, although how they ended up on the same flight is never explained, nor how this in-flight moment impacts the narrative. Thus the question is why, given the uncharacteristically heavy-handed plotting of DeLillo's fifth novel (we will track both a terrorist plot to detonate a bomb in Manhattan's financial district and a wrenching drama of a bisexual, just turning thirty, trapped between sexual identities who, in the end, destroys himself in a horrific act of immolation), why begin so deliberately suspended from action, so remote from characters within a lexical contrivance as obvious as the prologue? Why deny us entrance into the welcoming pleasure prison of this narrative?

Coming after the intricate enclosure of *Ratner's Star,* DeLillo clearly wants us out of this narrative. Coming off a work that rewarded retreat into its complexity, DeLillo offers a counterwork that keeps us distant—ironic, of course, given a narrative in which the two principal characters attempt what characters thus far in DeLillo's work have avoided: engaging the untidy realities of the freewheeling world they cannot control or contain. The narrative movement here is distinctly centrifugal. Thus far, characters, unaware of their own insufficiencies, have opted to retreat in a strategy manifestly unsanctioned by DeLillo-as-authority. Thus, wisdom rests outside those texts; whatever epiphanies they generate are clearly reserved for the reader. Characters in DeLillo's next two works, however, are not so savaged by irony; they struggle with the awareness of their own insufficiency; they are the contemporary wounded, the damaged souls of the late twentieth century, the inevitable product of the media-culture DeLillo scathingly critiques in his first four novels, characters who seek reclamation by rejecting the security of insulated private worlds and by daring forth into the same world that so compelled anxiety in DeLillo's first novels that it appeared to sanction self-destructive gestures of retreat.

Lyle and Pammy Wynant, the upscale Manhattan couple whose braided stories form the narrative line of *Players,* are certainly familiar to DeLillo readers. Bored, sustained by the rituals of professional success in a calculated retreat from the implications of vulnerability, imprisoned within a self-constructed lifestyle premised on the unacknowledged terror of unpredictability, addicted to the simplicity of artificially imposed order and the security of apartness, Lyle and Pammy live insulated from the real—suggested by his work on *Wall* Street and by her office in the massive enclosure of the World Trade Center north tower. Not surprisingly, DeLillo keeps us distanced from Lyle and Pammy: neither character is given any history or complicating emotional nuance—each stays a fetching surface, essentially contextless, a series of intriguing reactions within the narrative present, kept within the same sort of long-lens shot that records the prologue. Unlike previous DeLillo characters, however, Lyle and Pammy both come to sense their insufficiency, their detachment from life, and both will plot (disastrously, it turns out) to test disorder, to choose grief and to risk engagement in strategies that ultimately will give them the titillating thrill of mock passion (the shrugging indifference of their commitment is suggested by their last name—why not?), the shallow chance simply to play at the rich disorder of the unmediated immediate, a sorry charade that will leave them at narrative's end exploited, isolated, and abandoned.

Typical of DeLillo's characters thus far, Lyle Wynant, a successful stockbroker, is sustained by faith in an entirely artificial order, specifically the international financial markets that his brokerage firm monitors.[3] The continuous computer spew of teleprinter impulses, stock codes, and market prices ("the machine's coded model of exactitude" [70]) tidies the harsh realities of carnivorous capitalism that are inevitable, given the wildly uneven distribution of wealth—daily, Lyle passes indifferently among the indigent street people, the outcast victims of that same system, and in particular a protestor, past seventy, whose detailed placard, which he has tirelessly hoisted for seventeen years, actually enumerates historic crimes against the poor. That victimization, the passion and anger of capitalism's misbegotten, means no more to Lyle than the sweltering summer heat from which he seeks sanctuarial comfort on the floor of the Stock Exchange. A friend of his, a banker whose wife is struggling with a cancer diagnosis and who now sees "death masks" everywhere (23), cautions Lyle about that grief-world "outside," where "things" happen and "you're helpless" (65). But not so with Lyle. His life has settled into a programmed tidiness and a useful predictability—each night, he methodically separates his coins from his subway tokens and then stacks them according to denomination; he relishes the clean transaction of settling monthly bills; he "services" his wife without complicating passion (*he* uses that verb, even placing it within quotes); to entertain coworkers, he parrots routines memorized from popular comedy albums; he nightly surfs the television with the sound off, relishing the random shuffle of images, unable to muster sufficient commitment to a single program and dreading that hushed moment when he must turn it off; he dispassionately observes his own nose bleeding, intrigued by the color and sheen of the red; he memorizes passing license plates as part of a fantasy of being interrogated as a witness to a nonexistent crime; he shaves symmetrically, carefully controlling the distribution of lather; during the day, he repeatedly inventories his pockets. When he talks with Pammy in their apartment, their conversation creates a similarly intimate, privately controlled sphere with an original (and to the reader potentially annoying) patois of refurbished clichés, ethnic dialects and exaggerated accents, mock-baby chatter, bits of advertising slogans, and reinvented pronunciations. In short, Lyle cultivates a self apart ("a space between himself and most of the people he was likely to deal with in the course of daily events" [72]), ignores its inauthenticity, and relishes the perceived autonomy.

In alternating sections in each chapter of part 1, we likewise follow Pammy engaged in a similar life strategy of control and withdrawal. She blandly admits that she "hates her life" but that her unhappiness is a "minor thing . . . a small bother" (32). Thus, she contains/controls what for most would be a considerable anxiety.[4] After all, however, Pammy is a grief-management counselor (recall the Faulkner quote!). She spends her work days mollifying authentic expressions of grief by offering her clients sensible platitudes in a sensibly illustrated brochure that she is proud to have written (a "classic of dispassion and tact" [63]). Like earlier DeLillo characters, Pammy is at once intrigued and terrified by the implications of the manifestly imperfect body (she literally blocks her ears to avoid listening to a television interview with a man who stutters). She is repulsed by the press of the earthy and sensual. Her office on the seventy-eighth floor positions her safely above the complicated and unmanaged rush and push of street life, which she fears each evening when she must engage its oceanic seething; she is made anxious by the pull of crowds, discomfited by the awareness of bank security cameras tracking her; when she glimpses a man exposing himself in his car, she is horrified, violated by the man's carnality and by being implicated in the act as unwitting voyeur; Pammy disparages her own body (particularly her squarish jawline) but is quickly bored with the merest exertion of exercise; she is put off by talk of mucus and phlegm; she fears death (a passing headache in the shower, she is certain, is a metastasizing tumor); her marriage long settled into dinners of soup packets and nights of television, she is content with the routine frictions that pass for love-making. Her characteristic response to virtually every situation is a slow-drawn yawn—indeed, she continues eating in a restaurant even as a basement fire seeps smoke into the dining area. She is a control freak, distanced from her own body, fearing its unsponsored compulsions, its vulnerability to disease, its obvious structural imperfections, its unpredictable itch and pull, and its inevitable sorry concession to death. When she does decide to "unleash" her body, to sample the energy and force of the earthy and sensual, it is tellingly superficial: she buys bags full of fresh fruit at sidewalk stands or goes to her tap classes (where her body movements, of course, are tightly timed and scripted).

Then, within hours of each other, both Wynants are unexpectedly given the opportunity to touch authenticity, to engage the vulnerability of the immediate. When a colleague Lyle barely knows is gunned down on the Exchange floor in what is apparently a terrorist attack, Lyle suddenly glimpses the unbearable slightness of his being. He begins to suspect its very premise, feels inexplicably strangled within its logic. He is suddenly curious to engage genuine passion. Predictably, he indulges a standard office affair with a secretary, Rosemary Moore, whose intriguing physical presence momentarily stirs him—he compares her aura of deep loneliness to a figure in an Edward Hopper painting. The comparison proves telling as, despite the affair that tediously ensues, the two stay distanced from each other and from the complexity of authentic passion in a sort of staged play of adultery that follows with predictability the dreary routine from casual desk chat to impromptu lunches to after-work drinks and then, inevitably, to her apartment and to bed. Moore, in this case, is less. Devoid of emotional depth, their sex is predictably less than incendiary—Lyle is too caught up in his own performance and in his own embroidered fantasies drawn heavily from the cable porn he watches to care that Rosemary is left unsatisfied.

However, while at her apartment, Lyle chances to see pinned to a kitchen corkboard a photograph that shows Rosemary with the man killed in the Exchange attack along with a man who, it turns out, is the assailant himself. Pricked by the sudden implication of secrecy, Lyle inquires about the photo and will come to learn about a shadowy cell of urban terrorists bent on disrupting the world financial systems by detonating an explosive on the floor of the richly symbolic New York Stock Exchange itself. Lyle is intrigued by such a provocative guerrilla act, by its bold disorder and unsettling energy. But, even as he moves into the clandestine world, even as he is actually shown their considerable cache of weapons, he cannot conjure the intensity of conviction such an agenda demands. So, unable to be a real terrorist, like Godard's Michel, he will play one. Unable to choose grief, he will dabble in it. As he becomes involved with the underground ring, he will meet two characters who will set his shabby performance in hard relief. He first meets Marina Vilar, the beautiful sister of the dead terrorist, whose unapologetic commitment to mayhem and violence fascinates him. He next meets the mysterious, elusive J. Kinnear, the organization's master strategist, a man endlessly on the move, a philosopher who embodies the cunning cerebral passion of the revolutionary, maintaining a scrupulous middle position as a double agent, relentlessly theorizing (long ago, he taught speech at a junior college) about both the persistence and the vast organization of government evil and the ambiguity and disinformation necessary with any guerrilla underground. The paranoia of conspiracy structures his radical agenda (including his hints of involvement with the Kennedy assassination) and, in turn, demands that he not trust anyone entirely.

What Lyle discovers amid these terrorists, however, is not horror over the brutality of their intended mission or uneasiness over the murky uncertainties within their operations but rather what his drifting Wall Street existence so desperately lacks: meaning, direction, plot, structure. He decides to help arrange the second bombing attempt, but intrigued by the sheer play of plotting and unburdened by conscience or principles, he also feeds information to an enigmatic figure he assumes is a government contact (although the man may be an agent of Kinnear himself, who suspects a rat in the works). When Lyle agrees to provide $3,500 to Kinnear—to fund the second bombing attempt, he assumes—he and Marina end up in bed, a gesture Lyle sees less as an erotic experience (although he is compelled by the spaciousness of her physical prowess) and more as a sort of quid pro quo, payment for his risk and his investment—in any event, so unconcerned is he with the agenda of such urban terrorists or with the well-being of his lover that when he leaves Marina's bed, he immediately phones his government contact and relays all the information on the planned bombing, including Marina's address.

Unaware of Lyle's betrayal (or perhaps aware of it, given how little we know of his resources), Kinnear tells Lyle by phone to head to Toronto and to await there further instructions. At a pre-assigned time and place in the Canadian town of Brantford, Lyle rendezvous with Rosemary. They head to the hotel Lyle has selected as hideout to await instructions that we suspect will not be forthcoming. The reality of his sorry exploitation is underscored when Rosemary emerges from the hotel bathroom with a strap-on dildo, ready to "do" Lyle in a chilling parody of lovemaking. Lyle's narrative closes in an epilogue titled "The Motel" in which Lyle, now voided into a generic namelessness, is still waiting two days later for the phone call—from either Kinnear or his government contacts (it really makes no difference to him). Suspended from authenticity, this newfound life, manifestly a thin charade, nevertheless entertains him. "We watch him stand by the bed" (210); DeLillo suddenly introduces a distancing frame, the intrusive first-person plural pronoun, which recalls the long-lens shot of the prologue. We now watch Lyle waiting. Structuring the emptiness, he studies the tidy street grids of the Toronto city map (drawn, as always, to imposed order) and playing children's counting games (drawn, as always, to arithmetical tidiness). As the narrative ends, the morning sun suffuses the hotel room with a "luminous cleansing," suggesting the intrusion of the real world, the act—not the play—of authentic engagement. Not surprisingly, Lyle blurs in effortless dissolve: "The proper figure . . . is barely recognizable as male. Shedding capabilities and traits by the second." And then we are summarily dismissed by the narrative voice-over with a curt, "We know nothing else about him" (212), leaving us no option save, like those passengers on the airplane in the prologue, to go about the business of reengaging the world we had temporarily departed to engage this narrative.[5]

Against Lyle's ineffectual mock-Bond performance, we follow in narrative counterpoise Pammy's similarly disastrous play at engagement. Pammy is asked to share a getaway north to the deep woods of Deer Isle, off coastal Maine, with Ethan and Jack, a gay couple with whom she works. Initially, Pammy too easily reacts to the tonic wildness of the woods in patently superficial gestures (much as Lyle does, first with his tacky office romance and then with the terrorists). Impulsively she cuts her hair, she stands bare-breasted on the cabin's deck, she picnics under the stars, she listens to the seductive scratch and thump of animals beneath the floorboards, she drinks each night until she is giddy, she scarfs junk food, she critiques every sunrise, she revels in the sheer space of the rented cabin (comparing it to her cramped apartment), she even looks into a mirror and decides her lantern jaw is just fine. Ultimately, that logic of indulging fetching surfaces and superficial gestures will extend to her seduction of Jack in a sun-drenched open field, an experience that begins as low-grade "pleasant sex between friends" (165) but escalates unexpectedly into a passionate moment in which Pammy feels unity not with Jack but with the earth and her own body (her orgasm comes in "long, tolling strokes" [168]). Like her husband among the political fanatics, she is not prepared to engage the intensities or the complication of others, the genuine grief of either her own adultery or of Jack, who has not only betrayed Ethan but must now confront deep-seated questions over his sexual identity.

Like Lyle, then, Pammy maintains (much as she does in the World Trade Center) a steadying distance between herself and the more passionate others all around her. Throughout the Maine interlude, Pammy studies the untamed landscape either with binoculars, which maintain distance while offering the illusion of nearness (like the telephone that defines Lyle's involvement with the terrorists), or through sunglasses (her eyes are scored with raccoon rings from wearing them), which protect from raw exposure. She apprehends Jack in a similar gesture, their apparent intimacy testifying to a paradoxical intimacy of distance (after all, through her binoculars, Pammy mistakes a frogman in the surf for a seal). Making love with Jack Laws is an extension of the uncomplicated bumper-sticker platitudes that have long run, unexamined, through her head: "Follow your instincts, be yourself, act out your fantasies" (143). Jack himself, unwilling, as his last name suggests, to accept the limits implied by societal labels, lacks the critical self-esteem necessary for such a courageous stand. As his lover Ethan says, Jack has always been made "to feel expendable," "adorable useless Jack" (173, 19). Jack is thus left to struggle alone within this agonizing drama of self-definition—like the terrorists Lyle engages, passion is no game for Jack. Ethan and Pammy both dismiss Jack's interior anguish much as they ignore his anxious certainty over his recurring UFO sightings in the night skies over the island. Indeed, the day following their open-field encounter, when Pammy entreats a confused Jack to just "fuck" her again and he asks poignantly, "Where will I be then?" (175), she completely ignores his evident distress. For Pammy, despite her engaging in the complicated passion of adultery, the body remains an uncomplicated mechanism: when she is chilly, she reaches for a sweater; when she is hungry, she eats; when she is horny, she fucks. In short, she plays at adultery. Jack's issues will fix themselves, she happily decides, even as she watches from a distance boys negotiating the contrived complications of a miniature golf course.

It is, of course, not so simple: before they return to the city, Jack immolates himself in a desperate gesture of self-loathing. Pammy cannot deal with the precarious pitch toward emotional depth. As she approaches the burned body, she feels the awkward press of some unnameable "it," a "steady pressuring subroar" that she fends off by concentrating on nearby mossy rocks (199). After departing the charred stump (she wonders offhand how Jack managed to maintain the cross-legged position given the horrific devouring by the flames) and after offering a devastated Ethan the noncomfort of some of her much-rehearsed grief-management platitudes, Pammy does what characters have done in DeLillo since David Bell: she retreats. She buses back to New York (death terrorizes the margins of her awareness: she notes the disturbing number of dead elms along the highway) and retreats to her apartment, where she watches television to obliterate the possibility of awareness (ironically, she finds herself crying while she watches the contrived sentimentality of a late-night 1950s family melodrama). Hungry for roast beef, she decides to venture out to the neighborhood all-night deli (simple problem / simple solution—indeed, as if to confirm her suspicion, everyone on the street appears to be eating). On the walk back, keeping at a distance the insistent, demanding beauty of the street life, in but not of the crowd, she pauses at a flophouse marquee that reads "TRANSIENTS": the word, so multilayered (along with its homonym, transience), at once terrifying and compelling to those who genuinely engage the reality of the everyday but reduced, for one so casually playing at life, to an abstract noise. As her narrative closes, Pammy plays with the word as an engrossing aural event, separating it into two drawn-out nonsense syllables that act as "language units that had mysteriously evaded the responsibilities of content" (207). Absently, she sounds it out, relishing its abstract tonal makeup (recall Lyle in the hotel room with his counting games). Only then, as we leave Pammy, does she even bother to begin recovering the word's meaning.[6]

Both Lyle and Pammy move outward, then, heroically departing their pseudo-lives of structured order, but lacking the heart necessary to realize such a complicated gesture—the appalling passion of terrorism, on the one hand, and the appalling passion of love, on the other—they are Godardesque players, foredoomed to exploit those they encounter and ultimately to render ironic their own potential heroism. They are thus left suspended, denied revelation, their narratives abruptly dropped in moments of nonclosure. Unlike the characters in DeLillo's narratives of retreat, Lyle and Pammy are left in between: they are now unwilling to retreat, have both come to feel the pull of involvement, the rich reward of engagement. One waits by the phone, the other shuffles through the teeming otherness of streetlife Manhattan. But ultimately lacking the ample generosity of heart, they cannot turn the trick of connection. They dabble in risk, they play at vulnerability, they experiment with connection, they tease mortality. DeLillo underscores this distancing by actually separating the two storylines in part 2, Lyle and Pammy no longer even sharing chapter space. Finally, their attempts to engage are inauthentic simplifications—suggested by the recurring prowl of trucks peddling Mister Softee frozen desserts, a convincing confection that imitates ice cream but without the hard-sharpness of the real dairy product. Like the call and response of jazz, *Players* responds to DeLillo's narratives of retreat by exploring the risks of engagement, tracking two characters unwilling, unable, uninterested in the complications that engagement inevitably brings, the messy implications of passion—terrorism and love both—offering a frightening vulnerability that neither Lyle nor Pammy is ready to accept.

Running Dog (1978), Amazons (1980), and
The Engineer of Moonlight (1979)

There is something haunted, even doomed, about the narrative space of *Running Dog*. Despite DeLillo's disingenuous assessment of it as "damned funny" (LeClair 83), *Running Dog* remains DeLillo's least affirmative text—it is an oppressive dead-end narrative without even the implication of a saving counterforce argument, no rallying epiphany, no larger wisdom, no authorial satire, a text in which, for the first time in DeLillo's career, the central character dies at the close—no refuge afforded, not even the cozy privilege of Lyle Wynant's sham performance-life. *Running Dog* begins and ends with murders, both victims mutilated by the primitive, graceless work of a knife, and both executions, as it turns out, committed for bogus reasons. It is the narrative momentum toward the execution of Howard Glen Selvy, however, that locks *Running Dog* within an oppressive inevitability; and that death comes from a simple misunderstanding, a glitch in an otherwise massively efficient government surveillance system.

Although Selvy's narrative death is a singular event in the DeLillo oeuvre thus far, his narrative life is all too familiar. Like David Bell, Selvy has appropriated a life-role to mask a Prufrockian vulnerability (at one point he even eats the telling peach); he is a perceived self, a sustained bricolage of performance-ideas borrowed from spy movies and westerns, a conceptual self that denies him the experience of authentic depth and emotion. A real-life intelligence agent and trained mole (unlike Lyle Wynant, who merely plays one), Selvy, like the marionette-halfback Gary Harkness, accepts orders without question. Like Harkness's football regimen, Selvy's training contains the terrifying energy of animal violence within a tight choreography that ultimately divides the universe simply, if grandly, into a gameworld of us versus them, clear good versus clear evil. Like Bucky Wunderlick, Selvy is detached—he maintains an unfurnished apartment stacked with still-unpacked cartons in an African American neighborhood in Washington; he sleeps only with married women to "maintain an edge of maneuverability"[7]—a strategy of retreat, isolation, and transience that wholly abandons the responsibilities of the immediate. Like Billy Twillig, Selvy fears vulnerability and is uncomfortable with the body's evident imperfections manifested in the act of sex and the intrusion of death (Selvy describes sex inelegantly as a "bang, bang, bang," and he traffics in death unemotionally—even when he is the target of a hail of gunfire in a bar, he methodically notes salient physical descriptions of his two assailants). And like Lyle Wynant, Selvy, his background context only grudgingly revealed, lives solely in the present, compelled entirely by a fiercely strict routine. Whereas Lyle's obsessive rituals were self-generated, Selvy, a career soldier, is more like a creepy animé-machine assembled by the military, pure function disciplined by an imposed system of Pavlovian behaviors and a clear sequence of set-reactions that eliminates the risk of spontaneity. For instance, early in the novel, when Selvy and his lover want to play tennis in Central Park, they find only volleyball courts available—trained not to negotiate with the unexpected, Selvy typically insists they play tennis anyway, high net and all. Clearly, Selvy is that inevitability forecast in DeLillo's fiction since David Bell: a commodity. Text to text, DeLillo's central characters have not so much evolved as devolved, relinquishing narrative to narrative their context, psychology, choice, and integration until we reach the absolute zero of Selvy, a rudimentary gesture of an individual with the apparent shape and animation of a person but who opts for the frictionless comfort of a dimensionless, depthless existence. Selvy engages the world, yes—he is, after all, a globetrotting government agent—but he moves within the closed, protective box of his government training; thus, his instincts are more behavioral patterns, automatic and predictable, and his apparent engagement is another DeLilloesque variation on retreat. Selvy is comfortable with a worldview revealed by his fondness for assembling one of his guns: machine-tooled parts precisely connecting into a clear whole. "Things fit" (82).

What compels the deathward spiral of Glen Selvy's narrative? Selvy accepts the seductive fantasy of certainty, an unshaded universe of black and white. He accepts the dangerous life of a double agent because long ago he embraced the attractive idea of order represented by its regimen and by the integrity (and fetching simplicity) of its Manichean cold-war worldview. Selvy maintains that loyalty even after the clandestine outfit for which he works, Radial Matrix, splits off in the wake of the Vietnam debacle into unsanctioned covert operations under the direction of a Kurtz-like Korean War Air Force veteran named Earl Mudger. A special-operations advisor in Vietnam who came to control a massive network of black-market activities before the fall of Saigon, the dangerously eccentric Mudger (his legend in Vietnam included stories of a vast exotic zoo maintained deep in the jungle) now oversees, from his farm in northern Virginia, Radial Matrix's shadowy (and very successful) terrorist operations directed against countries whose political doctrines run contrary to American interests. Like David Bell's father or Harkness's coach or the terrorist J. Kinnear, Mudger centers his novel, a control freak whose sangfroid enables him to sustain the illusion of order via both the brute application of force and the charisma of his personality. That model-world denies the shading, the audacious eccentricity of paradox that, since *Americana*, DeLillo has counterargued is the very essence of the late-twentieth-century world. In his spare time, Mudger works on an invention: a small machine able to test not the hardness of steel (such machines, he indicates, already exist) but more its very physical content by use of a diamond tip "penetrator" that he has designed, indicating his belief in the ultimate knowability of the most impenetrable, unyielding surfaces. Inadvertently running afoul of Mudger's ordered network of interests, violating the tidy black-and-white assumptions of his private empire by introducing the inelegant shock of surprise, will doom Selvy.

That movement begins, oddly enough, with a thirty-year-old black-and-white home movie, a film that no one has ever actually watched. Within DeLillo's larger emphasis on centrifugal movement and engagement, *Running Dog* can be read as a quest narrative, a narrative of engagement that, naturally, skews the fundamental assumptions of the genre.[8] Traditionally in the genre, an obsessive, isolated central hero tracks a sacramental (and mysteriously attractive) grail-object and in the process contends with an often accidental conspiracy of superior (and generally malignant) forces and is ultimately rewarded, if not with the object itself, then with an enlarged sensibility, a grander awareness. If the hero's death ends such a quest (and most often it does), the reader recognizes that, in death, the hero has ennobled the human experience itself by illuminating the magnificent possibility of selfless, transcendent behavior. In *Running Dog,* however, there are no such heroics, no such spiritual vitality. What compels the quest that dooms Selvy is a tawdry pornographic home movie filmed, according to black-market buzz, in the final hours of Hitler's Third Reich in his bunker beneath the Reich Chancellery, an amateur film that promises grainy scenes of titillating debauchery to the plethora of agents vying for its possession. That group includes a prissy Manhattan art dealer with a trendy Soho porn gallery called Cosmic Erotics; a prominent United States senator with an extensive private pornography collection housed in a secret room behind the fireplace of his swanky Rock Creek residence; both the Mafia itself and a Mafia-like enterprise that controls a tentacled smut empire that reaches from Dallas to Toronto; and even Radial Matrix, which sees in pornography a promising opportunity to diversify into a lucrative new domestic enterprise.

Selvy is initially entangled in this quest for the film because of his role as a double agent: a junior administrative aide on the senator's staff, Selvy serves unofficially as buyer for the senator's smut collection while, as an agent for Radial Matrix, he is as well gathering potentially damaging dirt on the senator to head off the senator's much-ballyhooed public investigation into Radial Matrix's funding. During a visit to the Cosmic Erotics gallery auction, Selvy meets Moll Robbins, an investigative reporter researching an article on the porn industry for *Running Dog,* a left-wing underground newspaper known for the sort of conspiracy theorizing that panders to the connect-the-dots paranoia of the cold war. Moll, as part of a rebellion against her wealthy conservative upbringing, has come to indulge, as her first name suggests, a string of bad-boy lovers (including seven months on the lam with an infamous countercultural bomber-terrorist in the heyday of the '60s) and, of course, immediately finds the mysterious Selvy irresistible. Like Godard's Michel and Patricia, they quickly commence a sexual relationship—it stretches the definition to call it love, but the sex is compelling with an "element of resolve and fixed purpose" (35)—an involvement that violates Selvy's long-held code of relationships (Moll is not married) and thus marks a significant jolt from his protective routine.

He is quickly given a second jolt when his own outfit, Radial Matrix, puts out a hit on him. After Christoph Ludecke, the Holocaust survivor who actually owns the sole copy of the Hitler film, is knifed in a shadowy neighborhood of New York when he attempts to rendezvous with an unnamed buyer representing Radial Matrix (to protect his identity Ludecke is dressed as a woman), Selvy is sent by Mudger to negotiate with the widow. At her home, Selvy, trained to sweep any room for listening devices, uses a compact detector clipped to his belt to locate a hidden bug and, without thinking, disengages it. It is, he finds out later, a bug planted by Radial Matrix itself—and his unanticipated disabling of it raises unsettling questions within the organization's hierarchy about his loyalty (as does his ongoing affair with an investigative reporter), and he is made the object of an "adjustment," paramilitary parlance for assassination. Despite a long association with Selvy, Mudger himself dispassionately orders a two-man Vietnamese hit squad to eliminate Selvy. Trained to be loyal, however, and thus unwilling to tangle with the complications implicit in questioning his superiors, Selvy never challenges that decision even when given a chance by Mudger's flunky to explain why he disabled the bug. Following one failed hit in the early-morning hours in a nearly deserted Manhattan bar (after Selvy and Moll had attended a showing of Charlie Chaplin's *The Great Dictator* at an artsy theater), Selvy simply abandons Moll and, a step ahead of the hit squad, heads west in the company of a teenager actress/prostitute named Nadine Rademacher, whom he "rescues" from a Times Square porn theater with the promise to return her to her impoverished family in rural Arkansas.

It would appear that Selvy is breaking free of his routine, violating its programmed efficiency and engaging the freewheeling world in an ad-lib sort of improvisation that no character in the DeLillo canon had as yet even approached. He is, it would appear, choosing grief, and that with a vengeance. But it is not the case. Along the way, as Nadine studies Selvy's features by a hotel reading lamp, Selvy claims that he is actually Native American and that his given name is Running Dog. Although the outlandish appropriation plays to his fondness for the dignity of Native Americans in Hollywood westerns (after the shootout in the bar, the media dubs him "The Gunslinger")—and perhaps the name is meant to convey to Nadine his determination and his road savvy—the name suggests to the reader both a scared sense of retreat in the face of complexities as well as an unflattering sort of blind Pavlovian obedience (after all, in addition to several scenes involving leashed and trained dogs, Mudger's flunky drives about Washington in a limo accompanied by a brace of his trained St. Bernards who perpetually need to be run).[9] Indeed, with the blinded, homing instincts of a trained animal, Selvy is heading to a recently closed training facility in Texas, known as Marathon Mines, where he was long ago indoctrinated into the simplified universe of recognizable good and identifiable evil so seriously muddied by the clear evidence of his own outfit trying to kill him. Selvy is simply going home, specifically to the protective womblike space where the world made sense. In doing so, Selvy is curving his life to the tight arc of elected death. He will die like a soldier, as his training long ago had defined: "[That training] was a course in dying. In how to die violently. In how to be killed by your own side, in secret, no hard feelings" (183). Choice, he sees, is a "subtle form of disease" (192). Thus, as DeLillo told LeClair, the run to Texas is a "ritual suicide" (83), such a predictable move that the hit squad has no trouble tracking him, culminating in Selvy's execution and subsequent beheading, the agent certain, as he shoves Selvy's head in a duffel bag, that Mudger will want proof of Selvy's "adjustment."

So much for the heroic, transcendent death of the questing hero. Levi Blackwater, a Vietnam comrade of Selvy's who still lives in the abandoned training facility and who, after enduring months of torture and isolation as a POW, is now something of a "gringo mystic" (232), wants to comply with Selvy's frequent request by giving the body a traditional Native American "air burial": elevating the corpse on a wooden platform and thus offering it to the desert's predatory birds, thereby achieving a sort of ennobling transcendence, a symbolic reenactment of the spirit being released from the body. The effort fails: the ritual itself requires a strand of Selvy's hair, and his head is on its way to Virginia. And even the grail object itself disappoints: far from the anticipated S/M orgy, the black-market film (its private screening at Cosmic Erotics is related in the closing pages in contrapuntal quickcuts against Selvy's desert decapitation) shows a feeble Hitler, the twentieth century's defining monster, playing desperate clown for needful innocents, self-consciously pantomiming Chaplin's performance of him in The Great Dictator, cavorting, despite a sickly gait and palsied hands, for the delight of some Nazi children who will be compelled within hours, along with their parents, to take poison.

Pornography. Government intelligence. Paramilitary training. Organized crime. Communism. The cold war. Investigative journalism. Assassination squads. Nazism. The Holocaust. Jungle zoos. DeLillo introduces an overwhelming matrix of metaphoric structures that each testifies to a familiar DeLillo dilemma: the retreat from complexity, a Manichean either/or worldview that discourages speculation and accepts the concept of definition itself as unironic, embraces simplification and the commitment to clarity, specifically the arbitrary conjuring of an intricate but entirely fragile system of perception, a trapping environment of surfaces that frames a manageable, unshadowed model-world—and in turn reduces the self to a knowable commodity and dismisses as irrelevant even the premise of authenticity, specifically the freewheeling impulses of carnality and the inevitable intrusion of mortality. "I believe in codes," Selvy testifies early on (33).[10] Such design-perceptions collide with an entangling yin-yang world of Selvy's experience, a world of monster/clowns, victim/killers, and noble/fools. There are tenuous gestures toward engaging such a vibrant and contradictory immediate: Moll Robbins unexpectedly turns down the crude advances of the blue-eyed Earl Mudger, the very sort of uncomplicated, charismatic bad boy she had her whole adult life found irresistible, and she departs alone in the rain from their cab circling Central Park, breaking, as it were, the closed loop of her own habit; Nadine Rademacher, the porn actress / prostitute Selvy befriends, offers him a physical love that, despite her profession, is, for him, "wholesome and sweet," a love that suggests "healthiness" (182) and the possibility of the redemptive (underscored by a bracing river dip that Nadine invites Selvy to take the morning after they make love at her Arkansas farm); and Levi Blackwater engages Selvy briefly in a conversation before Selvy goes off to embrace a death that Blackwater cautions him is, finally, too easy, the sort of death that will disappoint, even as he counsels Selvy that living is far more difficult, an unending process without comforting truth, and that every person must be prepared to be reborn at every moment. Each slender presence, suggesting the difficulty in engaging the mystery of complexity, is dead-ended here—Moll is deeply depressed after departing the cab; Selvy finds Nadine's love unappealing and refuses her offer for a morning swim, staying dressed and on the shore; and Blackwater's intriguing advice is entirely unheeded as Selvy too intently watches the helicopter bearing the hit squad begin its whirring descent. Simplification here is simply too enticing.[11] There are, however, two striking narrative moments when Selvy confronts an unexpected Eastern presence, the sensibility that has, since *Americana,* posed a counterforce model-strategy for engaging complexity and mystery. Early on, while Selvy is being driven through a Washington park in one of Mudger's limos, he glimpses eight young Asians practicing in sync the slow motion of tai chi. Amid the park's graceless chaos, Selvy compares the stylized, fluid movement to branches adjusting to a sudden breeze, suggesting the grace necessary in the give-and-take of engagement. Later, after leaving his car in Arkansas as a farewell gift to Nadine, Selvy shares the bus bound for Texas with nine sleeping Japanese tourists, whose inscrutable calm amid the noise and commotion of other touristy types on the bus registers with Selvy: their "apartness," their "challenging sense of calm" (187). Such adjustment strategy is ultimately unavailable to a character who, tested by surprise, is unwilling, finally, to accept the risk of vulnerability.

And so we watch Selvy die. The fast approach of the particularly gruesome execution of a central character should play into the readerly inclination to identify with a doomed character, should generously complicate the reading experience by compelling sympathy. But such is not the case. DeLillo manipulates the reader into the identical position of distance and insulation that defines (and plagues) his characters. We are maneuvered—for what will prove to be the last time in DeLillo

—into the position of voyeur, suspended with Godardesque discretion between amusement and detachment. The novel, of course, begins in a considerably different tenor. It opens, uncharacteristically for DeLillo, in the compelling intimacy and unmediated subjectivity of the second person—"you" are thrown into the jolting immediacy of an unspecified panic; "you" are moving through the forbidding nightworld streets of a nameless city's rundown waterfront. "You" are dropped into the edgy intimacy of unfolding experience—enveloped by a literal and metaphoric darkness, uncertain of where "you" are going or why, only that "you" are hurrying and that "you" feel the disconcerting adrenaline rush of fear (a "dark elation" that triggers, inexplicably, a veiled reference to the Holocaust and, oddly, to lipstick and nylons [4]). "You" are thus positioned exactly where Selvy (and every character since David Bell) fears to be: within the hot vulnerability of the street-world, a promising uncertainty, fearful and yet thrilled by such enticing complication.

That promising intimacy, of course, is abruptly severed (literally, Ludecke, whose movements "you" are following, is knifed to death thirty-two lines into the book), and you are summarily repositioned outside the action (in third-person omniscience) for the remainder of the narrative. That leaves two reading strategies. Seasoned readers of serious fiction sense that they are reading a contrived narrative in which a writer of serious fiction is electing to manipulate the familiar formula of an established mass-market pop genre, specifically the political thriller: the strict attention to breathless pacing and episodic action; the overfondness for contrived and complicated paranoia; the indulgence of gratuitous violence; and the deployment of two-dimensional characters motivated by the simplest urges of greed and/or lust, all of it delivered in the pop genre's signature uncluttered, deadpan proseline. Intrigued by the sportive play of genre elements, such readers, uninvolved with the obviously hokey action or the two-dimensional characters, watch DeLillo slyly manipulate genre conventions. On the other hand, less sophisticated readers, products of a relentless media culture that has created a rage for solution and clarity and an addiction for superficiality and tidiness, can be entertained, even enthralled by the high-throttle action of the thriller-narrative. It is an untenable position, finally, a dead end for the reader: retreat or engagement, ironic detachment or ironic amusement.

In this regard, the Hitler film, the reputedly pornographic artifact for which so many so hotly contend and which is finally screened at Cosmic Erotics, can be helpful as a study on how an audience is to react to surprise and mystery. Three audiences "watch" the Hitler performance: the invited spectators at the porn gallery; the bunker audience in the film itself, and, of course, the reader, who "watches" the film via a series of italicized descriptions.

The film has four parts. The first focuses on the bunker audience: eleven unidentified people—six children and five adults—bring in folding chairs and then simply sit down. In the next scene, an unidentified woman presents a small white flower to another woman reading a magazine, a surprising tableau-gesture of unexpected sympathy, unmotivated generosity, and genuine tenderness, wholly out of place within the Third Reich context. In the next scene, with the camera now moving, suggesting instability and an intriguing dynamic, Hitler himself enters the room wearing an old derby and baggy pants, swinging a cane, and sweetly smiling, a game parody of Chaplin doing Hitler. It is a stunning act of contradiction—monster as slapstick comic, archfiend as generous paterfamilias of an extended and doomed family, monomaniac as self-deprecating parody, power-mad dictator as helpless little tramp—an intriguing knot of mystery, uncertainty, and surprise. It is not that we are to think Hitler was, after all, a kind fellow with a fondness for children.[12] Rather, this Hitler is suddenly a text uneasily suspended between simple readings, denied definition. Then, in the film's closing part, the camera is slowly trained on the audience itself, and we watch their exaggerated gestures of applause and amusement, we assume at the spectacle of der Führer's unexpected antics, revealing an audience unwilling to grapple with the considerable implications of what they are witnessing, an audience too content with surfaces, too eager for entertainment and the refuge of simplification. Two audiences—at the gallery and in the bunker—expect yin *or* yang, and neither is able to process the stunning evidence of contradiction and paradox. The gathering at the gallery, quickly sensing the film's lack of commercial appeal, drift out long before the screening is over. And those in the bunker, despite the imminent catastrophic collapse of their entire way of life and, incidentally, their own deaths, are content to be entertained by Hitler's clownish antics.

Thus there is ironic detachment or ironic amusement.

Readers of DeLillo's two narratives of failed engagement are accorded similar dead-end (Godardesque) options. Intolerant of the ad-lib openness of the unmediated real world, destroyed by any brush with passion, potent surprise, and knotty contradictions, the Wynants and Glen Selvy brought DeLillo himself, artistically, to something of an impasse. First withdrawal and now engagement, both grief and nothing, have failed. Because four years would pass before DeLillo's next novel, Selvy stands as something of a summary character, and his death gives him unsuspected presence in the DeLillo oeuvre. It signals far more than a mere narrative event—that death, in fact, signals a tectonic career shift for DeLillo, a movement in the 1980s out of the unwinnable endgame, the aesthetic limbo of endlessly (re)playing narrative variations on the disquieting dynamic of unworkable retreat and failed engagement. Even in "Creation," what would prove to be DeLillo's last published story for nearly four years, a simple vacation morphs into a ghastly limbo: the central character, stranded on a remote Edenic island in the Tobago Cays, unable to connect with a flight off, conducts a listless affair of a sort with a stranger in a depthless parody of Genesis.

Perhaps that alarming sense of endgame and diminishing narrative possibility contributed to the reckless terrorism and comic brio of *Amazons* (1980), a joyous and savvy sort of farewell text, a particularly unsubtle, even cathartic exercise in bridge-burning, a house-cleaning that would signal DeLillo's readiness to test heretofore unexamined narrative strategies. Because DeLillo has never publicly acknowledged authorship of *Amazons* (it is widely suspected the work is a collaborative effort, although the co-writer has never been publicly identified), any speculations about its evolution and intentions are, of course, tenuous at best. But the book, the purported memoirs of the first woman to play in the National Hockey League, a minor-leaguer who joins the New York Rangers midseason to help guide them to a playoff spot, is, save for a prose line that is unmistakably DeLillo, most defiantly, audaciously un-DeLillo, or better, anti-DeLillo. It is as if DeLillo with the arch eye of self-deprecation set about to upend one by one the assumptions his critics had come to make about his oeuvre: DeLillo cannot create a credible woman character (here is a first-person memoir of Cleo Birdwell in which DeLillo boldly colonizes the female psyche—the first trade publication featured a back-cover "Author's Photo" of a strikingly sexy woman in a Rangers uniform—a memoir that describes intimately the hazards and joys of being a woman, by her own admission an unapologetic connoisseur of the male form, a woman who continually defines herself against the stereotyping and malicious mayhem of the male-dominated world of professional hockey, and a woman who candidly comments on the curiously satisfying heft of her own breasts, the tingle of having her labia licked, the rushing wet of sexual arousal, and her appreciation of the correct way to manipulate an erect penis to discourage premature ejaculation); DeLillo lacks a sense of humor (here the humor is wild and broad, even slapstick, the dialogue snappy and charged with double entendres and trenchant sarcasm); DeLillo cannot construct even the simplest semblance of plot (here the narrative line freely exploits the inherent drama of a late-season run to the playoffs and the built-in tensions of the game itself to compel a plot that is breezy, episodic, and accessible); DeLillo abstains from the heat of sexuality and the provocative vulnerability of bedroom intimacies (Cleo Birdwell voraciously pursues intense, entirely gratuitous sexual encounters that are rendered here with the unblinking, salacious detailing of mass-market soft porn); DeLillo fashions intensely cerebral, complicated, inaccessible texts that disdain mass appeal (*Amazons* is a riotously slick commercial concoction, a narrative that struggles mightily—and successfully—to avoid complications, its obviously contrived premise an excuse to exploit broad humor, titillating sex, a cast of wildly idiosyncratic if entirely depthless two-dimensional secondary characters, and the inherent drama of sports and its spectacle violence—in short, piling up an impressive assortment of the standard conventions of mass-market novels).

Even thematically, *Amazons* unsubtly goofs with the dense, provocative themes that had defined each of DeLillo's previous texts: the insidious reach of commercial advertising and the reduction of the self to a commodity (*Americana*)—Cleo struggles through a riotous series of commercial endorsements; the debilitating stress of sustaining the performance piece known as celebrity (*Great Jones Street*)—Cleo quickly becomes an instant media event, a ticket boom, a sports-page gimmick; the dark appeal of the enclosed world of sports, with its clearly defined sense of purpose and the safe violence of its scripted execution (*End Zone*); the promise of scientific research and the daring projections of the scientific imagination (*Ratner's Star*)—a teammate suffers from an obscure spastic condition known as Jumping Frenchman Disease and Cleo visits a conference devoted to the disease that features hilarious spoofs on medical research; the gentle terrorism of betrayal (*Players*)—Cleo casually sleeps with her agent's lover; and the unsettling paranoia over vast conspiracies of global syndicate cabals (*Running Dog*)—in the closing pages, the Rangers are purchased by an Arab syndicate that wants to compel Cleo to skate with a veil. DeLillo even parodies his interest in the spiritual dimension, the earnest quest to validate a sustaining transcendent reality: Cleo responds deeply to the mystical blather of one Wadi Assad, a Kahlil Gibran–type guru whose slender best-sellers dispense fortune-cookie platitudes and innocuous faux parables. That DeLillo packs all these suggestive themes into a single narrative line is itself richly parodic. Given such a premise, it is irresistibly tempting to play with the pseudonym DeLillo here adopts—Cleo Birdwell—to suggest the novel's deliberately irreverent look back: Cleo, of course, recalls Clio, the muse of history; and the bird, of course, is a rude, disdainful gesture, an extravagant gesture of disapproval and broad rejection. Clearly, *Amazons* can be positioned as a sort of gaudy, bawdy indulgence that signals a necessary, generous gesture of closure, a bird well delivered, a tonic graduation-text that marks as much an end as a beginning, a termination / turning point.

A far more provocative indication of the direction DeLillo's artistic maturity would track can be found in the last work he published before heading to the Mediterranean. *The Engineer of Moonlight*, which appeared in the *Cornell Review* in 1979, is a closet drama that foregrounds the tension between withdrawal and engagement. Moreover, it argues, ultimately, the unworkability of systems that aim to create order amid the chaotic wonder of a grief-world that stubbornly refuses to concede itself to tidiness. The drama endorses, to paraphrase one character, the mysteries of the five-and-dime, the unsuspected deep of everyday things themselves. Appropriately, it is a play that need not be acted (indeed, it has eluded staging)—the characters talk (at times tediously), sunbathe, engage pointless games of trivia, and play a most esoteric board game whose rules, of course, the audience does not know. The plot itself is stripped and spare. Four characters gather in a secluded, spacious oceanfront retreat to tend to a brilliant mathematician, Eric Lighter, whose formidable intelligence has apparently cracked under the weight of his long struggle to curve the material universe into the neatness of an embracing system of data. Indeed, in that strange board game the characters play in the second act, Lighter is given the role of the Engineer of Moonlight, a title that neatly exposes the absurd contradiction of ordering the natural universe into some grand conjured design. Lighter has recently been released from a protracted stay at a recovery facility, and now, in between rounds of medication and bouts of insomnia (he whiles away the nights counting in different languages), he dictates a rambling memoir, part rant, part recollection, that reflects in its more lucid passages an unsuspected nostalgia for the unstructured immediate, for the difficult mess of family, home, and passion, and supremely a curiosity about the forbidding mystery of death itself. As his name indicates, since his hospitalization, Lighter is now unencumbered by the heavy imperative of understanding and explanation.

In his convalescence, he is being tended by two characters who do not promise much help in any effort to reengage the real world. One is Lighter's trusted factotum named James Case, who facilitates Lighter's retreat primarily as a career boon (a lapsed teacher, with its suggestion of engagement and involvement, he assists Lighter in transcribing his daily rants from tape to manuscript), a man so distanced from authenticity and so enamored with language that once, when he was left adrift at night in a dinghy in the midst of a terrifyingly strong current along the Maine coast, rather than simply cry out for help only said softly to himself, "Loud and prolonged cries for help," "Urgent shouts," and "Horrifying cries in the night."[13] Along with James Case is Lighter's much younger fourth wife, an innocuously shallow woman-child given to New Age mysticism and to long afternoons of sunbathing. Their guest, however, is Lighter's third wife, a savvy, strikingly sensual woman who dismisses mathematics as a leap of faith and who, consequently, represents Lighter's best chance to reconnect with the world and who must decide in the end whether to stay on to help her ex-husband's struggle toward recovery.

The character of the burned-out fifty-something mathematician is attractively suggestive of DeLillo himself and his own midcareer endgame as a novelist, an engineer overtired of the strategy of retreat, of fashioning elaborate text-worlds of contrived order, DeLillo himself an engineer of moonlight nearing not a tragic concession to the unstructured energy of moonlight so much as the dramatic decision to explore its wonder, its dreadful appeal. As the play closes, Lighter settles down to a typewriter to process the parts of his night ramblings that recall the elusive lure of ordinary objects. Amid a drama sustained by the self-consciously witty and polished verbal interplay of characters in self-elected retreat, the self-indulgent games of trivia and factoids, and the eccentric board game that so amuses the characters (and necessarily alienates the audience), DeLillo tunes into the unpolished and unfathomable world that looms just beyond this tidy ocean retreat: to the sunlight (characters, fearing it as carcinogenic, slather on protective liniment), the languorous midsummer animal heat the characters each disdain, and the surging ocean in which they never swim (Lighter had tried the week before, walking in backwards with his arms way out like a "hostage drama" [30])—in short, to the pull and call of the living earth itself. As Lighter concludes near the end, "Goddamn, goddamn. The world *is* beautiful" (45).

The novels that would follow DeLillo's return from his time overseas would be illuminated by an expansive generosity absent in these early works as his characters (and supremely his reader) move hesitatingly toward authenticity and community by embracing not merely the complicated mystery of the late-century world but rather by testing DeLillo's larger endorsement of the agency of language and the unsuspected potency of the reader-writer conspiracy. Indeed, it is to the enterprise of writing itself that DeLillo would turn. It is significant to note in passing that *Amazons* hints at this new direction: as her rookie season winds down, as she leaves the ice-world of winter hockey and moves into the green promise of a city spring, Cleo discusses with her agent an inexplicable urgency: "Lately I've been getting little urges to write down some of the things that have been happening these past months" (215). What we have witnessed, as it turns out, is the evolution not of a hockey star but of a writer—the very figure that will now assume stage center in DeLillo's landmark narratives of the 1980s and 1990s.

Part Two

The Word

People come through the gateway, people in streams and clusters, in mass assemblies. No one seems to be alone. This is a place to enter in crowds, seek company and talk. Everyone is talking. I move past the scaffolding and walk down the steps, hearing one language after another, rich, harsh, mysterious, strong. This is what we bring to the temple, not prayer or chant or slaughtered rams. Our offering is language.

—*The Names*

But he tried to write about the hostage. It was the only way he knew to think deeply in a subject. He missed his typewriter for the first time since leaving home. . . . He had to settle for pencil and pad, working in his hotel room through the long mornings, slowly building chains of thought, letting the words lead him into that basement room.

Find the places where you converge with him.

Read his poems again.

See his face and hands in words.

—*Mao II*

3

Narratives of Recovery

The Names (1982)

By DeLillo's own assessment, *The Names,* published in 1982, represented a dramatic shift in his authorial sensibility, a "new dedication" to craft.[1] The differences are striking. Unlike the earlier works, as we have seen rather loosely structured novels of ideas, DeLillo here works out, without irony, a traditional plot engined by suspense that centers on a character who actually moves toward an epiphanic closing. If it can be said to be a novel of ideas, *The Names* is an anatomy of language itself—letters, words, sentences, ultimately narrative itself—in which DeLillo, without intrusive irony or skewing cynicism, invests a fallen world with an abiding sense of meaning through the therapeutic application of language. For the three years he spent writing the novel, DeLillo lived abroad, in Greece, and traveled throughout a Mediterranean world awash in dialects, languages ancient and often inaccessible but hauntingly musical. "What I found was that all this traveling taught me how to see and hear all over again. . . . The simple fact that I was confronting new landscapes and fresh languages made me feel almost duty bound to get it right. I would see and hear more clearly than I could in more familiar places."[2] After the clipped-tight prose line of *Players* and *Running Dog,* language here is generously indulged—its sonic richness a supple acoustic gift, a pitch-perfect rendering of the color and sensual texture of an unfamiliar immediate. And, appropriately, characters here actually talk: the narrative is animated with dialogue—witty conversations, at times comically disjointed, that fashion a cozy community feel among the expatriate Americans in Athens: bankers, business executives, intelligence operatives, diplomats and their wives. Compared to DeLillo's earlier works, claustrophobic texts largely confined to narrow rooms or to the tight grid of inter-urban streets, *The Names* is a breathtakingly expansive narrative set in a number of sweeping locales, each vividly and lovingly conjured: the vibrant push of Athens street life, the austere majesty of exotic Aegean islands, the forbidding wastes of the Indian subcontinent, the rolling emptiness of the American prairie. It is an expansive, embracing sentiment emphasized in the first short story DeLillo published after his hiatus, "Human Moments in World War III." An astronaut, suspended above a world moving deliberately, recklessly toward nuclear self-extermination, sits mesmerized at the capsule's tiny cabin window stunned by the simple beauty, color, vulnerability, and strangeness of the world below. It is, he murmurs, so endlessly fulfilling, "so interesting" (126).

As narrative, *The Names* embraces rather than skews the premise of intimacy suggested by first-person narration. James Axton works as a risk analyst for a major insurance conglomerate in the volatile Mediterranean market, assessing terrorist threats to regional governments and to American industries, bookkeeping data on terrorist activity but staying detached from its context, avoiding even speculating on the passion behind such mayhem. As narrative authority (Axton worked as a freelance writer before joining the insurance conglomerate), Axton deploys narrative to assess his own experience, accepts the premise of revelation, and accords the structure of his narrative the feel and momentum of a traditional epiphanic experience and, in turn, emerges as a character capable of complication, intrigue, originality, and emotional depth, a man imperfect, even unpleasant at times, but redeemable by the jolting clarity of a cumulative, earned epiphany. We learn early on that Axton has accepted work in Athens to be near Kathryn, his estranged wife, who had taken their son to work as volunteers in an archaeological dig on a remote Aegean island. The eleven-year marriage had been rent by Axton's rather lackluster adultery, which his wife could not forgive largely because it so lacked passion. Axton will use his narrative to reveal gradually the painful details of his fractured marriage; his estrangement from his precocious nine-year-old son, Tap; and his uncertainties over an expatriate lifestyle that has left him, at midlife, rootless, bored, apart, perpetually out of place (he has never learned the Greek language and is appalled by the reckless, free-flowing Athens traffic). His is a peripatetic life of rented apartments, airport terminals, and forwarded telexes. That is, until reading Tap's novel-in-process rekindles Axton's conviction in the redemptive force of language with the stabbing suddenness akin to the Christian pentecostal experience (a metaphor DeLillo exploits). Language thus becomes a vehicle for revelation and observation, a force, felt and keen.[3] Unlike previous DeLillo narrators, Axton as authority engages the reader in a demanding confidence of communication, a violation of isolation that marks a radically new reader contract in DeLillo's fiction. In the closing pages, having quit his insurance work after being told that his data had been routinely back-channeled to the CIA, Axton returns to writing—not the technical writing or ghost writing he had churned out before but rather to the earnest enterprise of the book we have been reading, a book that reveals Axton's growth and shares his own secrets, in a stunning act of faith in language. *The Names,* then, is ultimately a book about its own gestation—as such it is a narrative about the reclamation of a writer (DeLillo himself as much as Axton), a turning-point narrative that establishes the premise for DeLillo's new phase: namely, that passion comes not from street engagement itself but rather from recording that complicating experience; not from grief itself but from recollecting it into lucid shape. Love, family, friendship, work—each in turn here frustrates, disappoints, or fails. Axton does not repair his marriage or bond with his son or find saving camaraderie among his expatriate friends. In a narrative in which the central character uses language at turns to fantasize, escape, analyze, assault, seduce, simplify, exploit, entertain, contain, tally, protect, and insulate, it is telling that in the end he uses it to connect—he bonds first with language itself; then with his son's clumsy, if audacious manuscript; and ultimately with an unnamed and unnameable reader, you, a surprisingly durable conspiracy of two isolates in separate rooms—writer and reader— that sustains the inexplicable intimacy of community despite unbroken, indeed unbreakable isolation.

Since *Americana,* as we have seen, DeLillo has suspected language, distrusted it as mediating strategy, an often inadequate vehicle for containing the evident chaos of experience within the too tidy logic of its too clean designs. When Owen Brademas, who heads Kathryn's archaeological dig, begins investigating a nomadic cult rumored to randomly bludgeon to death the crippled and the infirm, Axton is drawn to the mystery. After some investigation, Axton realizes that the killings are not random at all: the victims' initials match the initials of the locales where they are killed. Pattern, specifically a language pattern, furnishes a way to understand what is otherwise inexplicable—a rationale later confirmed when he actually meets members of the cult, self-described "abecedarians." It is a familiar DeLilloesque temptation: the gentle tyranny of language as an imposition of an arbitrary, albeit logical order, the alternative being to live within the inscrutability of the continuing crisis.[4] As one of the cult members calmly explains, "Madness has a structure. We might say madness is all structure."[5] The cult selects the infirm and the crippled, genetic mishaps and natural accidents, presumably to further tidy up experience. There is no larger rationale, no God-angle, no accompanying ritual—the chosen are dispatched with claw hammers inscribed with their initials, each killing an "austere calculation" (171), the victims objectified, denied humanity or context—inevitable, DeLillo has long argued, when language is valued solely for its ability to contain and control mystery. Thus, for the cult, language measures their deep fear of the immediate. Axton is tempted by the logic of the cult—early on he has more than appreciated the tidying power of language not only as a risk analyst but as a husband and a father and even as a son: he enrages his wife by actually listing twenty-seven of his character flaws that she is most likely to bring up in an argument; he bonds with his son largely by buying him books and by reading the boy's novel-in-progress; and he maintains a most puzzling relationship with his father, who apparently lives in Ohio with Axton's stepmother but who has for some time communicated only by sending his son postcards of Texas bearing generic nonmessages.

If the cult embraces a misguided faith in the power of language to contain mystery by providing some measure of order, by contrast, the archaeologist Owen

Brademas has come to experience erosion in just such a faith.[6] His earliest recollection is of attending an extreme church service in his native Kansas in which a young charismatic preacher encouraged the congregation to speak in tongues and in fact unleashed testimonies of such emotional force (including his own father's) that young Owen, tongue-tied and unmoved by what he apprehended as gibberish, ran from the church in fear. Since then, Brademas has doubted the spiritual dimension within the human character and even the value of emotions. Abandoning the immediate as stubbornly nonsuggestive, he has committed forty years to the nonlife of an academic and specifically to the study of long-dead civilizations and the dust-heavy quiet of archaeological digs, the work of meticulously shaping convincing narratives about dead civilizations by piecing together shattered artifacts salvaged from trenches cut into the earth. But, despite his current commission as head of the dig where Axton's wife volunteers, he confides in Axton that he has abandoned even his faith in archaeology itself; he finds dubious the notion that civilizations are capable of coherence, plot, or design. The writings he unearths now do not interest him—to him, they record the banalities of the immediate, bookkeeping records and merchandise inventories. Language, within such ledger logic, dulls into unalterable stillness. (Brademas admits to Kathryn that in his long university career it had never occurred to him to write poetry.) Words certainly fascinate the owl-eyed Brademas—he knows the etymological derivation of scores of words—but they do not compel him.

What is left now to compel Owen Brademas? Letters themselves, specifically the cut surfaces of those signature shapes carved into stone. It is the least involved level of language response—epigraphy. Brademas scours the libraries of the Mediterranean for examples of cut inscriptions, lovingly tracing the lines and curves of ancient lettering disentangled from the responsibility to mean anything. He travels to India, for example, to view a massive pavilion wherein an epic Sanskrit poem is displayed on twenty-five panels of ornamental marble (stretching roughly four city blocks), more than a thousand lines that recount the long history of the local people. But it is not the poem or its contents that enthrall Brademas; rather, it is the glyphs themselves, a joy in dusty forms, the "looped bands, scything curves, the sense of sacred architecture . . . those shapes, the secret aspect, the priestly, the aloof, the cruel" (284).[7] Importantly, he views the panels on the same day as a massive solar eclipse, suggesting that his vision may be obscured and imperfect.

This cold embrace of the intrigue of letters empties Brademas of his humanity. In this way he parallels the logic of the cult itself. Intellectually intrigued by rumors of the secret cult and convinced that he had actually met several members (mysterious strangers near caves who asked him, oddly, how many languages he knew and in turn found fascinating his work in epigraphy), Brademas journeys to the

Indian backcountry to find the cult, and he is with them for one of their killings in Hawa Mandir. Typically, he will not entangle himself in such raw immediacy and, far from acting to prevent the killing, retreats to the handy sanctuary of an earthen bin, used as a grain silo, while the actual killing is done. When he later relates the events to Axton, he recasts his account in the protective insulation of a third-person character. "In his memory he was a character in a story, a colored light" (304). Brademas consistently maintains such isolation. Throughout the narrative, his evident willingness to talk is less a passion for the ad-lib dynamics of conversation and more a vestigial fondness for lecturing and theorizing with rehearsed glibness (at one point he even discourses on the beautiful language of violence). Although his eccentric personality registers compellingly with both Kathryn and Tap (Tap will even use Brademas's long-ago prairie church experience as part of his novel-in-progress), Brademas never senses the vital potential of such human contact and remains detached from the risky implications of interactive bonding. While interred within the silo-sanctuary, Brademas recollects the prairie church experience, in retreat conjuring the signature experience that had convinced him long ago of the incipient danger of a raw universe beyond tidy explanation.

Consequently, his encounter with the cult and his near brush with the raw realities of mayhem and death destroy rather than invigorate him. When Axton arrives at the door of his apartment in Lahore, Brademas, still reeling from his encounter with the cult, mistakes Axton for the figure of death itself and says wearily that he is ready. "It's important," he later admits to Axton, "to get it right, to tell it correctly. Being precise is all that's left. But I don't think I can manage it now" (299). He confronts a universe that resists his most committed intellectual figurings—he is left tongue-tied in a grief-universe that will not sustain understanding, and rather than celebrate that mystery he rues the loss of his faith in design in such a manifestly imperfect world: "[The cult] mocks our need to structure and classify, to build a system against the terror in our souls" (308). Suspicious of emotions, intolerant of the disorder of surprise, intent on subduing and codifying a world unwilling to cooperate in such an absurd enterprise, more curious about the knowable past than the uncertain present and thus immured from the intensity of the unexamined immediate (his Indian apartment smells of sewage) and unavailable to the persuasion of community, Brademas would have comfortably centered any of DeLillo's first four novels. He becomes for Axton, however, a cautionary character, a retreat Axton (and, by extension, DeLillo) will not endorse.

Axton's reclamation begins with his decision to quit his position with the Northeast Group after he is told that the data he has been collecting to assess Mediterranean governments and American industries according to their vulnerability to terrorist attacks has become an information conduit for the CIA and that Axton had consequently been an unwitting dupe for the government agency. If the alphabet cult and Brademas both use language as a system of control, shadowy agencies such as the CIA project that logic into the international arena, use language to create artificial boundaries, to divide the globe using an unambiguous East versus West logic, and to provide theoretical justification for such arbitrary divisions by propagating the sort of propaganda that fans jingoism and xenophobia. Conversations throughout the narrative testify to the simmering civil unrest in Greece fed by government agencies, domestic and international, intent on deploying language as a weapon for fomenting parochial interests and for making religious and economic inequities appear inevitable, violence acceptable, and secrecy critical. Language in such hands is hardly a vehicle for expression or even exchange but rather of systematic oppression, rabid paranoia, and enforced division. Axton taps a far different sensibility. After he returns to Athens from his disturbing encounter with Brademas in India, Axton finds himself missing Kathryn and Tap, who are now in British Columbia for Kathryn's new museum job. He misses the simplicity and depth of conversation, "the seeping love of small talk and family chat" (312), language used to create generous intimacy by sharing space. When he finds out the next day the truth of his job, Axton resigns his position to return to the States to write, to freelance, an option that suggests his own determination to assert an individual voice and his willingness to engage the difficult ad-lib of the immediate—he will no longer assess risk but rather engage risk, a monumental turn for a man who had earlier swum in the Aegean with his clothes on and who, as a cloud of bees descended on his helpless son, was momentarily enthralled by the beauty of the angry insects.

And risk happens almost immediately. On an early-morning jog with a banker friend the day after he resigns, Axton is the target of what appears to be a botched shooting. He is not sure if he is the object of the shots—his jogging companion's bank had financially supported Turkish enterprises, but he is, after all, an American. However, the experience—the surprise and proximity of death and the stunning recognition of the implications of his own national identity, which he had long ago marginalized—is sufficient to convince him that government agencies manipulate language to guarantee fear, mayhem, and brutality, a logic that, like the other secret cult, ultimately reduces people to objects, diminishes the potential for individuality, and subjects all events to a rigid system of imposed understanding. He rejects it—and by extension the forbidding persuasion of the cult and Brademas's infatuation with letters—the only way he can: he reclaims a "second life" (329), his long-abandoned status as a writer, and thus reasserts an individual voice that, in turn, affirms language's privileged ability to embrace rather than simplify the immediate (specifically, the book we have been reading). That saving movement is completed in two dramatic events: Axton's long-delayed visit to the Acropolis and his subsequent reading of his son's novel-in-progress, a brief chapter of which Axton uses to close his own narrative.

Axton had, by his own admission, long avoided the steep Acropolis and the imposing temple of the Parthenon as oppressively somber, a consecrated space that privileged "beauty, dignity, order, proportion" apart from the unruly street-life immediate far below (3). Shaken by the shooting, however, he makes the climb at last to the Parthenon, seeking just such a rescue from the press of the immediate. Once there, however, he is immersed in an ongoing celebration of dialects and languages, the dense, ad-libbed music of a living community of voices animated by the intricate webbing of the ceaseless jazz of conversation; its fluid, sonic weave enthralls Axton (an earlier, similar experience in the streets of Jerusalem had disturbed him), an aural epiphany that language, without meaning (Axton cannot understand any of it), can render the curve and delight of music itself, its "open cry" an improvised recitative (330). "This is what we bring to the temple, not prayer or chant or slaughtered rams. Our offering is language" (331).

It is not enough, however. As the chapter ends, Axton notices an untended box camera mounted on a tripod and, curious where its owner might be, decides too quickly that the owner is irrelevant. Rather, Axton conjures an owner from the resources of his own imagination, thus indicating a dangerous willingness to indulge language as evasion, to abdicate language's joint connection with the immediate that DeLillo has long endorsed. Furthermore, this powerful experience on the Acropolis cannot suffice because Axton does not understand what he hears. Like a Catholic who attends a seder ceremony (or like Owen Brademas at the prairie church meeting), Axton is aware of the implications of the language event and is moved to an appropriate awe but cannot fully involve himself, denied the intimacy of communication. It is, finally, exclusionary, the forbidding implications of the curse of Babel.

What, then, would complete Axton's evolution as a writer? We close Axton's narrative with a chapter from his young son's manuscript, the retelling of the story of Brademas's prairie church experience. The young Tap is surely promising as an author-figure—throughout the narrative he has been fascinated by words and has been absorbed by his exotic surroundings, his keen eye rescuing the slenderest details that pass by Axton unnoticed. And at nine, he is writing already—indeed, he is midway through a first novel. That manuscript celebrates the privilege of language to create, unlike the passing music of conversation atop the Acropolis, a viable, substantive structure, the vibrant and suggestive form of narrative. And unlike Axton's fanciful conjuring of the absent photographer, here Tap wrestles Brademas's real-world experience into the serious business of form by manipulating the elements of setting, character, suspense, and tension.

But Tap's manuscript is not the resolution text.[8] The manuscript chapter is rendered in the uncorrected prose line of the nine-year-old, unchecked by the mechanics of conventional spellings and paragraphing and syntax, and thus undisciplined, unstructured, playful and teasing perhaps, but whose delightful Joycean puns are manifestly unintentionally suggestive. Its apparent creativity is mere unanchored subjectivity, its levels of play more sophisticated than the nine-year-old could realize; language thus is ultimately privatized. It is at best a process text, a kind of written variation of speaking in tongues, ultimately inaccessible to an audience without significant intervention and translation. Like Tap's invented language, "Ob" (in which he inserts that syllable into words), this sort of prose intrigues, even delights for a while but eventually grows irksome (there is a point in which Axton snaps at Tap to stop talking in the nonsense language) because it closes down the loop of communication; its writer-friendly prose, so terminally original, is ultimately clumsy and messy rather than inventive, restricting access to only the most patient and creative readers. It recalls a moment in the text when Axton and his friends need to invent a word for an impromptu late-night swim and decide to call it a "Keller" after the friend who just took such a swim—inventive perhaps, but restrictive in its ability to enjoin a community.

More to the point, with attention so focused on the words, what is lost amid the play and game of Tap's writing is the trauma and anxiety recounted in the narrative itself, the fictitious child's free fall into the terror of an imperfect world. And that trauma is further distanced because it is not even Tap's to share—he inhabits Brademas's experience in an act of narrative colonization that is more exploitation than exploration, more projection than examination. It is an odd gesture of appropriation given the rich (and often unsettling) experiences of Tap's own life—his global shuttling, his parents' fractured marriage, the awkward estrangement from his father. Importantly, the manuscript's closing image—a terrified child in a cold rain, left in a nightmarish world—suggests a far darker vision than what Axton himself endorses.

Whereas the Acropolis visit consecrates the immediacy of spoken language, Tap's manuscript celebrates the bracing viability of written language, and that manuscript, crude as it is, is the ignition text for Axton's own reclamation and as such provides a fitting close to Axton's own manuscript, the text we have been reading. It is as if an astronaut, grown weary of flight and lost to its wonder, rediscovers the joy of ascent and gravity-busting buoyancy by watching a child play with a crudely made kite. Axton's own manuscript, conservatively executed compared to Tap's, completes Axton's dramatic endorsement of language as a vehicle for difficult self-revelation that ultimately connects to a responsive, participatory, if unnameable reader. As a character notes, the word *book* is derived from *box,* something designed to be opened. In a story of boundaries and borders, performances and deceptions, silence and isolation, the narrative Axton offers is itself a gesture of honest disclosure and authentic exchange, a gesture unprecedented in DeLillo's fiction to this point. In a story busy with those determined to contain and simplify the world's pressing mystery, Axton uses language to reveal the uncertainties that haunt the everyday immediate, Faulkner's grief-world, without thinning that richness or simplifying its implications—indeed, in an aside, Axton says that he has given up alcohol, suggesting his movement toward honest clarity.

Thus DeLillo, himself the writer renewed, appropriately begins this new phase by defining what a writer is not, assessing and rejecting a variety of templates. The writer is not some archaeologist, piecing into coherent and tidy narratives unearthed fragments of experience; nor is the writer a historian, too eagerly imposing explanation and motive onto the mess of event; the writer is not a preacher, exploiting the emotions to deal in the inaccessible and the unseen; the writer is not a filmmaker (in a subplot, an experimental-film director named Volterra plans a film of the cult, a film without a script), bound to a technology that renders experience as detached images; and a writer is surely not a risk analyst, one step removed from the impact and passion, the depth of gains and losses inevitable within the unscripted immediate. Rather, the writer draws on each but is ultimately the sum that is greater than its parts. Narrative, DeLillo argues, is that rare aesthetic system which permits, indeed factors, ambiguity, openness, flux and accepts its own limits and, indeed, embraces, like the universe itself, the rich suggestivity of mystery. Like the universe itself, the narrative is a fluid architecture in which coherence does not mean clarity and whose patterns do not imply meaning. Language, as DeLillo will pointedly argue in succeeding novels, is the sole aesthetic vehicle able to both defy the casual contemporary assumptions of alienation amid the contingency of a world beyond our shaping and at the same time to give shape to that mystery without flattening it, thus preserving the radiant awe over our every step into the immediate when the time comes to close up Axton's (or anybody's) book and return to its roiling unpredictability.

White Noise (1985) and *The Day Room* (1987)

It is deceptively easy to move from the closing of *The Names* to the opening of *White Noise*: from James Axton atop the Acropolis amid the carnival noise of strangers, overlooking Athens, to Professor Jack Gladney atop the College-on-the-Hill amid the carnival noise of strangers, overlooking the industrial town of Blacksmith. Like Axton, Gladney revels in the reassuring press of a crowd, in his case the students returning for the fall term, the snaking lines of full-laden station wagons, the campus abuzz with the random blather of separations and reunions among the "spiritually akin."[9] Yet something here disturbs. Whereas Axton is exuberant and revived by his intuited intimacy with the community spontaneously forged by the casual conspiracy of dozens of dialects, Gladney maintains a calculated privacy, more apart than a part. Unlike Axton, who relishes the crowd with unironic sincerity, Jack Gladney exploits crowds, seeks them out, content to burrow within them with a parasitic resolve—whether on the grandly dubbed "day of the station wagons," during the school term in his packed lecture halls, in the vast neighborhood supermarket, in the local ten-story Mid-Village Mall, or even at home, embunkered amid his extended family, a massive complex constructed of five children from five marriages (5). *White Noise* examines the threat implicit in Axton's tonic affirmation of the crowd; here, crowds become seductive, the collective mundane that nullifies the self, makes irrelevant the discovery of identity, and suppresses the inclination to reflect.

Gladney, despite his considerable bulk, is a fragile little creature surrounded by cold fact, a man calmed only by feeling part of something large—for instance, he draws validation when the ATM machine confirms the balance he had estimated on his own. What most terrifies Gladney as he edges into late middle age is the unassailable inevitability of his own death. Consider, DeLillo poses, what makes possible the luxury of Axton's generous epiphany atop the Acropolis: whomever the Athens shooters may have been targeting during Axton's early-morning run, they *missed* Axton. Consider, DeLillo now proposes, attempting to sustain the weight of Axton's luminous affirmation had a bullet actually hit. What then to do with Axton's generous gift of language if he had tapped, as we all must, the reality of the peculiarly human condition of waiting for the clumsy intrusion of death, to be so aware (the only species cursed/blessed to put into words this inevitability) and so vividly helpless?

The Day Room, an experimental two-act metatheatrical piece that DeLillo completed (and had staged) during this same time, centers on this same anxious confrontation with mortality. Although DeLillo draws out a number of theatrical metaphors to suggest his perceptions of the late twentieth century—among them the unreliability of appearances, the shifting nature of identity (the same actors play different roles), the need we have to fill the awkward silences between us with the most banal blather—he investigates most prominently how the theater and the ritual of acting itself can suggest the performance we each undertake every moment of every day in an admixture of dignity, comedy, and desperation: specifically, how we choose to pretend that every moment is not stolen from an inevitable and imminent death. We go about our daily busyness unwilling to acknowledge what we know is true; thus, we live perforce in a grand sort of day room, like patients pretending not to be patients, engaged in daylong therapeutic play and structured busy work, pretending we are anything but terminal and anywhere but in a hospital-with-no-walls in a strategy of protective, elective ignorance.

The first act takes place in a nondescript hospital room, where a man who has come only for routine tests must tolerate first a garrulous roommate and then a procession of nurses and doctors who are apparently imposters, other patients who have wandered out of the hospital's psychiatric wing. In the second act, the same theater space is altered (indeed before our eyes, DeLillo refuses to allow the theater its artifice) to become a nondescript motel room where, as a television babbles (played by a patient from act 1 now bound in a straightjacket), a couple talks about their pursuit of an avant-garde touring company known for conducting performance pieces in unlikely public places, performances so real that they alter the very emotional makeup of those fortunate enough to catch the show. Of course, we come to realize that we have been watching that traveling theater group all along. DeLillo plays on the familiar world-as-theater conceit to suggest ultimately how we are all actors refusing the implication of authenticity, specifically the intrusion of death. As the play closes, DeLillo offers two familiar alternatives: elaborate retreat or stoic engagement. On the television, a commentator reviews how to safely watch an imminent solar eclipse by wearing a shoebox contrivance with a pin prick in it and then recommends, without irony, keeping the box on even after the eclipse has passed. Meanwhile, against that chatter, a patient moves into the shadowy background of the stage space and quietly strikes a number of tai chi poses, the stylized Oriental body stances that suggest (as they did in *Running Dog*) a radical spiritual balance and earned emotional clarity in the face of oppressive, stressful external forces. That interior calm, beyond the explication of language, stands as a most attractive alternative in the face of a terrifying death that we cannot soften, cannot deny, and cannot afford to ignore. It is such an enviable peace that Gladney must struggle to earn.

At the outset, Gladney is certainly far from such peace. At fifty, despite middle-class comforts and professional security, Gladney cannot sleep at night; he is certain something is living in his basement; although healthy, he broods about his death. As we begin to see, Gladney occupies the fragile edges of a placid sitcom-styled world precariously poised near catastrophe (suggested by his well-appointed suburban home positioned above a deep ravine and along a busy highway), a tidy world that routinely shudders with inexplicable surprises (the smoke alarm keeps going off; the trash compactor suddenly blows out; the town's elementary school is closed without explanation and then swept by Mylex-suited scientists, one of whom, it is rumored, drops dead in the hallways; an elderly blind man and his sister are lost for days in the local mall, a disappearance for which a psychic is enlisted; Gladney's four-year-old stepson, Wilder, suddenly vanishes in a supermarket; a colleague, reassuringly portly, simply disappears into the surf off Malibu, while another drops to his death off a ski lift in Austria; the town's asylum burns to the ground; subjected to hypnosis, a local policeman recounts seeing a dead body being tossed from a UFO; rummaging through his garbage, Gladney finds a mysterious pair of men's underwear, shredded with lipstick markings). Within such an environment, Jack Gladney clings to crowds because he is haunted by vulnerability —he studies obituary columns and compares the ages of the dead against his own; when a myoclonic jerk shakes him awake, he wonders if his death will be as violent; traffic on the highway behind his snug home sounds to him like "dead souls babbling at the edge of a dream" (4); on a curious (and altogether morbid) whim, he stops at an abandoned cemetery, and as he studies the tilted, mossy tombstones and touches the cracked stone surfaces, he actually feels a creepy presence, the "level of energy composed solely of the dead" (98); his sleep is regularly disturbed by agonizing sweats; he often wonders whether he will die before his wife, the ample and confident Babette with her unshakable faith that nature can be amended, a woman who is always wearing running suits, who exercises strenuously, and who conducts senior-citizen education classes on proper posture and healthy diet.

Gladney's hanging dread is considerably exacerbated when, after a railroad car derails near Blacksmith and releases a huge cloud of an insecticide derivative known as Nyodene-D, he is exposed to the slow-moving airborne toxic event for two and a half minutes as he furiously pumps gas at an abandoned filling station during the town's chaotic evacuation. His fear suddenly becomes intolerably real— death the noun, distant and abstract, becomes dying the verb, ongoing and immediate. "I've got death inside me" (150). Panicked, he will participate in a battery of medical tests to determine the exact impact of his contamination—but the data will stay exasperatingly ambiguous (a medical technician at the evacuation site tells him they will know more in fifteen years—if Gladney is still alive). Thus Gladney is left exposed, alone, and uncertain. *White Noise,* then, serves as something of a companion piece to *The Names,* a necessary counterargument to that narrative's ascendant affirmation of community and participation. If *The Names* expands, *White Noise* contracts; if *The Names* is a novel of revelation and epiphany, *White Noise* is a novel of exposure and confusion; if *The Names* permits a salvaging community that upends late-century assumptions of isolation, *White Noise* invades a solitary self; a first-person narrative like Axton's, *White Noise* is charged not by the mystery of community but rather by the mystery of inviolable privacy, DeLillo reminding us that if narrative can embrace, it can as well enclose. If James Axton uses the self to discover language, Jack Gladney uses language to discover the self. Gladney reverses the normative arc of the epiphanic experience that Axton so neatly undergoes: from confusion, suspended amid mystery, through a shattering moment and ultimately to the contentment of clear sight. Gladney, on the other hand, will move from the contentment of clear sight through a shattering moment that leaves him confused, suspended amid mystery.

Like Ishmael, another first-person narrator whose traumatic experience exposes him to the suasive beauty of mystery but maroons him alone within that terrifying epiphany, Gladney relates his narrative uncertainly;[10] the narrative is told in a sort of first-person angular that lacks the conviction of community and the joy of confluence that so compels Axton. Clearly testing Axton's hard-earned epiphany, DeLillo here privileges isolation and the vulnerability of the self, fixed within the rich confusions of a fluid reality that is subtly patterned yet entirely meaningless (unlike Axton, who narrates after the experience, Gladney narrates in an unnerving, unfolding immediacy). In an irony that would surely not be lost on its author, the novel that exposes the self separated from the comforting noise of the crowd would prove to be DeLillo's breakthrough work, finding not only wide acceptance in universities as a "teachable" DeLillo text but garnering the author unprecedented market success as well, not only because the novel treats the timely issue of ecological disasters—it was published within a month of the catastrophic chemical spill in Bhopal, India—but also because it so apparently unironically engages the comfortable feel of traditional domestic realism, Gladney the first DeLillo character grounded in his community and committed to his work, happily married and surrounded by kids. Yet Jack Gladney is a massively conceived performance piece, a career fraud, who moves by the end of the novel to a position apart, accepting the vulnerability implicit in mortality and rejecting the insulation of domesticity and the seductive illusion of invincibility he had found within his comfy bunker of middle-class plenty.

Ever the cultural anatomist, DeLillo uses Gladney's first-person narrative to examine the impact of three late-century cultural pressures—the cult of Adolf Hitler, the addiction to television, and the faith in science—that have conspired to cheapen death of its mesmerizing density and stark mystery and that, in turn, have created a generation terrified of vulnerability and inevitability and thus disconnected from the fullest embrace of the immediate, that strange and compelling vastness that Gladney is determined simply to ignore. Indeed, white noise itself is a common acoustic phenomena, a kind of all sound / no sound event in which crowds of random sound waves of varying frequency intensities simultaneously combine into a sort of pitchless hum, the low-level background din that people routinely block out.

As a professor of Hitler Studies (a discipline he himself invented twenty years earlier), Gladney has tamed the inexplicable event of Hitler into the reassuring logic of tidy journal papers and mesmerizing seminar lectures. Without emotional outrage, Gladney has crowded himself within the protective penumbra of the myth of the charismatic monster who comes to us, as a colleague of Gladney's observes, not larger than life but "larger than death" (287), who centered the twentieth century largely because he trafficked so confidently in death, calling into being both a world war of unprecedented scale and the obscenity of the chillingly euphemistic Final Solution, the century's two defining events that numb by their very weight, rendering generic twentieth-century death (and by extension life). Gladney, however, has processed the Führer into a creepy kitsch, reconstructing Hitler into the blandest kind of celebrity, a depthless commodity (in a darkly comic point-counterpoint joint lecture delivered with a colleague, Gladney compares Hitler to Elvis); Hitler becomes for Gladney a career-maker and for the College-on-the-Hill another quirky syllabus topic to complement a Popular Culture department that also offers seminars on car crashes, cereal boxes, and public toilets. Gladney offers his students not moral sensibility or ethical critique but rather mesmerizing films of Hitler's stadium rallies that emphasize the spectacle but do not encourage speculation on the forbidding evil that the man unleashed. The Hitler myth provides Gladney a protective refuge. On the advice of the university chancellor, Gladney long ago bulked up to "grow out" into Hitler (17); like all department chairs, he wears full academic regalia around campus but has added a careless beard and heavy-framed dark glasses (even though they bother his eyes), thus fabricating a protective bunker of his own, a public persona he has dubbed J. A. K. Gladney—its laughable fraudulence underscored by his desperate attempts to learn just enough German to impress international scholars during a fast-approaching Hitler Studies conference. When a colleague meets Gladney sans regalia and glasses in a hardware store, he is surprised to find that Gladney is really a "big, harmless, aging, indistinct sort of guy" (83), an innocuous enough remark but so near the truth that it touches off a reckless spending spree, Gladney even encouraging his kids to pick out their Christmas gifts early, a panicked strategy of insulating his suddenly exposed self within the protective bunker of satisfying stacks of material goods.

In addition to analyzing the Hitler effect, DeLillo returns to his long interest in the thick influence of television, specifically the news with its nightly assault of calamity that makes catastrophic events overwhelmingly generic.[11] As Murray Jay Siskind—a visiting lecturer of popular culture at the college—observes, television with its "waves and radiation" has permeated our domestic sphere, "a primal force in the American home . . . like a myth being born right there in our living room" (51), an aesthetic force that—unlike books or painting or music or even film—has become an unprecedented invasive force. Effortlessly, the technology of images has displaced concern—indeed interest—for the unrecorded world that unfolds all around its tight frame. When Siskind and Gladney visit a tourist trap outside Blacksmith—The Most Photographed Barn in America—Siskind observes that the tourists, their cameras aclick, are not really seeing the barn itself but rather are re-recording it, maintaining its celebrated image, validating only that in a gesture of "spiritual surrender" (12). To counter the isolating effects of such domestic image-technology, Babette compels the family to eat their dinner while watching the nightly news—hoping to "de-glamorize the medium" and combat its narcotic pull (16).

Still, the news compels. And because the news has always been about how we die, how we maim each other, its relentless and indiscriminate procession of images becomes a ghastly narrative of catastrophe, a carnival excess of shootings, plane crashes, bar fights, house fires, traffic accidents, and murders periodically cut with commercials and packaged with the same marketing savvy as any entertainment programming. Denied privacy or dignity, death on the air becomes performance; looped endlessly, it becomes spectacle, even entertainment, an aesthetic anesthetic, rendering us insensitive, even indifferent to the complicated and often gruesome reality of what we are viewing (consider the horrific events recorded—and then endlessly replayed—from the Zapruder film to the *Challenger* explosion to the World Trade Center attacks). Worse, the accumulation of shock footage creates addiction for progressively more sensational coverage, a condition Siskind terms "brain fade" (67)—for instance, a breaking news story of two bodies unearthed in a backyard quickly disappoints when it is clear there are *only* the two corpses.

Not surprisingly, television pervades Gladney's narrative consciousness—Gladney's first-person narration is even periodically interrupted by triads of name-brand products, like commercial breaks, unrelated to the ongoing narrative events. Such commercial breaks reflect how television has permeated Gladney's thoughts, becoming part of the logic of his narrative processes.[12] Indeed, amid the confusions at the evacuation site and in a moment of particular tenderness as Gladney watches his daughter sleep, she murmurs, "*Toyota Celica,*" and Gladney feels an immediate validation—"the utterance was beautiful and mysterious, gold-shot with looming wonder" (155)—a comforting tie to the vast collective fashioned by commercial advertising. Television alone has come to validate experience, to give it weight and substance—when the airplane carrying Gladney's twelve-year-old daughter, Bee, experiences a dramatic altitude loss, she is disappointed that upon deplaning she finds no local media to confirm the magnitude of the experience. "They went through all that for nothing" (92). Later, when the evacuation following the airborne toxic event stretches into days, disgruntled residents forced to stay in primitive conditions at evac stations begin to grumble that they have been abandoned by the local media, that their plight has lost its depth and drama because it is no longer on television.

Finally, DeLillo scrutinizes the premise of contemporary science. He finds that, like Hitler's legacy and television news, science denies the nuance of mystery to the immediate. Science and the practical applications of technology routinely damage the delicate integrity of the natural world, disregard its intricacies, treating it as a simple commodity. The churning toxic cloud that pushes glacially across Blacksmith is just one reminder of the damage so casually, so steadily inflicted by science and technology on a fragile ecowebbing, our species behaving like some blind virus stupidly, relentlessly destroying the very thing that gives it life, condoning a slow-motion environmental holocaust that has yet to generate the level of concern that would indicate its implications are even vaguely apprehended. The tap water in Blacksmith tastes funny, and the town is told without explanation to start boiling its water. A foul odor hangs about the streets. Without clear explanation, the local school must be evacuated. Gladney's kids, despite their young ages, do not delight in their world, they understand the world is charged with carcinogens and bombarded with low-level radiation from radios, televisions, power lines, and microwaves and that particle pollution has rendered even sunlight toxic. Gladney wonders if the town's chemical dump may be responsible for his teenage son's odd hair loss.

If science and technology destroy, they also meddle by extending to a needful people the illusion that nature can be controlled (Gladney's German teacher, after the death of his mother, finds particular solace in meteorology), that the body's deficiencies can be corrected, life extended indefinitely, thus canceling the responsibility to accept the difficult arc of mortality, encouraging a dedicated denial of its reality. Dylar, an experimental synthetic psychobiological drug that Babette first hears about when she is reading supermarket tabloids to an elderly blind man, is designed to depress the part of the brain responsible for death-anxiety. As a shocked Gladney will himself find out when he confronts his wife with the empty prescription bottle, Babette, who despite her reassuring girth and healthy lifestyle had long harbored a fear of death as profound as her husband's, had responded more than a year earlier to the tabloid ad and had volunteered to serve as a test subject. When the small drug company pursuing the research decided the drug was not ready for human testing, however, Babette arranged to secure a sample of the medication by having sex over a period of six months with a project manager. But the medication has not worked—its only noticeable effect is a diminishment of Babette's memory. Still, her need persists: during the height of the panicked evacuation, amid the air-raid sirens and swooping helicopters, Gladney notices Babette slipping something into her mouth—she tells him it is a Life Saver.

When the evacuation and subsequent exposure so completely rob Gladney of his fabricated persona and force him to confront the grief-world that lurks just beyond the fringes of his comfortably tidy middle-class world, Gladney is presented an array of strategies for confronting the invasive immediacy of death. In the first part of the narrative, Gladney's strategy had been clear: calculated denial.

As he decides during his stop at the cemetery, he will allow the days their drift ("Do not advance the action according to a plan" [98]), ignore the gradual movement toward death by pretending such aimlessness resists ending. Indeed, there is even an appropriate drift to the unfolding narrative Gladney constructs in the first part—it is episodic, mimicking aimlessness and permitting the endearing illusion of never necessarily curving toward closure, each chapter a fragment of discrete narrative that collectively resists the gravitational pull of a coherent plot. After all, as Gladney tells his Hitler majors in his Advanced Nazism course, all "plots tend to move deathward" (26).[13]

That strategy is shattered, of course, by the Nyodene-D exposure. Afterward, Gladney must sort through options. He might try acceptance: Winnie Richards, the reclusive neurochemist at the college, is stumped by the Dylar sample Gladney brings her to analyze until Gladney tells her what he knows of the drug's intended effect. Then she counsels him to accept his fear, that the vastness of fear alone provides a "fresh awareness of the self" and that fear of death is the ultimate self-education (229). Or Gladney can try disengagement: the brooding Heinrich, Gladney's only son, at fourteen his hairline already receding, simply withdraws from any engagement with the natural world (he compares the world to a landfill), doubts the evidence of his own senses (he and his father conduct a disturbing— if hilarious—debate one rainy morning on the way to school on whether it is verifiably raining), dismisses emotions as chemical and/or neural misfires, and not surprisingly lives almost entirely behind closed doors within the shadows of his bedroom, playing chess by mail with an imprisoned serial killer in Texas. During the airborne toxic event, Heinrich is stimulated by the experience of large-scale doom—dressed in camouflage, he thrives amid the apocalyptic confusions of the evac station, comforted by the natural world's lurch into chaos. Or Gladney can try reckless defiance: Heinrich's friend, Orest Mercator, plans to set a world record for staying in a cage of poisonous snakes, an extreme gesture that cheapens the genuine mystery of death and underscores a careless arrogance that denies the physical its fullest measure. Or Gladney can try containing the fear of death via information overload: his daughter Denise, who worries early on that Babette may be having medical trauma and who first finds the empty prescription bottle of Dylar in the trash compactor, carefully combs her massive medical tomes to find something on the medicine; she is well-versed in the pathology of symptoms, recognizes carcinogens, scores high on television cancer quizzes, and can recite a catalog of illnesses and treatments. Death for her becomes another medical event, decidedly inglorious, a prosaic data transaction, with all the mystery of, say, an appendectomy. And, of course, Gladney can always try blissful ignorance: at the age of four, Babette's youngest child, Wilder, has evidenced no interest in language and thus enjoys (as his name suggests) an immediate involvement with the moment and with the natural world, uncomplicated by the sort of awareness that troubles his elders—pure receptor, he can stare endlessly into an oven window; he can study water boiling; he is easily confused when he sees Babette interviewed on television, lovingly caressing the television screen and ultimately crying, unable to separate the image from the real thing even when the sound malfunctions; he can sit quietly amid the noise of the Gladney dinner table with Buddha-like serenity; and he can go on a seven-hour crying jag without motivation. Such blithe aimlessness may be attractive, but later Wilder will happily pedal off on his tricycle across the busy highway behind the Gladney house, a disturbing episode that underscores the threat of living unaware.

Clearly, however, the most tempting strategy Gladney tests is the argument offered by Siskind. A Mephistophelean figure (he comes from the city, which he disparages for its oppressive heat; he is an amateur student of comparative religions; he is continually wreathed in smoke, always puffing on a pipe; he has a stiff goatee and wisps of hair that curl, hornlike, along his neck), Siskind is a most persuasive, most articulate creature of the flesh, a proponent of the thrall of the senses—he loves the smell of a woman's hair, the staticky slide of nylon-stockinged legs being crossed and uncrossed; he attempts only half in jest to seduce Babette; he overloads his grocery cart with generic goods, he sniffs the groceries in Gladney's cart; he defends car crashes in a seminar as upbeat expressions of American competitive spirit; he relishes the company of prostitutes during the evacuation, even attempts to negotiate for services. During a looping stroll around campus after Gladney has been exposed, Siskind masterfully manipulates a troubled Gladney, counseling him that anxiety over death is only natural, that death offers no wonder, that it will always be premature and invasive and that regret is therefore inevitable, that the reality of death leaves every life incomplete, awareness making impossible any attempt to live fully (a three-day scream, he says glibly, is about the most intelligent response). Helpless, we therefore fashion some believable afterlife, a desperate fantasy of survival. But, Siskind theorizes a tempting way around helplessness: you can be a die-er, he tells Gladney, and accept death, or you can be a killer and thereby gain life credits, a kind of scorecard contest (Siskind is a sportswriter by trade—indeed, he first appeared in *Amazons*); by controlling others, you buy yourself time, defy the law—both natural and juridical—by indulging the violence and energy of assertion. "To plot is to live" (291). Siskind, of course, dismisses the implications of his argument as just a theory (indeed, its implications horrify the reader—it justifies everything from drive-by shootings to the Holocaust). Gladney, however, is persuaded by its compelling simplicity. As Gladney begins to conceive of this sort of end run around death, his visiting father-in-law, ailing and nearing a death that he accepts with grim humor (a welcome counterargument to Gladney's manic terror), gives him an unexpected gift, a .25-caliber Zumwalt, a small German-made automatic.

Armed and feeling empowered, Gladney will follow Siskind's advice and take control: he fashions himself a plot—cuckolded husband kills his wife's lover—that is at once grandly operatic and baldly clichéd. He will track down the drug company executive—whose name, he learns from Winnie Richards, is Willie Mink and who has been fired from the drug company both for advertising for human test subjects and for his liaison with Babette. Richards tells Gladney that Mink is still staying at the same nearby hotel where he had met with Babette. Calmly, Gladney decides he will go the hotel, shoot the man three times in the stomach (certain that will inflict the greatest suffering), wipe the gun clean, put the gun in Mink's hand, and then scrawl a suicide note on the bathroom mirror with a handy crayon or lipstick tube—and, of course, take whatever samples of Dylar he may find. He is not troubled by the absurdity of a suicide to the stomach or multiple self-inflicted shots or by the assumed availability of a crayon or lipstick. Gladney boldly heads for the seedy hotel where Mink is staying in a parody of lawlessness and breaking free— he steals a neighbor's car (sort of—the keys are in the ignition), he exceeds the speed limit, he does not yield as he moves off the expressway ramp, he runs three stoplights, he does not pay his toll, each gesture a thin parody of his decision to step away from limits. His plot, however, begins almost immediately to unravel. He finds that Mink has grown stupid from ingesting Dylar—a pathetic Mink, dressed in a Hawaiian shirt and Budweiser shorts, mumbles incoherently as he stares blankly into the hotel-room television and shovels handfuls of Dylar into his droolly mouth. A side effect of his abuse of Dylar, the real world has lost its immediacy: Mink can no longer distinguish the word from the reality; thus, when Gladney yells, "Hail of bullets" (311), the hapless Mink ducks in panic. Gladney nevertheless fires twice, hitting Mink in the stomach. Then the plan collapses of its own irony: Gladney puts the gun in Mink's hand to create the appearance of a suicide, and Mink promptly shoots Gladney in the wrist.

His plot gone awry, Gladney quickly ad-libs a new one: he opts to be overwhelmed by an inspired rush of compassion, a convenient and unconvincing lurch toward a Hollywood happy ending.[13] After assuring the barely coherent Mink that he had in fact shot himself, Gladney first performs mouth-to-mouth and then hustles the wounded Mink off to a nearby night clinic, staffed entirely by German nuns. A happy ending, à la *The Names*, appears ready to break out—Gladney even engages the nuns in playful German-language exercises, language forging a contentment of belonging. But then Gladney's wounds are treated by Sister Hermann Marie, an imposing and unforgiving nun who ministers without compassion or gentleness. As Gladney inquires in passing about a picture on the clinic wall showing

John Kennedy and Pope John XXIII holding hands in heaven, the nun testily reveals that she has no faith in the Christian afterlife ("Do you think we are stupid?" [317]); indeed, marginalized medieval curiosities such as herself pretend to believe only to give significance to the world's abandonment of faith. By the time of Gladney's departure, she is so miffed that she is reduced to spitting at him angrily in German, pressing her face into his and spraying him with a wet hail of guttural invective that Gladney cannot understand in ways that recall Axton atop the Acropolis unavailable to the meaning of the language around him. The implications, however, are manifestly different. Although Gladney finds the unintelligible harangue arresting, even "beautiful" (320), the nun's cadenced assault rudely strips Gladney of any illusion of community—it is a far cry from the consoling and generous webbing Axton feels amid the disparate dialects atop the Acropolis.

Gladney, then, offers a closing chapter that is less a narrative ending than a series of suggestive vignettes that each confirm Gladney's isolation and apartness—death cannot be ignored, it cannot be indulged with self-pity; it cannot be contained or understood; and within its sweeping energy, each must stand alone. First, Gladney relates Wilder's harrowing tricycle ride across six lanes of crowded expressway traffic and how he ended up howling in the murky shallows of a watery ditch—a cautionary tale about the risks of living too blithely in the moment without awareness of death as a parameter. Embrace limits: and so Gladney moves his narrative to a highway overpass where, each evening, residents of Blacksmith have begun to gather just to watch the sun set, mesmerized into a reverent hush by the striking colorations that have lingered since the toxic cloud. All ages gather, exposed to the ringing bronze of the sunset; with folding chairs and thermoses, they look westward, react uncertainly to the vivid spectacle in a tonic mingling of dread, awe, and elation, compelled by the sheer drama of ending, each sunset an event that is (like death itself) paradoxically generic and yet extraordinary, beautiful yet terrifying. Confronting it, Gladney acknowledges, must be done alone. "This waiting is introverted, uneven, almost backward and shy, tending toward silence" (324). Despite the throng that gathers, Gladney notes that after darkness has fallen the people break off from the crowd and return slowly to their cars, to the isolation of their "separate and defensible selves" (325)—a sobering reminder that confirms isolation as inevitable. So compelled by the drama of ending, Gladney rejects his desperate faith in science and medical technology: he decides not to open sealed medical test results that would likely give him the clearest indication of the effects of his Nyodene exposure, and he opts not to return the persistent phone calls from his doctor—he decides, in short, to live amid the unfolding immediate, decides that the real mystery is not sickness or even death but rather wellness, each day that we do not concede to the inevitable collapse into disease. Accept the moment, Gladney tells us.

Gladney's narrative will twist a final turn, however. Accepting uncertainty, we wait, together yet apart, uneasy but compelled by our awareness to respect the condition of vulnerability. So we close in that refuge where Gladney had earlier found such easy security: the massive labyrinth of the local supermarket. But Gladney discovers that the store's long-reliable shelving scheme has been unaccountably shuffled; now patrons wander about, uncertain and lost, vaguely heading, each one alone with carts full, toward the terminal checkout. Amid the exercise of mortality, the reality of its casual and inevitable intrusion, Gladney chooses grief, elects awareness necessarily yoked to confusion, taps into the mesmerizing beauty of a clear logic: we are each heading alone toward the terminal, moving deliberately through an uneasy and fluid reality, working through the confusions—life, metaphorically, a neighborhood store teeming with goods yet subject to constant change, and death, metaphorically, the slow-moving checkout at the register. As he closes his narration, Gladney dismisses once, for all the tempting lure of the tabloids whose cunning, oppressive hype first introduced the panacea of Dylar; he scans the garish headlines at the checkout line, those that promise miracle vitamins, cancer cures, and the remedies for obesity and those that exploit our obsession with dead celebrities. Each represents an absurd tampering with what is the stunning natural order of living and dying, ultimately the same process. Gladney accepts what he has long resisted, the privilege of being generic; he accepts, despite heroic efforts to conjure relationships that last, the complex gift of isolation, which in the end allows his narrative to bless the obligation of vulnerability, which James Axton never confronted in his heady celebration of the community forged by language. DeLillo himself suggests such a position of both isolation and unsuspected strength in a short story from the same time. In "The Ivory Acrobat," a woman living in Athens is traumatized by the severity of an earthquake and struggles in the aftermath to adjust to her anxieties until a friend presents her with a carved Minoan statue of an ancient traditional figure, a bull-leaper, a young person who would hurl over charging bulls. The ivory figure is of a young woman suspended in space, her curved, lean, supple form in exultant and lonely somersault over the danger and thunder of the unseen bulls—a potent suggestion of the unexpected litheness of the human soul, alone and strong, suddenly, dramatically confronting genuine fear.

4

Narratives of Redemption

A part and apart, Axton at the Acropolis and Gladney in the supermarket: DeLillo examines two sides of a decidedly contemporary sort of awakening, the elevating confidence that comes from the difficult gesture of accepting the mysterious draw of uncertainty and the problematic positioning of the individual within a freewheeling universe that science and television, despite their sustained efforts, cannot diminish into predictability or banality. But DeLillo as administrator of language understands that the invigorating discovery of this confidence cannot entirely satisfy; the fragile moment cannot suffice. Passion, it turns out, is not in the experience of the immediate. Rather, passion is in the work of shaping that experience into language, the determination to record it, sharing that experience with an unnameable but genuine audience using the aesthetic technologies of narrative: observation, pattern-making, plot-shaping, design, and invention. The spell must be spelled out or it is pointless ecstasy, a momentary intensity cooling inevitably into private recollection until dispersing ultimately into the thin recesses of the forgotten. Thus, in the confident voice of his most accomplished works—*Libra, Mao II,* and most dramatically *Underworld*—DeLillo focuses ultimately on narration itself, specifically on the role of the writer and of writing in an electronic age so stunningly, so overwhelmingly visual that it threatens the word with irrelevancy. In each work, he tracks in intricate counterplay characters drawn to the notion of engagement against other characters, writers or writer-figures, who use the technology of words to invest that struggle with weight and presence by organizing its struggle into designed discourse, setting the chilling wonder of experience to the available music of language.

Libra (1988)

DeLillo has often cited the ambush in Dealey Plaza as a cultural trauma, a national epiphany that would leave his generation suspended between outrage and fear. DeLillo has connected his own development as a writer to the shootings in Dallas. "I don't think my books could have been written in the world that existed before the Kennedy assassination. . . . It's conceivable that this made me the writer I am—for better or worse."[1] Indeed, the assassination dramatically plays on themes that have long engaged DeLillo: the confrontation with the sudden immediacy of mortality; the clumsy play of chance; the fascination with the hacksaw intrusion of violence. Moreover, for DeLillo, the assassination marked the street-birth of the media age—specifically, of television news and the rush to bring catastrophe into living rooms. The eighteen-second Zapruder home movie, initially circulated underground but ultimately appropriated by mainstream media and replayed ad nauseam, revealed within its enhanced and blurred stopped-frames the shocking eggshell fragility of the human frame (it is, after all, a film record of a man's head being splattered), as did the live broadcast two days later of the shooting in the basement of Dallas police headquarters of the suspected assassin—an image burned into a nation's collective memory: the sweatered Oswald, his mouth an ago-nized oval, gripping his stomach, there next to an imposing Dallas police detective, helpless, implausibly enough dressed in a heroic white hat. Here, DeLillo sees a culture begin its unsettling addiction to spectacle violence, the deep thrill of graphic film sequences that, from Vietnam (only a handful of months from com-mencing its slow-burn ignition) to the World Trade Center attacks, has deadened any ability to react to the private privilege of pain and death.

By itself, the shooting in Dealey Plaza makes poor narrative material: its plot is riven by coincidence; it lacks a believable culprit, a stable hero, definable motiva-tion, a clear conflict, reliable themes, a clean line of action, and, most troubling, a final page. It is complexity without purpose, agony without meaning, violence with-out justice, a riddle without answer—in a short story DeLillo published the same year as *Libra* ("The Runner"), a man on his usual run through the park, witnesses, helpless, the swift abduction of a child and assumes it must be a desperate father, only to find out later from police that the snatching was an entirely random crime—the implications terrify him. When DeLillo, nearly twenty-five years after the fact, turned to the materials of the Kennedy shooting for narrative treatment, he would come to it not to resolve its entangling questions by constructing a sound reading of the events. These historic fictions (so-called "docu-fictions," such as Norman Mailer's *The Executioner's Song* or Truman Capote's *In Cold Blood*) methodically impose order on the scatter of events and enchant bare history with the fiction writer's gift for detail and observation; uncertainty morphs into in-evitability, mystery into hard-edged clarity, the inexplicable into the inevitable, and harrowing contingency into satisfying causality. Rather, under DeLillo's treat-ment, the assassination speaks to the depth of our need for such plotting, our hunger for plausibility. Dealey Plaza instructed DeLillo's generation that despite being empowered by centuries of Enlightenment assumptions about the sheer power of the speculative imagination to render solutions and despite an event that has engendered a dense florescence of interpretation and explication, we have been left no closer to surety. Facts—even in such intimidating volume—have constituted only competing truths. Despite 692 eyewitnesses and the unblinking testimony of more than seventy cameras crowding a tight triangle of streets beneath a nondescript six-story brick schoolbook warehouse (DeLillo would spend three years researching the evidence), the shootings on that Friday noon, awash in the clarifying glare of the noon sun of a late Texas autumn, remain in shadows. After Dealey Plaza, we have been left to the elaborate exercise of craft and deceit, conspiracy and paranoia that, if divorced from the horrific execution that actually took place at 12:30:52 on November 22, 1963, reveals the imagination engaged full throttle in the face of persistent mystery, reveals how perfect facts perfectly pieced together make perfect fictions.

In a narrative that seeks to constellate a plausible reading of the Kennedy assassination, Lee Harvey Oswald naturally commands the narrative center. More than forty years after the shooting, Oswald has become a familiar, if troubling, text, the template for a subculture of disaffected misfits, ranging from next week's neighborhood nonentity who inexplicably sprays gunfire at the workplace to the more dramatic examples of John Hinckley or David Berkowitz, Ted Kaczynski or John Mohammed, Eric Rudolph or Dennis Rader: the Ur-loner, the alienated maladjusted nobody, raised amid difficult familial pressures, unmoved by affection, fed on the tough-guy fantasies of television, paperback novels, and movies and determined to secure a place within history, to become an event, a domestic terrorist fueled, not so much by any political fanaticism or any commitment to mayhem, but by the need to be known, by the need to be more than ordinary, the need to shake free of the banality of middle-class satisfactions (like work, love, family) by attaching the isolate self to the sweeping movements of history itself. That reading of Oswald makes reassuring sense—the "lone Texas gunman" drawn as much from Hollywood westerns as from conspiracy theorists. We have made from unpromising materials a persuasively coherent form named Lee Harvey Oswald, a three-name, two-dimensional bricolage of television footage, grainy black-and-white photographs, diary entries, police records, and sound bites; we have substituted accessibility for speculation, repetition for clarity, and the attractive glint of surface for depth. Oswald, after all, was given to us amid the shock and whirl of an unfolding trauma, manufactured on the spot by television itself—we had received no foreshadowing, had tracked no motivation, no complicated ascent toward that trigger moment. Stunned by the cold testimony of contingency, we fashioned an uncomplicated heavy, a conjure summoned by the crack of a rifle, to carry the deep burden of plausibility and plot.

We made that Lee Harvey Oswald—and DeLillo audaciously unmakes it, returns Lee Oswald to compelling uncertainties, gives depth to the accessible image that the media rendered as history, re-complicates *history* with *his story,* not to generate sympathy for Oswald (in the narrative, he is a violent loner and a hapless failure—his three shots at the motorcade are each ineffective) but rather to reclaim the privilege of uncertainty itself and to remind us that definitive form and stable certainties are the dreary, distracting inevitabilities of the surface-culture of the media age. As a child in the Tremont section of the Bronx (within blocks of DeLillo's own childhood haunts), Oswald is most compelled by the underground subway system. We first meet him hurtling through the tunnels, tuned to the power of the dark and the tantalizing suggestion of a world beneath a world, a secret world purer, truer than the bald, obvious surface world. In school, the young Oswald loves to read about animals, but he studies burrowing animals and cave dwellers, lair-bound creatures inaccessible to intrusive observation. Oswald maintains just such a distance from the reader—inaccessible, contradictory—as the truancy board concludes, in their psychological profile of Oswald as an underachieving teen: "He feels almost as if there is a veil between him and other people through which they cannot reach him, but he prefers this veil to remain intact."[2] *Libra's* Oswald thus stubbornly resists coherence or even definition, his identity subject to multiple drafts and versions, a matrix of maddening contradictions and inconsistencies—in short, a dense text open to interpretation.[3]

To construct and reconstruct Oswald, DeLillo, as governing authority, structures two parallel plots: in one (each chapter headed by a geographic locale), DeLillo meticulously recreates a plausible fictional biography of Oswald, tracking the paradox of Oswald's contradictory commitments to both the political left and right, to both the Soviet Union and the Marines, to the austere doctrine of Marxism and the opulent rhetoric of the American Dream—balancing these evident contradictions into a convincing psychological narrative that leads with gathering momentum to the sixth-floor window of the Texas School Book Depository. In a counternarrative (each chapter headed by dates in 1963 moving inexorably toward November 22), DeLillo fashions a fictional conspiracy, conceived by a retired CIA agent named Win Everett, his career in ruins after the 1961 Bay of Pigs debacle and now exiled to the indignity of a teaching post in history and economics at Texas Woman's University. Everett first conceives of an intrigue to be carried out by other disaffected agency renegades from the Bay of Pigs: a spectacular miss of the American president that would be blamed on pro-Castro fanatics and would, in turn, ignite national outrage and rekindle a renewed (and genuine) effort to overthrow the hated Castro. But the charade-assassination, even as it is planned, evolves (Everett unable to control his own plot) into the very real execution eventually carried out in Dealey Plaza. These conspirators, of course, need a dupe "to extend their fiction into the world" (50), a credible lone gunman, a redundant shooter to take the fall, a shadow player who would be apprehended and, of course, killed by local police while the real shooters would vanish. Even as the conspirators sketch out the requirements of such a figure, they are introduced by chance to the attractive figure of Oswald, already familiar to government information

agencies: at twenty-four, a drifter without steady employment, a troubled and troublesome ex-Marine, a communist sympathizer, a one-time defector now with a
Russian wife, a vocal political agitator with grandiose self-delusions (who had
apparently masterminded the botched April 1963 shooting of Major General
Edwin Walker, a controversial right-wing firebrand living in Dallas), and, best of all,
a Castro supporter with a penchant for mail-order rifles. Although the intersecting
drama between conspirators and the unsuspecting Oswald is mesmerizing (indeed,
some initial critical reaction to *Libra* blasted DeLillo for confecting history), a plausible theory of the Kennedy shooting is clearly not DeLillo's aim. *Libra* is more
a theory about theorizing, a narrative about narrating, a plot about plotting. The
novel foregrounds its own presence. Indeed, four writer/plotters—Win Everett,
Lee Harvey Oswald, Nicholas Branch, and ultimately DeLillo himself—contest
the narrative, and within the tension of their creative efforts DeLillo clarifies his
own thematic concern: the therapeutic energy of the imagination able to accept,
rather than resolve, uncertainty, instability, and mystery.

As originating author of the assassination plot, Win Everett relishes the elegance of design and the illusion of control: he sees the elaborate staging of a faux-
assassination as justified retribution for the administration's mishandling of the Bay
of Pigs. His plot will right that evident wrong, like some contrived vengeance
drama—the faux assassination will "happen" to take place in Miami on the second
anniversary of the Bay of Pigs fiasco. Everett must conjure a convincing pro-
Castro assassin and then plant a clear paper trail of forged documents, doctored
photographs, and bogus letters, a profile that, as it emerges, fits Oswald—Everett
delights in such detail work; his plot is history as it should be, with clean lines of
responsibility and predictable consequences. He sequesters himself in his basement, literally cutting and pasting photographs of Oswald to enhance the background of Oswald as a credible shooter. Like a meticulous novelist storyboarding a
massive plotline, Everett fashions linearity, designs causality, and recovers account-
ability from the figures he manipulates—he finds it difficult even to accept that
Oswald exists separate from his control. In a telling aside, Everett's young daughter, waiting for her parents to fall asleep, brings out what she calls her Little Figures, two clay dolls of Native Americans that she keeps hidden in her closet, not
as toys but as surrogate parents should her own prove someday to be bogus. They
protect her, she believes, from the world. Certainly, her father's bravura basement
conjuring suggests a similar refuge. The plotting itself insulates him—he cannot
confide to his loving wife, cannot enjoy the simplest mealtimes with his family, and
feels particular estrangement from the uncomplicated openness of his young
daughter.

In his sanctuarial basement, however, Everett feels the centripetal acceleration as
his plot, with its elegant and abstract intricacy, being commandeered into mayhem

by accomplice T. J. Mackey, a "cowboy type" who resents Kennedy's blundering and the subsequent softening of the administration's anti-Castro rhetoric as a condition of the High Noon victory during the Cuban Missile Crisis (24). As such, Mackey represents, unlike the ivory-towered Everett, plotters who crave not elegance but power, not invention but execution (pun intended), the terrorist figure that had long moved about the shadows of DeLillo's fiction. Dangerous because they are passionate, ruthless because they are certain, noble because they are single-minded, such terrorists invade event itself with the muscle of intentionality. They do not conjure—they deploy. Unlike Everett, with his gluepot and razor, his talent for detailing, and his fondness for locking cause to effect, these men suggest the mess and tangle of engagement. They calculate with single-minded purpose, strong-arm chance and event to a limited agenda, and then clear away from the maelstrom of consequences. There are other terrorist plotters here: Castro himself, whose revolution and calculated ascent to power are recalled in narrative asides among the shooters recruited for the Dallas hit; Kennedy and the doomed Bay of Pigs mission; Jack Ruby, who with chilling moxie and a vigilante's sense of justice (and in front of millions of eyewitnesses) executes the "smirky bastard" responsible for a nation's inconsolable grief (419). They are the doers. If Everett sees Oswald as a suggestive pattern, to Mackey, Oswald is merely a convenience— Mackey arranges for one of the assassination squad to rendezvous with Oswald at the Texas Theater after the shooting, not to effect, as Oswald believes, his escape to Mexico (and ultimately to Cuba and to what he imagines will be his heroic reception) but rather to shoot Oswald and thus deliver to Dallas police the "lone gunman," killed presumably by the mysterious Castro agents who had used the communist sympathizer to kill the president. Tidy and tight. Like Everett's basement storyboarding, however, Mackey's plot does not ultimately succeed—Oswald, panicking when he realizes that he has been set up to take the fall for the assassination, shoots a police officer en route to the theater. The police swarm the theater and arrest Oswald before he can be dispatched.

Long before he is the subject of such plottings, however, Oswald himself has struggled to construct a reliable, satisfying, stable version of himself.[4] When the conspirators break into Oswald's New Orleans apartment to secure a sample of his handwriting, they are stunned to discover a cache of forged documents—passports, driver's licenses, draft cards, and political membership cards—that testify to Oswald's creepy fascination with inventing identities. Indeed, Oswald answers to a different name in virtually every place he lives. Among them is an elaborate sort of alter ego, named Hidell, whom Oswald invents while stationed as a Marine radar operator in Japan in an elaborate gesture at secrecy that coincides with his decision to engage the clandestine world of espionage as part of his planned defection to the Soviet Union. Like other DeLillo characters of the media age, Oswald is absent a core self; he thus sees himself from the outside, audience to his own efforts to create a significant self (or selves, in his case). Oswald will thus play clumsy author to his own identity; he claims on a form for study overseas that he wants to be a short-story writer, despite a severe language disorder that renders even simple handwriting nearly impossible. The young Oswald dreams of becoming consequential, a nondescript kind of guy deformed, like so many of his postwar generation, by the fantasies he has absorbed uncritically from television and westerns, from movie posters and James Bond novels—indeed, he dreams of having his stature confirmed by being on the cover of *Time* and, supremely, of being on television (he is momentarily mesmerized when he and his wife are caught on screen by a department-store display camera). He lives apart from his own life, watching it. Despairing over evidence of his inconsequentiality after defecting (Soviet officials are uncertain how to take the American, their polygraphs on him come up inconclusive), Oswald prepares to slash his wrists—but as he does, he thinks of a Gillette razor blade commercial. Then he consciously mimics the wrist-slashing process as he has seen it played out in the movies (he even imagines appropriate soundtrack violin music as a camera follows his blood-swirl down the sink). A month before the Kennedy shooting, he spends the night of his twenty-fourth birthday watching a late-night double feature on television: *Suddenly,* in which Frank Sinatra, as a burned-out combat veteran, attempts to shoot an Eisenhower-styled president, and *We Were Strangers,* in which John Garfield, as a heroic and doomed American revolutionary, plots to kill a ruthless Cuban dictator. Oswald believes the films speak to him. "They were running a message through the night into his skin" (370).

What he disdains is his ordinary self, the surface consolations of home, family, work, love (in a particularly affective moment, he wanders about his Dallas neighborhood lugging his garbage, unable to afford the pickup fee, looking for an empty can to use). He resists the pedestrian implications of his own unhappy childhood —the death of his father shortly before he is born, the difficult poverty, the aimless wandering with a smothering mother, the struggle to maintain interest in school, the routine abuse of the schoolyards. "Happiness," he writes in a letter to his brother that DeLillo uses as an epigraph to part 1, "is taking part in the struggle, where there is no borderline between one's own personal world, and the world in general." Oswald wants to grandly project his manifestly inconsequential self into something far bigger. Embedded within the grind of poverty that has left inaccessible the American Dream, he is persuaded early on by the communist vision, a faith triggered when at fifteen he is handed on the street a pamphlet about the fast-approaching execution of the Rosenbergs for alleged spying activity. Within the refuge of neighborhood libraries in New Orleans, he is mesmerized by accounts of the charismatic figures of Lenin and Trotsky ("History means to merge.

The purpose of history is to climb out of your own skin" [101]). Later, while stationed in Japan, he is thrilled glimpsing a visiting John Wayne, feeling the aura of
the big-screen projection. Intoxicated by the poetry of Walt Whitman, which celebrates the ever-widening horizon of an expanding self, Oswald begins at twenty
what he self-consciously designates as his Historic Diary, in which he writes himself into the Big Picture for a posterity he assumes will be interested in his journey
into history (the passages we read are labored and fractured). While in the Soviet
Union, he is particularly riveted by news of the downed American U-2 pilot Fran-
cis Gary Powers, an unlikely nobody who quite literally dropped into history to
become what Oswald so hungers to be: a media-text, a historic vector, that unanticipated juncture in which the nondescript merges with history itself. Even as the
oxygen-masked Oswald lays dying in the ambulance that takes him from Dallas
police headquarters, certain now that he has become a vector, he identifies with
Powers, ejected from his plane, dropping slowly, unstoppably into the Russian
countryside and into history. "Me-too and you-too. He is a stranger, in a mask,
falling" (440).

Oswald will try to find this tantalizing premise of self-projection first within the
military—by eighteen, he is stationed with the Marines in Japan. He does not
respond, however, to the indignities of the harsh system—we follow the harrowing
twenty-eight days he spends in the brig, where he must forsake any sense of individuality amid the guards' routine beatings. It becomes for him an Orwellian
metaphor for a military system that he sees is as oppressive as the capitalist system
back home. He plots then to defect, to join his puny self to a Soviet collective
whose sheer geographic expanse and commensurate sense of historic moment
mesmerize him. In Moscow, however, he finds little interest in his defection—his
security clearance had long been invalidated, making his value as an informant
minimal—and he is assigned a low-level factory job in Minsk. Frustrated, Citizen
Oswald returns to the States and finds himself mired in dreary domesticity, still a
zero in the system, unable to hold even a dead-end job and prone to abusing his
wife in his frustration. After the botched Walker shooting, he discovers he is a subject of interest to the FBI and is given the chance to play secret agent, to gather
information on leftist pro-Castro agitators in New Orleans by posing as a right-
wing anti-Castro fanatic. It is this involvement that will lead him to the eccentric
homosexual pilot named David Ferrie, one of the conspirators (whom Oswald
already knows from his high-school days in the Civil Air Patrol), who in turn per-
suades Oswald to participate in the shooting of the president. It is when he is jailed
after the shooting that he understands that now he has a mission: to validate and
explicate this radical media-text named Lee Harvey Oswald, to dismiss the patsy
defense and claim the privileged status of the "lone gunman" (426). He finally
achieves the status of third-person commodity, an image—as he himself is shot in

the basement of police headquarters he conceives of the shooting as a televised event (shot as much by Ruby's pistol as by the news cameras); through the pain, he imagines himself on television, reacting to the pistol shot. So who *is* Lee Harvey Oswald? In the closing chapter, the grim burial of Oswald (he is buried under the name William Bobo, a last alias, a final reminder of his inaccessibility), a grieving Marguerite Oswald confirms the status of her son as compelling cipher: she vows to someday write extensively about her son, volumes, she promises, full of a mother's recollections and not part of the ongoing national record of her son as a misfit assassin. "Who," she demands, "arranged the life of Lee Harvey Oswald? It goes on and on and on" (455).

In a spare narrative presence, DeLillo introduces a third author, a fictitious retired CIA analyst named Nicholas Branch, hired by the agency fifteen years after Dallas to write a definitive "secret" history of the shootings. As historian, Branch seeks the convincing read, the unassailable solidity of plot, the harmonics of cause and effect, motivation and resolution. But Branch is entombed in a forbidding, fire-proof subbasement teeming with documents from the assassination, an accumulating inundation of grisly photographs, boxes of physical evidence and cassette tapes, binders of testimony, all supplied by a vaguely malevolent provider identified only as the Curator. Like Everett, like Oswald, Branch is another lonely man in a small room, an isolate sustained by theories and facts. We learn nothing about Branch, we are not even given physical detailing (save the protective gloves he wears)—he is thus the disembodied imperative to understand, the principle of historic explanation itself made ironic, even parodic, by Dallas. As historian, Branch is detached and curious, and quietly overwhelmed, consequently, by the massive plotlessness of the accumulated data (his name suggests the tortuous connections—or are they coincidences?—he comes to see within the data, even as he struggles to resist the easy lure of paranoia). Even simple facts—Oswald's eye color, whether he drove a car, his height—are inconsistent. Branch will come to concede that any coherence shaped from such mass will always be premature and finally abdicates the imperative entirely by lamely concluding that the Kennedy shooting was a "rambling affair that succeeded in the short term due mainly to chance" (441): coincidental meetings between those involved, the choice of the motorcade route, Oswald's employment in the book depository along that route and his work schedule that would put him on the sixth floor, alone, just as the motorcade passed, and even the unseasonable weather in Dallas that encouraged an open car. Thus, the historian despairs—Branch concedes after fifteen years he has "precious little" actually written (59)—or goes about fashioning towering improbabilities that deny complexity, like the twenty-six volumes of the Warren Commission Report, which Branch describes as "the megaton novel

James Joyce would have written if he'd moved to Iowa City and lived to be a hundred" (181).

It is left finally to DeLillo himself to participate as the narrative's fourth plotter, ultimately the sole successful author-agency. Unlike the frustrated Branch, DeLillo seeks to surround the inelegant moment in Dallas with a comforting plausibility, to provide what he terms in the author's note to the first edition, a "refuge," a shelter in which events play out with the solid construction of inevitability even as those events themselves reveal the puzzling intrusion of chance and thus accept the plot's necessarily provisional nature, its susceptibility, indeed invitation, to later revision. DeLillo as novelist co-opts inevitability and provides the very events that frustrate Branch with the richness of a plot that privileges its own instability. It is both form and antiform. Unlike visual media, which so casually appropriate the presumption of final arbiter by virtue of the "real" data of the recorded image, narrative redeems history from its evident confusion but at the same time refuses to accept any of its patternings as final—certain, yet flexible; clear, yet ambiguous, that is the mission of narrative, stabilizing into a manageable line the difficult onrush of circumstances, content with the rush and feel of causality, content with a serviceable—rather than an inviolable—truth.[5] Resolution is not the goal but merely the incentive. *Libra* thus is a revelation of its own logic, a sort of first draft of a plot, coaxing its momentary spell, a compelling confidence in the exertion itself that shapes in a reasonable facsimile of probability the satisfying texture of (re)created voices, revealing details and compelling a story, which renders, finally, the only sort of order possible in the late-century universe defined by the unnerving realities of uncertainty, fluidity, and chaos. Much contemporary cultural anxiety emerges because history despairs over such a premise and because the media presumes a patently bogus authority to stabilize event; it is narrative art alone that thrives confidently within such freedom and thus extends the difficult solace of a temporary harmony.

Here the title comes into significant play. When conspirator Clay Shaw first meets Oswald, he immediately asks his astrological sign. He then describes Oswald's character via the astrological reading of a Libran: "We have the positive Libran who has achieved self-mastery. He is well balanced, levelheaded, a sensible fellow respected by all. We have the negative Libran who is, let's say, somewhat unsteady and impulsive. Easily, easily, easily influenced" (315). Both, of course, define Oswald. Either extreme, DeLillo cautions, violates the purity of the impenetrable yin-yang construction not only of Oswald's contradictory character(s) but of any human psyche. Subjecting any event, even the most mundane, to the massive scrutiny that Dealey Plaza has received, DeLillo suggests, would be to confirm inevitably the tricky play of coincidence, the spell of mystery, the intrusion of chance, and still the reassuring suasion of inevitability and apparent design, sustaining both structural balance and irony. Thus, after engaging the narrative dynamic of community and isolation in *The Names* and *White Noise,* DeLillo furthers his investigation into narrative by affirming as therapeutic the exercise of speculation itself, its reconstruction of possibilities, the agency of invention, in short confirming the imagination's central position in a media age that has otherwise ushered to the margins those still engaged in the act (and art) of writing.

Mao II (1991)

If contemporary authors linger in the margins, amid the self-enclosing delight of narratives they generously construct against and amid the careless mayhem of contingency, DeLillo cautions in his follow-up work that such isolation can bring insuperable loneliness and violate the humane need for others, leaving the entire writing enterprise precious and narrow. What obligation does the writer have to engage, resist, or at least confront those very contemporary forces that have come to render individuality and identity—long the sustaining grails of narrative inquiry—as irrelevant? How comforting, finally, is the bunker? *Mao II* boldly interrogates this dynamic, the tension between isolation and community that defines the reader-writer dynamic amid the special pressures of a late-century media culture.

We begin in a ballpark, emerald bold with efficient white lines and uniformed players all in place, an entirely conjured environment that is the innocent evocation of a young Willard Skansey Jr., a socially retarded nine-year-old midwestern farmchild who behind a locked bedroom door joyously announces imaginary baseball games. At once player, announcer, audience, and radio, the child is gratefully disengaged from the relentless emptiness of long Iowa afternoons. Spontaneous, free-flowing, immediate, the pretend games suspend the isolation that hangs heavily about the child who is already distant from an older sister and awkward with parents who practice the gentle terrorism of relentless constructive criticism, a child unable to process the implications of his own apartness but able nevertheless to revel in the surprising exercise of a mind consoling its own anxieties within the spun-green reach of a made-up ball diamond, a child caught up by the splendid technology of invention and by the grateful enclosure of a fragile hiding place. Some fifty years later, this same Willard Skansey will die far from the retreat of a locked bedroom; in fact, he will die in a sterile public arena—on the deck of a Mediterranean ferry on his way to effect a heroic (and doomed) rescue of a United Nations worker and minor poet kidnapped by Middle Eastern terrorists. Amid a crowd of indifferent foreigners, Skansey will die unnoticed, from untreated internal injuries sustained days earlier in a freakish hit-and-run accident in which he was struck by a careening car, the victim (although the term is itself inappropriately dramatic) of the same dreary contingency that he had sought long ago to escape within the friendly confines of a made-up ballpark.

Not entirely surprising, in the intervening fifty years, Willard Skansey, that lonely prodigy with the full-throttle imagination, had become a writer of fiction who had published under the pen name Bill Gray (such a strategy of identity displacement suggesting a telling dislocation from his authentic self, indeed the generic name itself is so thin in character as to be near anonymous). He had authored two slender midcentury novels—thus he was among the last generation of writers to deploy the narrative before the chill descent of the shallow distractions of the media culture—film, television, commercial advertising, assorted cyber-environments—in short, the last generation of writers able to shape the grand narrative of their culture before writers would have to face the stark implications of their own gathering irrelevancy as audiences turned to the innocuous accessibility of the image. Thus, for DeLillo, Willard Skansey is particularly intriguing, a writer still able to recollect how observation (his last name merges two verbs that both mean "to look at"), pattern-making, the enthralling suggestivity of plot and character, and the music of designed articulation could create a moral force able in turn to strike, alter, bury, and lift readers one vulnerable heart, one epiphanic awakening at a time.[6]

Skansey's two books had indeed shaken their cultural moment in ways that a scant thirty years later would appear quaintly nostalgic. But there is powerful testimony of this critical dynamic. DeLillo tells of a twenty-something man-child in the late 1970s named Scott Martineau, indifferent to his college commitment, adrift in the reckless and dead-end pursuit of chic spirituality (pharmaceuticals and hokey pilgrimages to the Himalayas), who, while selling shoes in Minneapolis, is given Skansey's first book to read and who feels his life suddenly clarified, his isolation cut into, his self at once violated and rendered whole—still, of course, manifestly alone, he feels nevertheless shared. Fiction clarifies his identity. That is the critical dynamic of DeLillo's reader-writer contract: two strangers, isolates in separate rooms, writer and reader, sharing the comforts of a conjured voice, the luxury of design, the reassuring rhythms of sentences, the steadying engine of made-up actions of convincing word-chord characters, the essential ventriloquism of text production summoning that accidental conspiracy between two fragile individuals, writer and reader, who stumble upon each other within the narrative space and who find in that rich, inexplicable interaction, that mysterious community, the redemptive validation of mutual consequentiality. Unlike the centripetal exercise of the imaginary ball game that enthralls the young Willard, the narrative act, which presses voice into stable form, is a reaching outward, an intrusive gesture of engagement that makes possible the sole unit among all human relationships—friendship, marriage, love, family—that here does not come under DeLillo's harsh scrutiny.

DeLillo has always suspected tidiness, however; indeed, here he interrogates the premise of this mutually sustaining writer-reader dynamic. Like the young Willard Skansey, the adult Bill Gray has withdrawn to a sort of antilife behind locked doors. After the initial flush of success, Skansey, pursued by predatory fans enamored by the cheap aura of his celebrity, the market commodity named Bill Gray, retreats for more than thirty years to a rural compound outside Manhattan, becomes the "lost man of letters,"[7] a virtual prisoner of his own quirky eccentricity (ironically, like J. D. Salinger, he becomes an even greater celebrity by his withdrawal, famous for not writing, famous for not appearing, a culture's literary gimmick).[8] With romantic grandness, he sees himself as a vestige of integrity in a commodity world (he is struck by the intriguing wisdom of a fragmentary bit he recalls from the hat page of a Sears catalog: "Measure your head before ordering," a suggestion of the traditional narrative imperative to prize the individual); he perceives himself as the curmudgeonly arch-individualist, the last holdout (he still uses a typewriter, relishing the hard push on the keys, the clacking strike of ink on blank paper), a defined and defining voice whose long self-exile underscores dramatically how narrative, ultimately language itself, had lost its place in the contemporary surface environment defined by the image, the terrifying blandness inevitably engendered by an era of relentless electronic herdspeak that condones, even necessitates surrendering the rich complications and responsibilities of defining identity and instead encourages distracting the lonely self with the image-glut of television, its pleasant diversion of surfaces, its illusion of presence, and the easy comfort of its false sense of immediacy and community. Fiction, apparently, has lost its cultural clout. As Bill Gray himself is told by George Haddad, a political scientist and cultural theoretician who will help Gray contact the terrorists responsible for the Swiss poet's kidnapping, if books are to have a centering effect on their culture any longer, it would only be books such as *The Quotations of Chairman Mao*, Mao's Little Red Book, that are to be "studied, repeated, memorized by an entire nation" (161), the written word now deployed to enforce totalitarian uniformity, crush individuality, and justify recasting the individual into two-dimensional facsimiles that dress and think alike. Thus, Bill Gray would appear to be justified in his retreat—lonely exile is the last, best refuge available for the contemporary writer in the electronic age.

But there is something amiss that indicates how passionately DeLillo himself disputes that rationale.[9] Gray is more a monitory character, a caution against the easy concession to unearned pessimism, the retreat into the cold solace of silence and isolation. Unlike DeLillo himself, who has published steadily and prodigiously over four decades despite his perception of contemporary culture as progressively more indifferent to the individual and progressively more enamored by the image, Gray, thinned by his long exile, has stopped writing. The authentic voice

that animated his initial efforts has been long lost to a public persona, to the distracting drain of celebrity; his exile sustained by a steadying ingestion of sedatives,
antidepressants, and alcohol, Gray has wrestled for twenty-three years to complete
a novel-in-perpetual-progress (a "shitpile of hopeless prose" [122]) that molders as
scribbled typescripts in stacked boxes and some two hundred numbered binders,
its execution an exercise in isolation behind a locked door that darkly recalls
the open-ended baseball games indulged by the lonely child forty years earlier. The
manuscript has become a dead issue—in both senses. (At one point, Gray's ex-
editor tells Gray of prostate problems that have left him sterile.) Alone for decades,
Gray has peopled his isolation with two virtual strangers (the fan Scott Martineau
and his lover, an ex-Moonie named Karen Janney) whom he hires solely to maintain his household-bunker. Over two decades, luxuriating within self-sustaining
aesthetic futility, Gray has opted entirely out of living, has inelegantly dodged the
responsibilities of family, passing through shattered marriages and maintaining a
distant intimacy with three grown children (he stops in Boston to visit his lesbian
daughter only to find out when the taxi drops him off in her neighborhood that he
knows neither her phone number nor her address).

Unpublished now for twenty years, denied the vibrant dynamic of the reader-
writer conspiracy, trapped within the self-sustaining enterprise of endless revision
and thus disenfranchised and rendered impotent, Gray has been thinged—left
alone, aging, indistinct and inconsequential, a fading voice without the solace of
an ear, like that nine-year-old announcing a ball game to pillows and stuffed animals. Not surprisingly, his relationship to his manuscript is hostile, even apprehensive—it has become a slobbering mutant whose monstrous bulk haunts his days.
In a novel that develops a subplot involving the political kidnapping of the Swiss
United Nations relief worker and minor poet named Jean-Claude Julien, DeLillo
parallels Gray's elective captivity to just such terrorism. In those vivid moments
when the narrative shifts to the captive poet, hooded and fastened by plastic wire
to a water-supply pipe in some bomb-shaken back street of Beirut, we watch as
Julien's sense of his own identity slowly erodes, we feel the insidious creep of
anonymity as each mental game, each invented diversion he structures to pass the
endless captivity, ultimately fails (recall young Willard amid the Iowa emptiness).
Julien's cache of memories, so individual and vivid, blurs into hackneyed fantasies
as he talks himself slowly into the unrelieved blank of nonidentity, concedes to the
creep of thingness—ultimately, the poet himself will be traded off like a black-
market commodity to a rival terrorist organization. That deterioration, that forfei-
ture of identity against the tiring drone of the single voice, surely approximates
Gray's own self-imposed captivity; his long struggle with his unfinishable manuscript measures how dramatically he has lost contact, has lost his audience—
indeed, how, desperate, he has grown terminally transfixed by the entertaining

suasion of his own voice: "I have grown a second self, a self-important fool" (37). At one point, he compares himself poignantly to a television left on in an empty room.

Until 1989, the narrative present, that is, when Bill Gray, overtired of monkish isolation, this "wretched hiding" (45), determines to reengage the world he had so entirely fled—a process that will begin with his agreeing to sit for a professional photo shoot. Photographer Brita Nilsson, who for four years has been compiling portraits of writers, is invited to the Gray compound. In the extraordinary evening she spends photographing the reluctant recluse, DeLillo juxtaposes the soul-taking implied metaphorically by the ghastly intrusion of the open lens (Gray compares the session to a wake) with the soul-sharing that is undertaken so effortlessly by the two strangers.[10] They talk. They share a level of unexpected conversational intimacy that shatters Bill Gray's hard isolation and reanimates that part of him, long denied, that hungers for the sort of connection that his early writing had supplied—the authentic wonder of the narrative act, the striking intimacy of a voice being heard. At dinner before Brita departs, Gray toasts his guest: "This place feels like home tonight. There's a wholeness, isn't there. . . . Here's to guests and what they mean to civilization" (67). Indeed, when Brita later departs for New York with Scott Martineau as her driver, Bill Gray, stirred by the reanimation of intimacy, will conduct a sexual encounter, albeit of an uninspired sort, with Karen Janney. Stirred by Brita's gently invasive presence, however, he will phone her the following morning on impulse and leave a meandering message on her machine (although she is in her apartment, half asleep, listening) that becomes in fact a poignant, evocative description of the cryptic beauty of an ongoing sunrise, his voice-message, like his manuscript narratives (like any fiction, for that matter), an artful and heartfelt message that must wait, suspended and uncertain, for the validation of being heard, a voice thus speaking out of and against its own echoing isolation. The message indeed stirs Brita—in the murky morning light, she will accept the sexual advances of Martineau who, too tired to drive back to the compound, had spent the night on her sofa.

Gray is now pulled by the centrifugal imperative. Part 1 closes with Gray actually venturing into Manhattan for lunch with an ex-editor—who will, in turn, enlist Gray's help to free the kidnapped Swiss poet. Determined to commit himself to the efforts to secure Julien's release from war-savaged Beirut, Gray will carefully slip out of the restaurant unobserved by the waiting Martineau and will join the "surge of the noontime crowd" (103). And in the second part, the narrative opens to the unsavory world from which Gray had withdrawn for nearly twenty years. DeLillo introduces the disturbing presence of the terrorist that here represents the cultural counterforce that accounts for the growing irrelevancy of the writer.[11] When the narrative ultimately shifts to Beirut in the epilogue (long after Gray himself is dead) and we confront face-to-face DeLillo's terrorists, we find that they are not particularly compelled by religious conviction or political fanaticism: they scheme largely to be on television. Unlike the contemporary writer of fiction bound to the slowburn effects of language, the terrorist, proficient in image technologies and savvy in media propaganda, now dictates the world's narrative by manipulating the accessibility and frictionless immediacy of the evening news (and the public's disquieting addiction for its simplifications and its bogus clarity), plays to the shock-register of a well-conceived image strategically fed to the world-media technologies; and, in turn, the terrorist—and the image—now shapes, drives, and directs the public consciousness in ways that writers—and the word—formerly commanded.

That image-culture with its pervasive reach and its oppressive immediacy has made the crowd—rather than the individual—the defining unit of contemporary culture. DeLillo draws into his narrative abundant evidence from 1989 of the menacing charisma of crowds that nullify the potential of individuality, that sacrifice its difficult uncertainties to a smooth and disturbing mass-unit: there is the spring wedding ceremony in Yankee Stadium of 13,000 followers of the Reverend Sun Myung Moon; the April catastrophe at the Hillsborough Stadium outside Sheffield, England, where dozens of panicking soccer fans were pressed to death against the stadium's locked fences; the doomed summer protests in Beijing's Tiananmen Square; the frenzied mobs of Iranian Shiites at the state funeral of the Ayatollah Khomeini in July; the measureless numbers of the New York City homeless living in packing crates and on subway grates just beyond the reach of George Bush's kinder, gentler America. In each case, the individual is invalidated, rendered an irrelevancy. The late-century self is here what is has always been in DeLillo: embattled, vulnerable, uncertain, doubting its own relevancy and scouring its immediate cultural environment for validation. Narrative has long privileged such weakness and elevated such confusion (recall Faulkner's grief-world), accepted, indeed enchanted the immediate with uncertainty, stoked the rage for complexity, sustained the spell of the human dilemma and the attendant privileging of mystery, and ultimately respected the borders of identity, in fact demanded that the individual—reader and writer—participate in the act and yet maintain integrity, violated and yet inviolate. If poetry presumes the give and take of public recitation, if painting defines its most dramatic effect by the sharing implicit in public viewing, if theater and cinema are places visited not artifacts experienced, and if television coldly exploits isolation, narrative alone maintains, respects, even demands loneliness as terrifying precondition, permitting the graceful and paradoxical preservation/ravishment of that lonely self within the aesthetic experience.

Of course, readers become a problematic pressure if they seek to make literal this metaphoric confederacy with the writer. Scott Martineau, whose long-ago epiphany reading Bill Gray's novel reanimated his life and gave direction to its stubborn drift, pursued his obsession with the reclusive novelist, methodically tracked him through Gray's publisher (getting a job in the mail room and then cross-checking postmarks from the recluse's infrequent letters), and after accosting the stunned writer (caught unprepared in front of a hardware store) persuaded Gray to hire him as a sort of general assistant. Left to maintain the novelist's sprawling archives, manage his finances, and run the household affairs, Martineau has become in the eight years of his service the ultimate sycophant, an obsessive control freak, a domineering pseudo-captor—and more disturbing he has abandoned any necessity of defining his own self and has become, as Gray's devoted factotum, a creepy parasite. Therein lies the threat of attempting to make real the aesthetic intimacy—the reader surrenders identity to the persuasive enchantment of the authority. Martineau maintains no life distinct from his function as Bill Gray's handler; although he conducts a tepid relationship with Karen Janney, an ex-Moonie he first encounters wandering the streets of a small Kansas town (Martineau is visiting his sister and Karen is in mid-deprogramming), he gets involved with her largely because she reminds him of a character from a Gray novel. The casualness of their "passion" is underscored by her willingness to service Bill on the quiet. Martineau is too-content to dust and tidy Gray's world, to enable his extended exile, to provide him a perfectly-appointed refuge.

Witness the only moment in the novel that Martineau must briefly act apart from his function as Gray's keeper. Coming out of a Manhattan bookstore (yet another protective haven), Martineau is suddenly seized upon by a stranger who claims only to want to talk to him. Typically he hurries away from her, away from such unpredictability; but at a curb, the persistent woman tries to hand Martineau a wrapped bundle that he thinks initially must be some sort of wounded animal (he only thinks later it might actually have been a sick baby). She begs him cryptically to give it a home, a chance to live outside the city—confronted by such vast untidiness and the responsibility to engage another amid its suddenly-surging energy, Martineau will not even make eye contact, turns from the evident distress of the street woman, and heads for the protective security of an uptown hotel bar to keep his appointment with the photographer Brita Nilsson. But if he is vulnerable on the streets, he is lord of Gray's compound. In a particularly uncomfortable moment, Martineau will actually order Gray back to his typewriter like some delinquent child sent off to attend to overdue homework. Ironically, Martineau has already dismissed the novel-in-progress as compromising to Gray's reputation, has in fact argued that it is best left unpublished (most likely because its publication would jeopardize the fragile dynamic Martineau sustains in the household). Gray has begun to resist his imprisonment ("Kid thinks he owns my soul" [73]): when Martineau delivers a particularly cutting comment about the diminished quality of Gray's writing in the new novel, Gray hurls a butter dish lid at his head. When Gray ultimately breaks free of this self-imposed captivity and heads to London to participate in a public reading for the captured Swiss poet, departs in fact without Martineau's knowledge, the reader/disciple is left predictably devastated. We watch uneasily as he obsessively cleans and recleans Gray's typewriter by repeatedly putting his face to the keyboard and blowing, suggesting the useless, and ironic struggle to reanimate, literally re-inspire the keys.[12] But after Gray's disappearance, Martineau never feels compelled to reclaim his abandoned position outside the compound; indeed, the protective isolation that he and Karen define is cut only by dead words (Gray's sought-after manuscript, which Martineau predictably decides to leave unpublished) and unshared images (the contact sheets from Gray's photo session).

It is that photo shoot that commences Bill Gray's reengagement. The shoot (even the terminology is predatory and menacing) is a risk, of course—a photo will flatten him instantly into a commodity (after the session, Gray despairs, "I'm a picture now, flat as birdshit on a Buick" [54]). After all, the characters here study the canvases of Andy Warhol who pioneered (and indeed lived) the embrace of such superficiality, the avant-garde High 60s conception of the contemporary artist as celebrity/commodity. With his uncanny sense of the implications of the technological revolution in easily reproducible images, Warhol unsettled traditional notions of portraiture as a privileging of individuality; by deliberately accentuating the two-dimensionality of the camera image to suggest a thinning of individuality, Warhol satirized the self-as-commodity with his trademark silkscreen prints that would stack row upon row of distorted gaudy images of cult figures such as Marilyn Monroe and Elvis Presley until the image—not the person—would become the subject. *Mao II* in fact comes from a Warhol pencil drawing of the Chinese dictator (a reproduction of which Martineau gives to Karen after his trip to a New York gallery) that is part of a larger study that extracts the Communist leader's notorious image from its troublesome historic context—"Photocopy Mao, silk screen Mao, wallpaper Mao, synthetic-polymer Mao" (21)—and freefloats it as a mass of reproduced images until the proliferation of images, not the person, becomes the subject—a second Mao. Warhol's own performance-art lifestyle compelled a generation of his artistic contemporaries (among them DeLillo) to consider the implicit threat/promise of image reproduction, how the technology of circulation and mass production threatened the very concept of multi-layered identity, long the privileged concern of narratives, by giving it over to the easy clean of two-dimensionality. The image then is DeLillo's specific targeted inquiry: what to do with the writer, indeed with narrative in a culture that now unfolds before the camera, its every moment, public and private, pedestrian and spectacle, sustained amid an environment relentlessly aclick, depressed into two-dimensionality by unblinking, unrelenting lenses. Unlike the narrative experience, which sustains individuality and coerces the probing exploration of identity, the image offers simple surface immediacy, replaces speculation and analysis with accessibility and casual identi-fication.

Uneasy with the late-century implications of its evident vulnerability and denied examination by the glitzy persuasion of an image-inundated cultural envi-ronment, the fragmented self searches for easy strategies of displacement, searches for the charismatic embrace of a collective that would simply make irrelevant con-cerns over individual identity or its development. Through the character of Karen Janney, DeLillo explores the exhilarating attraction of the collective, specifically Karen's years of self-erasure as a disciple of Sun Myung Moon, years of working the streets and shopping malls, tirelessly soliciting donations because of her con-viction that she had found in this "chunky man in a business suit from the Repub-lic of Korea" (186) a messiah, a totalizing presence of spiritual magnitude sufficient to burst the hard parameters of her self and to allow her to feel as reassuring the meld of group identity. The novel begins in the sunny April wash of Yankee Sta-dium as Karen, along with 13,000 other Moonies, participates in a communal wed-ding ceremony (she met her selected husband two days earlier and understands their commitment is to missionary work that makes concerns over love irrelevant, even petty). Even as thousands of cameras record the spectacle, even as the fol-lowers' individual voices swell into a single chanting voice (the liturgical "Mass" engendering a new uneasy sense of mass), DeLillo captures the disturbing impli-cations of so much self-surrendering, the loss of intimacy, the abandonment of per-sonality. That her parents, watching helpless from the stadium grandstand, find Karen's commitment odd, indeed a sort of radical brainwashing, and that, desper-ate, they will be compelled ultimately to kidnap her and to force her to undergo eight days of intensive round-the-clock reprogramming in a seedy hotel in the Mid-west suggests DeLillo's uneasiness.

Three years after her reprogramming, however, Karen cannot entirely set aside her need for a larger authority to give her self its shape and direction, its definition and assertion. She cannot find an authentic self, no sustained exertion of her own consciousness—when DeLillo follows her character as she moves through the har-rowing night-world of Manhattan's homeless after Gray disappears, she feels "all drift and spin" (142) with her authority now suddenly absent. The narrative voice appropriately flatlines into non sequiturs and disjointed observations, childlike syn-tax and diction, garbled fragments and clichés. She is particularly compelled by television ("She took it all in, she believed it all, pain, ecstasy, dog food, all the seraphic matter, the baby bliss that falls from the air" [119]), susceptible to its fric-tionless immediacy, willing to identify and sympathize with its mesmerizing surface images. She indulges an extravagant sympathy for what she watches on the evening news: those sorrowing at the Khomeini funeral (although she knows little of the Iranian culture), those snagged within the killing press of the soccer panic, those gunned down in the government assault on Tiananmen Square. She cannot sustain loneliness, cannot tolerate isolation (she tells Martineau he should have brought the wrapped baby back to the compound); her casual assignations with both Martineau and Gray indicate her need for the reassuring press of others. In New York, she will offer to hordes of ragged indigents living in a Tompkins Square band shell the banal consolation typical of the rhetoric of any fundamentalist collective: the leveling descent of the approaching apocalypse, the ultimate scoring through of individuality. Her impromptu offer to become their charismatic authority is a missionary endeavor that hinges, as all such religious enterprises, on effacing her bothersome self in a gesture of promiscuous (and futile) compassion—no one listens, hers is another voice lost to an audience. She will eventually return to the compound and to the quiet work of helping Scott Martineau tend the ghost of Bill Gray.

When Gray flies to London to participate in the public reading that is to be part of consciousness-raising event for the kidnapped Swiss poet, that gesture goes awry (the event is cancelled when a bomb goes off in the hall, evidently part of larger scheme to kidnap Gray himself). After talking with the political theoretician Haddad, who maintains considerable ties to the terrorist factions operating in Beirut, Gray determines to head to Lebanon to negotiate firsthand with the terrorists, indeed to offer himself in a swap. It is a bold gesture of outreach. But while that gesture hopelessly flounders as gracelessly literal (indeed, DeLillo deflates its misdirection in the ignominious death that Gray endures on the crowded ferry bound to Beirut, his body never claimed, his identity papers filched presumably for black market sale), another far quieter liberation does occur. Willard Skansey will shake free of the stifling casing of Bill Gray, will build on the implications of that taped phone message to Brita Nilsson, indeed will tap into his long dormant imagination and finally defy the logic that has long deemed isolation, silence, and endless drafting as the inevitable way of the contemporary writer.[13] Gray begins to write about Julien, opens his imagination to the particular conditions of such notoriously unimaginable captivity. He invents his way into a dramatic gesture of simpatico with the held poet; he studies each line of the fifteen poems Julien had published; he clears his head: stops his medication, stops drinking. It is a far cry from young Willard Skansey's conjured ball game—those invented games consoled a lonely boy by peopling an imaginary space with the faux-companionship of conjured images—here the imagination is a centripetal force, a hopeful gesture outward, a compassionate premise. "Find the places," he encourages himself, "where you converge with him" (160). Far from his Manhattan bunker, reduced to using pen and paper, thrown back on the most primitive sort of expression and the barest sort of need to touch, to violate the self, Gray writes nevertheless, violates his isolation as well as that of the captive poet, struggling to record how captivity oppresses, recreating the captive poet's conditions in an unforced confederacy, the self both apart and a part: "a writer creates a character as a way to reveal consciousness, increase the flow of meaning. This is how we reply to power and beat back our fear. By extending the pitch of consciousness and human possibility" (200). Ultimately, after the traffic accident, even as he faces what he fears are life-threatening injuries, he comes to see Bill Gray as a character that he is in the process of killing off—in a darkly humorous scene, Gray, concerned about the degree of injuries from his hit and run, will solicit medical advice from drunken British veterinarians who are holding a conference at his hotel by telling them he is a writer doing research on a character who suspects similar internal injuries.

Of course, Gray fails. So long unused, his imagination finally cannot sustain his reach, he falters trying to particularize the details of the captivity tableau, and slowly, he succumbs to the nagging drain of his physical injuries. But failure does not diminish his heroic revival (he dies on the deck of a ferry pointed defiantly toward sunrise). He does, finally, free one captive: Willard Skansey. That gesture of liberation sets the foundation for the ultimate affirmation of the text: the reach and scope of DeLillo's narrative itself (the writer is dead, long live the writer). DeLillo's narrative voice pitches with unforced ease into the reach and swell of the minds of these disparate characters, a promiscuous omniscience that testifies not merely to an author's elegant, unforced ventriloquism but suggests the moral energy of the narrative act is what it has always been: to counter loneliness, to violate the self, to project the I into the consolation of a linked series of unforced confederacies, first author to character and then character to reader and ultimately (gloriously) author to reader.

The contemporary author, DeLillo argues, can claim finally no clear community function, must in fact concede the public arena in the late century to the terrifying invasion of totalitarian forces that range from the cheap blather and sloganeering of politics to the dark, charismatic draw of fanatic religions, from the dehumanizing implications of mass-technology to the pervasive pornographies and virtual realities of unchecked media. The writer cannot stop such encroachment —suggested here by the shadowy figures of the terrorists who close the novel. In the epilogue, more than a year after Gray's disappearance, we learn that Brita Nilsson has since abandoned her writers project and has now accepted an assignment to photograph the elusive terrorist Abu Rashid. When she is taken to his hideout, Brita observes his fanatic minions, all boys, their young faces hooded and each wearing Rashid's photograph on t-shirts as a sort of collective identity—their youth testifying to the unthinking ease of their indoctrination, the ease with which they have surrendered to the collective. Brita rejects such a premise—she boldly lifts one boy's hood and photographs his face, in essence restoring his identity—only to find her valiant (and quixotic) gesture roundly rejected by the young boy himself who instinctively attacks the photographer and tries to confiscate her camera.

But we close with a demonstration of how narrative can withstand the lure of the collective in the age of the image: that night, Brita, unable to sleep, positioned on a hotel balcony overlooking the Beirut streets, watches an impromptu wedding celebration wind joyously through the streets, its drunken revelry, innocent energy, and authentic passion a telling comparison to the joyless choreographed Yankee Stadium ceremony that had begun the novel. As Brita watches and pours herself a drink to join from her balcony in the happy chaos of the street celebrations, the giddy intoxicated feel is momentarily threatened by the unexpected intrusion of an unescorted Soviet tank—a potential showdown that surely recalls the lone protestor and the government tank in Tiananmen Square. But here the menacing tank proves harmless, indeed its turret is swung by its unidentified occupants in a wild, comic mimicry of the outlandish street dancing. The scene becomes a freighted moment, preserved within the generous clarity of language, that suspends itself between simplifications, participates for the reader in simultaneous, multiple levels of apprehension, at once mimetic and symbolic, tender and streetwise, provocative and consoling, romantic and parodic, ironic and affirmative, pessimistic and joyous, vivid and mysterious. The moment becomes a defiant complex shattering of distance, a demonstration of the intimacy between a hopeful author and a promised participatory reader—DeLillo and you—two lonely isolates in separate rooms. The novel ends with the flash and shatter of cameras illuminating the Beirut night sky—cameras dryly recording the dead city. "The dead city photographed one more time" (241). Against such a flattened sort of record, the narrative thrives, able to coordinate the intricate tension of suggestive images, able to testify to how the chaotic world conjures nevertheless the accidental collision of random moments that touch the mysterious, thus refusing the destructive simplifications of the open lens (indeed DeLillo's descriptions of the garish flash of the cameras in the Beirut night suggest the staccato flash of gunfire) and articulating within the elegant capture of prose the freewheeling chaos of the immediate without sacrificing its tension between clarity and mystery, the rich offering of suggestivity, an uncompromising rear-guard action, a furious commitment to maintaining the integrity of the language-reading of the world, part of the writer and reader's ongoing joint struggle toward authenticity, identity, and meaning. Scrutiny becomes plot; language itself becomes suspense; reader becomes character; and mystery becomes solution. Writers, finally, cannot afford the luxury of silence; and readers cannot tolerate the isolation such unshattered silence would make inevitable.

Underworld (1997)

As if to affirm that position of the writer, DeLillo would follow *Mao II* with a monumental assertion of the viability of narrative. At eight-hundred-plus pages, *Underworld* is an anaconda text with a labyrinthine crosshatch of plotlines and dozens of characters—historical and fictional—scored across five decades, an intimidating intricacy in which plot summary is not merely impossible but inappropriate. Indeed, any stab at defining *Underworld* must be immediately qualified by "yet." It is, most obviously, an ambitious cultural biography, a wide-lens look at fifty years of the American experience, specifically the Nuclear Age, from the apocalyptic anxieties of the early cold war through the tense brinkmanship of the Cuban Missile Crisis and the doomed containment crusade of Vietnam and, ultimately, to the giddy flush that followed the speechlessly swift collapse of the Soviet empire and the late-century emergence of capitalist commodity-culture as the defining world market. Yet if *Underworld* is ambitious in its scope, it is as well intensely intimate, a generous excavation into the life of a successful fiftyish Arizona waste-management executive named Nick Shay, who must make peace with a difficult adolescence and with a growing realization of a disturbing loss of vitality; he is that nondescript late-century Every-Executive who, slipping into the quiet terror of a suburban late middle age and feeling the chill approach of mortality, interrogates the cumulative value of his marriage, his infidelities, his career success, and his friendships, even as he comes to realize that life can go on far longer than living.

Still, if *Underworld* is a nuanced work of psychological realism, it is also a caustic broad-stroke satire of American late-century culture that is at turns hilarious and despairing, indulging even as it indicts our addiction to violence, our willingness to displace history with the evening news, our relentless devastation of our own environment, our cheapening of the binding promise of marriage and the reward of family, our unshakable faith in the propaganda of capitalism and the fetching gospel of materialism, our tolerance of the wonderland logic of nuclear warfare, our curious indulgence of fanaticism (both religious and political), our abiding fascination with the titanic trivia of sports. Nevertheless, if *Underworld* despairs and indicts, it celebrates as well. It is a daring novel that validates our need to touch transcendence, DeLillo's most direct investigation to date of a spiritual overlay capable of redeeming the intricate oppression of our physical nature —the narrative draws unironically on the deep appeal of traditional ritual Catholicism, the mysterious vocabulary of paranormal miracles, the attraction of New Age spirituality, even the intriguing appeal of numerology (particularly the number thirteen). Indeed, the narrative's visionary peroration is nothing less than a refulgent re-visioning, without clear irony, of the Internet itself as a vast embracing system that both grants transcendence from bothersome physical limitations and offers the generous webbing of an immeasurable community, both long the privileges of the Christian afterlife. A narrative that aspires to such transcendent realms as well lovingly indulges the press of the street; *Underworld* is DeLillo's most affective gesture at autobiography, an intimate recollection of the working-class Italian American environs of the Bronx in the early 1950s.

If *Underworld* appears to promise the nostalgic warmth of autobiography (DeLillo never before used so directly materials from his own life), it is as well maddeningly cool, a cerebral exercise in language engineered by a master stylist who with élan creates a stunning collage of styles and a montage of pitch-perfect voices, a massive assemblage that ultimately focuses attention on the medium, not on the mesh of events chronicled but rather on the implications of transcribing that mesh into the music, force, and energy of language, the virtual reality of word, sentence, and paragraph. The nameless narrator, a felt rather than heard presence, shifts voices with the confidence of a master ventriloquist, capturing at turns the smart rhythms of the street, the coded paranoid jargon of government and corporations, the hip slang of 1960s bohemian artists, the contrived discipline of theological discourse, the disjointed conversations of kitchen realism—such prose stylings, juxtaposed section to section, delight as a sonic complex. Despite such foregrounding of style, the novel is a sentimental, even mawkish jock novel, a sort of *Field of Dreams*–ish (melo)drama that explores how effortlessly we coin heroes and conjure community magic from the ephemera of the playing field—the prologue recreates the October 3, 1951, epochal showdown at the fabled Polo Grounds that decided the National League pennant between the New York Giants and the Brooklyn Dodgers, which culminated in Bobby Thomson's last-inning home-run blast. That captivating set piece signals a narrative-long speculation over the fate of that ball, historically never recovered. In addition, *Underworld* plays on the missing father–wounded son tension so critical to the male-weepy sports-fiction genre—Nick Shay lingers for nearly fifty years within the trauma of the abandonment by his father, a charismatic small-time numbers runner who went out for cigarettes and never returned. If it is sentimental (at least by DeLillo's standards), *Underworld* also bristles with the hard-edged tension of a gothic novel of sensation in which a shadowy central character spends a lifetime struggling to bury an indiscretion, the plot accelerating toward the revelation of that devastating secret as the gathering momentum of duplicity yields ultimately to the difficult redemption of a halting confession (Nick's closing admission to his wife of more than twenty years that, while still in his teens, he had shot point-blank a neighborhood heroin addict).

As a text, then, *Underworld* provokes rather than abides boundaries, challenging, teasing the reader whose presumed mission is to contain such a text within the logic of a reading. If *Mao II* explores the challenges, frustrations, and dimensions of the writer imperiled by and within the media age, then *Underworld* is a necessary complement-text that explores the challenges, frustrations, and dimensions of the reader within that same cultural context. If *Mao II* is a writer's text, *Underworld* is supremely a reader's text. Like the World Trade Center whose towers were pictured on the first-edition dust jacket and whose construction mesmerizes characters during an interlude set in the early 1970s, *Underworld* is a structure conceived on an excessive scale, a daring engineering feat of dense architecture that is at once efficient and expansive, enclosing and forbidding. *Underworld* achieves the feel of coherence, the integrity of plot from echoes and fragments that confirm attractive patterns—suggestive character doublings, recurring numbers, tantalizing coincidences (some historic, some invented), intriguing juxtapositions and jump-cuts, resonating symbol-patterns and viable motifs, parallel situations—that accumulate in re-readings and begin to suggest tissues of connections that in turn justify, even demand the diligent exercise of readerly speculation. Although its dominant character, Nick Shay, certainly undergoes the expected psychological validation of the narrative epiphany, surely the grander epiphany is the slow-fuse awakening reserved for the persevering, participatory reader who is necessarily dropped into this honeycomb text and then challenged to become a system-maker, to coax an arrangement, to contain the narrative within a form, a "reading." *Underworld* invites invention, challenges the reader to both relish—and ultimately reject—the gentle privilege of understanding.

So grandly imposing, *Underworld* immediately recalls *Ratner's Star*—but that text's daunting, mathematically derived design is deliberately alienating to even the most willing reader; we are invited to admire it like some astronomical phenomenon, from a distance. But from its remarkable opening re-creation of the Polo Grounds, *Underworld* invites entrance; not coincidentally, the prologue begins with a young boy, truant from school, jumping the turnstiles to steal *into* the stadium. It is a text engineered to be, in turn, engineered. We are given a text crowded with intriguing, attractive side narratives and set pieces that can be ordered and reordered into efficient and suasive readings. Page to page, the accumulation of evidence intrigues: what to do with Martin Mannion, Nick's friend who, on a school field trip to the Bronx Zoo, urinates into the buffalo enclosure, frustrated over the animals' shaggy docility; with Erica Deming's recipe for Jell-O chicken mousse; with the mysterious woman dressed like a raven who dances so provocatively with J. Edgar Hoover's longtime companion Clyde Tolson at Truman Capote's 1966 Black and White Ball; with the African American street preacher who comic Lenny Bruce suddenly "channels" during a nightclub act; with the abortion of Nick's first child; or with the formidable German philosophy student who, on a disastrous first date with Nick, battles a rat in his apartment bathtub, etc., etc. In turn, what are we to do with all the different types of "shots," all the "targets," the "towers," the cancers, the games, all the walls, the different types of waste, all the Edgars, all the orange, all the thirteens, etc., etc. Such abundance of details entices, demands involvement: where does each detail "fit," can each one be related ultimately to some Grand Unifying Theme? What emerges as a narrative refrain—"everything is connected" (it appears in the text, no kidding, thirteen times)—functions as the intriguing instruction from the narrator-authority, as much encouraging as frustrating.[14]

The narrative thus rewards ingenuity and diligence; like Nicholas Branch without the despair, we recycle evidentiary bits (the central motif of the text is the rigid economy of waste management) even as we realize the scale of the task (characters ponder the unlimited inundation of the landfills)—simply, the text never surrenders itself to any reading; indeed, it subverts even the premise of an ultimate "reading." It stays positioned in the between, or more appropriately in the among: tantalizing, the text thus simultaneously denies and invites explication (how many thirteens can *you* find in the text—does it "mean" something, for instance, that Nick's infamous rat date occurs the night he and his date are to see Charles Mingus, whose name has, gulp, thirteen letters). Here, clarity and mystery are not antagonists but rather the identical complex intellectual motion. Consider the World Trade Center: *two* monumental towers despite their curiously singular name, two separate entities that nevertheless realized an unforced, mesmerizing symmetry, indeed became a single entity, one tower completed by the other (eerily, their eventual destruction would be joint as well). Similarly, in *Underworld,* form and surprise merge—on the dust jacket of the first edition, the stunning André Kertész study of the fog-shrouded towers on the front merges seamlessly into its haunting negative on the back. The more diligently the reader constructs a viable reading, the deeper the excavation into the text, the more the text yields contradictory evidence, significant asides, paradoxical data—in short, the more the reading asserts its authority, the more the reading subverts it.

Far from taunting the reader or diminishing that participation, such a text becomes an empowering experience. Traditionally, a reader has always been something of a paranoid, tracking (at times trudging) through an alien text, recovering evidence "planted" by a shadowy authority, struggling amid a conspiracy of symbols, crossed behavioral patterns, and webbed motifs to recover sufficient evidence to sustain a convincing reading presumably endorsed by the author-creator. As evidenced by the considerable number of published explications *Underworld* has already generated in its relatively brief shelf life, we certainly can do this: trace patterns and satisfy this traditional reader contract; with Talmudic resilience and dedication, we can create a system of design (trace, for instance, a thematic pattern, character doublings, a resonating symbol-matrix), unbury a clutch of secrets from the text, contain it, and depress it into a satisfying argument. Like the narrative's considerable number of crafters and orderers—among them, FBI director J. Edgar Hoover, Nick's childhood teacher Sister Alma Edgar, his Jesuit confessor Father Paulus, Giants announcer Russ Hodges, Texas serial killer Richard Henry Gilkey, Dallas dressmaker Abraham Zapruder, Los Angeles artist Sabato Rodia, junk artist Klara Sax, avant-garde film director Sergei Eisenstein—the reader can opt for form, can unironically recover a viable and attractive clarity but one that, amid a narrative that embeds layers of potential exculpatory evidence on every page, quickly becomes an exercise that is at once reassuring and splendidly ironic.

Thus, even as we recover a convincing reading, we must relish the play, the generous glimpses of additional links that ultimately privilege readings; we must relish such persuasive openness, the sheer dimension, the thumping energy, the scale, the audacious intricacy of the narrator-authority. As reader-participants, we are compelled then to be simultaneously like the narrative's junk artists—who resiliently conjure from fragments riveting and sustaining monuments to form—and the narrative's jazz aficionados (among them Nick Shay)—who appreciate the dazzling ad-lib and the eruption of surprise, the crazy immediacy and vibrant openness that shatters the polite pretense of form. Design complements fluidity; structure invites contingency; clarity assumes mystery; density relies on surprise. The text lurks among the endeavors, contained yet elusive, caught yet promiscuous, a strategy that conjoins the narrator-authority and the reader-conspirator and that, in turn, continually revitalizes this private textual space, a shared authority that celebrates, ultimately, the imaginative release of both labors: like a bop jam, an intriguing kinetic of composition (the writer who constructs) and improvisation (the reader who glimpses).

As readers, then, we cannot resist playing out the implications of an attractive narrative argument, tracking a single thread through the labyrinth (it is, after all, an invitatory text). We could consider, for instance, one patterning: the narrative of Nick Shay, the text's dominant presence, read against the narrative of Sister Alma Edgar, the authoritarian old-school nun who teaches Nick and his brother Matt in the 1950s and whose death in the early 1990s serves as the narrative's closing event. What might such a juxtaposition yield?

Nick Shay, at fifty-seven, begins the narrative at that inevitable point when a lived life has begun to cool into form, settling into an expensive clarity that trims mystery and accepts as sufficient the sustained, strategic containment that comes with the banal busyness of routine, the ordering imperative of a career, and the comforts of a settled domesticity. "I live a quiet life in an unassuming house in a suburb of Phoenix. Pause. Like someone in the Witness Protection Plan."[15] The practiced joke lamely reveals a depth of quiet desperation, how an individual can be planed into a nonentity. The chaotic energy of Nick's past, particularly his tumultuous adolescence in the immigrant neighborhoods of the Bronx, has now been buried (he entertains co-workers with cheesy imitations of Hollywood-styled Mafia stereotypes). Like the sort of God Nick respects—distant and mysterious—Nick has spent a lifetime in uneasy negotiation with his own past. But, entowered in corporate headquarters high above a sweltering Phoenix, Nick has, like the mythical bird itself, risen from the smoke and ruin of his past; a teenage delinquent, he is now a successful executive for an international waste-management enterprise that is itself in the business of tidying up and burying.

We will watch in the narrative present as Nick goes about tidying up his emotional life; he will expose what few secrets linger to complicate his strategic containment, and he will concede, finally, to the attractive trim of tidiness. Nick's narrative, for instance, begins when he decides impulsively to confront the lingering ghosts of his adolescent affair with his science teacher's wife—he drives out into the New Mexico desert to attempt what turns out to be an awkward reunion with the woman, now a legendary junk artist who is in the process of converting hundreds of decommissioned B-52s into a massive work of installation art. There are, of course, other secrets Nick will expose. On a business trip to Kazakhstan to inspect a facility where the Russians are disposing of hazardous wastes using radiation, he will confront his wife's lover, an associate and long-time friend, even striking him, each "token blow" improving his mood, until the requisite energy spends itself in its own irony (797). Then, on his return to Phoenix, Nick will finally accept that his father was not the victim of a mob hit—an enthralling speculation that has long allowed him to romanticize his father—but rather that Jimmy Costanza was just another dime-a-dozen deadbeat who abandoned a needful family. Ultimately, Nick will reveal to his wife of some twenty years his closest secret, his arrest and conviction when he was seventeen for the accidental shooting of his friend, George Manza. But as Nick's narrative ends, as secrecy yields to revelation, mystery to clarity, chaos to tidiness, Nick feels a striking loss of momentum, a collapse into banality. As he departs the narrative, he bleakly assesses how dearly he misses the mystery of the uncontained moment, those "days of disarray" (806), their hot immediacy and sweet urgency. "I want them back, the days when I was alive on the earth, rippling in the quick of my skin, heedless and real. I was dumb-muscled and angry and real . . . a danger to others and a distant mystery to myself" (810).

Far from a mystery, Nick's life finally makes sense; what is left of it (and he is haunted by the approach of death) will now be Prufrocked, measured out carefully and cleanly: he attends Mass not out of faith but because of the appeal of the practiced ritual; he slathers on sunblock; every morning he runs a carefully measured metric mile; in his spare time, he arranges and rearranges books on his shelves; he fastidiously separates his household garbage and bundles his newspapers; he takes his granddaughter on a tour of a recycling plant. He closes the narrative defined and contained, a hard and entirely evident surface (ironically listening to the free-souled noise of jazz), he is a "crisp" suit surrounded by the "drone of computers and the fax machines" (806). When, as a self-described "executive emeritus" (804), he travels to conferences on the growing crisis in landfill availability, he senses that the problem has been rendered oddly unreal, dispensed to and contained by in-house reports and journal articles that, like his own life, never touch the terrifying "actual pulsing thing" (805). His, ultimately, is a narrative of separation and loss. After all, as a Brooklyn Dodgers fan, he remembers the emptying heartache of the Thomson blast. Thus, according to the logic of that legendary 1951 game, he is destined for loss; indeed, he has spent $34,500 to secure the Thomson home-run ball (despite its dubious lineage) not because he is a fan of the game but because the ball is, to him, a powerful symbol of loss itself.

To underscore that movement to loss, Nick's settling into tidy form, the narrator-authority relates Nick's narrative backward, begins it in 1992 when, uncharacteristically on impulse, Nick decides during a business trip in Texas to drive to New Mexico and surprise Klara Sax, his long-ago lover. The specifics of that affair, however, will not be recounted in the narrative until some six hundred pages later. Decade by decade, Nick's narrative will move backward (like a voice-over countdown to an explosion) until in part 6 the narrative detonates amid the sound and movement of the Bronx streets with Nick at seventeen, a section that crackles with the hard brio of street language, the stripped click and vulgar spark of overheard conversations, a section shattered into clipped and urgent fragments of action, violent and carnal, reckless with menace and joy, a section that climaxes with Nick's incendiary affair with a much-older married neighbor and then in the shooting of George Manza, both defining experiences of shattering surprise. Part 6 is a breathless record of living moment to moment, of spontaneity (a tough-talking Nicky moves in and out of street fights, chain-smokes, shoots pool, cruises the night streets, vandalizes cars, romances available women, works uninspiring blue-collar jobs, and stays unfettered to school). It is that chaos that Nick, nearly a half century later, will come to crave.

After his arrest for the shooting of the waiter / pool shark George Manza (addled on heroin, Manza offers Nick a shotgun and inexplicably tells Nick it is not loaded even as Nick levels the shotgun and fires point-blank), Nick is dispatched to juvenile detention in an upstate facility amid the forbidding Catskills. He yearns for clarity, understanding, control. "All that winter I shoveled snow and read books. The lines of print, the alphabetic characters, the strokes of the shovel when I cleared a walk, the linear arrangement of words on a page, the shovel strokes, the rote exercises in school texts, the novels I read, the dictionaries I found in the tiny library, the nature and shape of books, the routine of shovel strokes in deep snow—this was how I began to build an individual" (503). A staff psychologist probes the shooting of George Manza with Nick and concludes with suspect Freudian neatness that Nick's shooting of the much-older man was a ritual expression of his repressed rage at his father's disappearance—mystery cleared up, clean and neat. When Nick is unexpectedly remanded to complete his sentence among the Jesuits at a remote reform school in Minnesota, the Jesuits offer him a cold vision (appropriate to the climate) of the universe defined, analyzed, essentially cured of mystery—Nick is, at one point, taken through the naming of all the parts of an ordinary shoe—a resilient indoctrination, finally, into the persuasion of order. Years later, this clarity, this contentment with analysis will have rendered that so-carefully built individual, the unbearably slight construction of the closing pages.

Good. But what about Sister Edgar—how does she "fit"? The reader gathers, speculates, juxtaposes. We notice that as Nick loses mystery and gains order, Sister Alma Edgar loses order and gains mystery—there, we have recovered a tantalizing pattern. Sister Edgar's long joyless life, ironically devoted to a ministry of faith that is for her uncomplicated by compassion or actual belief, has been an exercise in unyielding regimen. She is the clichéd iron-fisted nun (within the narrative, her name and her mannerisms are deftly paralleled to J. Edgar Hoover's—she calls herself a "junior G-man protecting laws" [249]). Her classroom is a rigidly maintained authoritarian state, her teaching style sustained by fear and compelled by the tight, syllable-crisp Q&A format of the *Baltimore Catechism* ("true or false, yes or no, fill in the blanks" [244]), with its implicit argument that the universe's mysteries can be tidily resolved into a black-and-white world (long after Vatican II, Sister Edgar retains by special permission the regimental white veil and black habit, itself offset by her skin's bony-whiteness). She bravely (if absurdly) crusades against a world seething with unseen microbes: she is constantly cleaning and scrubbing, even wearing protective latex gloves. We watch Sister Edgar fastidiously scrubbing a series of brushes (each time to disinfect the brush she has just used). She concedes to no mystery: at the height of the cold war, she matter-of-factly handles the insanity of Mutual Assured Destruction by calmly conducting class-time civil-defense drills, helpfully instructing her terrified students to wear dog tags to help identify their bodies after the attack and even lining her classroom with aluminum foil to block the radiation fallout. Years later, she does not fear even the difficult approach of her death: "She was not sentimental about fatal diseases. Dying was just an extended version of Ash Wednesday. She intended to meet her own end with senses intact, grasp it, know it finally, open herself to the mystery that others mistake for something freakish and unspeakable" (245). Hers, like Nick's, is a dimensionless life of solution, containment, clarity, and understanding.

Sister Edgar closes the novel (and her life) ministering in the early 1990s in the impoverished ghetto of the South Bronx, the neighborhood of Nick's childhood. Amid the crumbling buildings, she (with her friend, Sister Gracie) delivers food and attempts to provide minimal medical service to the drug addicts, the AIDS patients, the sidewalk clutter, the addled indigent. When a twelve-year-old homeless girl, the stunningly beautiful Esmeralda, is raped and then thrown to her death from a rooftop in the neighborhood, Sister Edgar, edging toward a keen despair over such unfathomable mayhem, forces herself to recite quietly the reassuring Q&A from her *Baltimore Catechism*. Yet in the weeks after the murder, Sister Edgar teeters near an unfamiliar despair, the long "serenity of immense design" suddenly disturbed (817), her unquestioned (and largely unexamined) faith now cut by doubt. She is intrigued when rumors sweep the neighborhood that when early evening commuter trains illuminate a billboard advertising Minute Maid orange juice, the shadowy face of the dead girl can be seen. When she decides to investigate (over Sister Gracie's objections to such "tabloid superstition" [819]), Sister Edgar gathers near the billboard along with a neighborhood crowd to await the train's headlights. She finds herself caught up in the experience, feels the approaching shatter of an epiphany, and then sees confirmation of the illumination as a train's lights sweep over the billboard for the briefest of seconds. Even as Sister Gracie dismisses it as an optical illusion (importantly, her explanation is muddled by her dental corrective device), Sister Edgar "feels something break upon her. An angelus of clearest joy" (822). In a burst of inexplicable openheartedness, she abandons boundaries, spontaneously casts off her rubber gloves and moves about the raw sprawl of the throng, shaking hands and embracing those she had avoided moments earlier as diseased and threatening. Even days later, when the juice ad is taken down and the illuminations stop, she carries the image with her, a transfiguring experience that confirms the sort of faith that does not provide answers but rather sustains mystery. As a reader, we connect the dots, indulge a clever summary-reading: even as Nick Shay becomes a unit, his life defined and contained, Sister Edgar becomes an un-it, her defined and contained life rent by the intrusion of surprise. When she dies soon after the billboard is changed, she "awakes" into cyberspace, her veil and habit now shed. She taps into a "glow, a lustrous rushing force that seems to flow from a billion distant net nodes" (825)—a transcendent reality that challenges the tidy deciphering of explication.

Thus, as empowered reader we have constructed an attractive interpretative pattern: Nick's joyless surrender to a thinned life of pedestrian banality erected opposite to (recall the World Trade Center) Sister Edgar's joyous confirmation of depth and paranormal excitation. If Nick Shay is more dead alive, then surely Sister Edgar is more alive dead. Of course, other similarly empowered readers skeptical about things spiritual will find Sister Edgar's lurch into that breathtaking cyber-expanse difficult to accept—such readers, of course, have less trouble accepting Nick's late-life surrender to smoldering regret—which raises the inevitable question: which ending does the narrator-authority endorse? Which is intended to be ironic? It is, finally, not a matter of choice: here, despair and hope, anxiety and comedy, horror and irony are—like the twin WTC towers—complementary enterprises, like Bobby Thomson and Ralph Branca, on different teams but part of the same game; or like the impoverished neighborhoods of Sister Edgar's Bronx that are also a popular stop on a bus tour for camera-toting foreigners interested in seeing American urban decay up close; or like the long-lost Sergei

Eisenstein film, *Unterweldt,* that treats within its dark futuristic vision the deepest fears of the nuclear age, a civilian population mutated into ghastly deformities and enslaved by a totalitarian state, yet whose Manhattan premiere is highlighted by the Radio City Rockettes dressed in military costuming in a cheesy kickline set to campy military music. Examples proliferate. It is as if DeLillo himself had moved to an endgame, proffering both grief and nothing, sorrow and irony. In the closing page, the narrator-authority generously provides a way to understand this readerly opportunity, this provocative tension. Reeling from the billboard miracle, Sister Edgar accesses a Web site where she is enthralled by a hydrogen bomb explosion, rendering tidy and safe a terrifying reality that had haunted the narrative since the late afternoon of the Thomson home run when, amid the celebrations, an attending Hoover is informed of a Soviet nuclear test. Now, Sister Edgar "detonates" bomb after bomb, each explosion a dazzling radiance that leaves her "vague, drained, docile" (826), at which point she is seamlessly projected into that very cyberspace—she apparently dies at her computer keyboard.

Invoking the provocative intimacy of second person, the narrator-authority then intrudes and invites the reader to ponder a single unidentified word on the same computer monitor. We are asked to examine the thing as a simple combination of letters, blinking impulses on a screen, a bald construction, a glyph tidy and clean, with available links that would track the word's etymology (the "tunneled under-world of its ancestral roots" [826]) and even translate it into dozens of obscure languages (forms piled upon forms). Then, dramatically, the narrator-authority invites "you" to turn from the mesmerizing screen and consider the world there outside the window, there on the scatter-strewn desk on which "your" computer rests, evidence of an "unwebbed" off-screen world thick with the tenor of the everyday (827), the casual argument of things that resists containment, that is alive with the crazy toss of the moment, the density of a random glance, the largeness of things themselves. We are challenged to enlarge our focus, to contain both order and mystery—both Nick Shay and Sister Edgar. Only then is the screen word identified—it is the word *peace*—a gesture now of both genuine hope and ironic contentment. The word and/or the world, peace and/or pieces, the twin towers of perception, clarity and mystery, system and surprise, one engendering an inevitable longing for the other, one completing the other. Should we be content with our tidy reading of Nick Shay and Sister Edgar? Hardly—the text, after all, delivers sufficient evidence to argue that Nick's autumnal angst is in fact liberating wisdom and that Sister Edgar's luminous cyber-heaven is in fact a terrifying, enclosing bogus-system that ironically traps her.

Ultimately, the design implied by this (or any) "reading" of *Underworld* is necessarily suspect, a tidying into form of a massive bank of data (consider the cast of intriguing secondary characters herein ignored, the numerous plotlines untracked, the considerable gathering of symbols and motifs left unexplicated, the stunning passages left untouched), a projection of an engaged ingenuity that is born of the conviction that design is tenable even if revelation and concealment are, finally, synonyms. Design succeeds only ironically, by its willingness to concede its own vulnerability, its provisional nature, its inevitable amendment. Arrangement and expression do not dispel mystery, do not insist on understanding, do not flatten the text but rather provide the fragile, finite reassurance of invention itself—and invite successive explorations, entirely new constructions of understanding. It is a strategy of inexhaustible invitation recalling Hawthorne's Surveyor in "The Custom-House" sketch that opens *The Scarlet Letter* in which, fired from his dead-end ledger job and suddenly freed to indulge his imagination in the oriental embroidering of the elaborate tale we are about to commence, he confidently extends to willing readers the invitation to embroider their own scarlet letter, their own account of the origins and import of that compelling, mysterious ragged letter that he had recovered (or did he?) amid the moon shadows and yellowed parchments of the Custom-House's second floor. With similar generosity, DeLillo's narrator-authority liberates the contemporary reader into complexity, offers not essential truths for the reader to grasp but rather the essential, sustaining truth of grasping itself, the reader as invested in and as rewarded by the text as the writer.

Part Three

The Soul

The noblest thing, a bridge across a river, with the sun beginning to roar
behind it. He watched a hundred gulls trail a wobbling scow downriver.
They had large strong hearts. He'd been interested once and had mastered
the teeming details of bird anatomy. Birds have hollow bones. He mastered
the steepest matters in half an afternoon. . . . He stood a while longer,
watching a single gull lift and ripple in a furl of air, admiring the bird, thinking into it, trying to know the bird, feeling the sturdy earnest beat of its
scavenger's ravenous heart.

—*Cosmopolis*

In the rolls of the dead of September 11, all these vital differences were
surrendered to the impact and flash. The bodies themselves are missing
in large numbers. For the survivors, more grief. But the dead are their
own nation and race, one identity, young and old, devout or unbelieving—
a union of souls.

—"In the Ruins of the Future"

M'illumino
d'immenso.

—"Mattina," Giuseppe Ungaretti

5

Parables of Resurrection

After the monumental edifice of *Underworld*—with its joyful, elegant privileging of the act and art of explication, its robust affirmation of the grasping ingenuity of both the reader and the writer, and its confident narrator-authority so deftly tapping into the vital sufficiency of the aesthetic enterprise—DeLillo, perhaps sensing that the infinite jest of massive texts that forever resist final readings might become tiresome diversions, perhaps sobered by the larger cultural movement toward the dawn of a new millennium, itself inevitably freighted with spiritual significance, perhaps engaged by confrontation with his own mortality (inevitable as he passed the age his own father had died), returned to the unsponsored immediate in a tetralogy of sorts that would reveal a fearless evolution into a frank confrontation with spirituality, a movement beyond the stubborn opposition of grief and nothing, toward a decidedly unironic embrace of transcendence, beyond the street, beyond the word. We must be careful, however. It is not as if DeLillo, late in his career, suddenly embraced the visionary plane of experience with hokey, suspicious suddenness, a too dramatic, born-again road-to-Damascus conversion that would appear parodic. The possibility has edged DeLillo's work since David Bell, adrift in the Christmas season (like so many other DeLillo characters), toyed with Eastern sensibilities. The impulse has animated DeLillo's works in subtle (and unironic) play since his first story, his very first character a radical street preacher in contemporary Manhattan. We recall those gentle, wide-eyed hippies David Bell encounters in the desert wastes with their unshakable certainty in a cosmos of love; Harkness's looping desert meditation walks; Opel's dramatic childhood river baptism that alone gives her character (and her offer of protective love) the authority as that novel's moral center; the astronomer Ratner's mystical epiphany gazing into the night sky over Pittsburgh; Jack's agonizing Gethsemanic gesture of self-destruction; the gringo mystic Levi Blackwater with his cryptic assurances to a doomed Selvy; Wadi Assad's best-selling inspirational wisdom; Owen Brademas's wild-fire pentecostal church service; Steffie Gladney's eerily calming Toyota Celica mantra; Win Everett's daughter's Native American clay figures in that box under her narrow bed; Karen Janney's ministry among the homeless in Tompkins Square; the urban lost clustering about a Minute Maid billboard watching for miracles.

But even given DeLillo's Catholicism, his formative studies in theology and philosophy, and his long fascination with the vertical vision, his later works can surprise (even unsettle) with their forthright address. They can seem inaccessible, even forbidding despite their slender heft—together, they are barely half the size of *Underworld*—spare, Zen-like parables that can frustrate reader involvement, appearing at times to be gnomic meditations rather than traditional narratives. The tetralogy, however, describes an imperfect arc of a hesitant ascent as each central character defines a different relationship with the immediate that has long tested DeLillo's characters: first, a retreat from its disquieting implications (Michael Majeski, *Valparaiso*); then, an embrace of its devastating splendor and difficult beauty (Lauren Hartke, *The Body Artist*); and a violent transcendence from its oppressive limitations (Eric Packer, *Cosmopolis*); and finally the celebration of the difficult embrace of the self unbound, freed at last to feel the immensity of the soul itself, the nothingness that has haunted DeLillo's fiction since the desert wastes of his earliest fictions reconfigured into infinity itself (Alex Macklin, *Love-Lies-Bleeding*). The characters each commence among DeLillo's comfortable urban elect—thirtyish, confident, successful, content—but in quick order each must confront the stark implications of a life spent stubbornly on the horizontal plane. Each will make a difficult, terribly public journey toward authenticity and toward the discovery of an unsuspected identity, a process of self-interrogation that comes inevitably to involve the daring vocabulary of spirituality that has intrigued DeLillo since his first published story.

Valparaiso (1999)

Because of a travel agent's glitch and a string of unintentionally comic misunderstandings at two airports, system analyst Michael Majeski's routine business trip to Chicago (specifically to nearby Valparaiso, Indiana) turns into an absurd misadventure in which Majeski ends up routed first to Miami (specifically to nearby Valparaiso, Florida) and then ultimately to Valparaiso, Chile. The scale of the error attracts immediate media attention, and Majeski finds himself a hastily manufactured Warholic. Rather than resisting such attention, however, he welcomes the opportunity to become a celebrity-commodity. For most of act 1, DeLillo deliciously satirizes the inane superficiality of such fifteen-minute celebrity as Majeski tirelessly engages endless rounds of interviews ("67 interviews in $4^{1}/_{2}$ days in $3^{1}/_{2}$ cities") in which he responds to the same questions with what quickly become prepackaged answers. Without specificity, he glibly tells interviewers that since his journey, he has become a "complete man," that his otherwise dreary, upscale suburban lifestyle has found a new "clarity," a "luminous quality."[1] He revels in the media attention, even quits his lucrative job to join the celebrity circuit: paid appearances, book deals, film projects, motivational seminars, autograph shows (for a fee, he will sign boarding passes and airline coupons). As his fifteen minutes near their inevitable clickover, however, Majeski begins to scrutinize the starker implications of his flight, and we begin to sense the terror that lurks unsettlingly about the easy comedy of this wild ride and how Majeski has sought the hot glare of media attention largely to dodge the disconcerting epiphany that had shaken him during the long cold descent into Chile.

In the second act, under the relentless prodding of talk-show maven Delfina Treadwell ("the shining soul of daytime America" [64]), a media caricature so devoid of an authentic self that she feels animated only through the vampiric suctioning of energy from her studio audience, Majeski begins to recount that descent. It is an ironic juxtaposition: on the studio set, abuzz with the carnival excess of high-tech spectacle effects, Majeski quietly, with mounting distress, recounts his descent into an identity crisis. Suspended high above the bleak spine of the Andes, Majeski undergoes an unanticipated, uninvited moment of anxious self-assessment. Under Delfina's interrogation, he recalls confronting the irrefutable evidence of his own inconsequentiality: bound for a destination he did not choose, six thousand miles from where he intended to be, feeling acutely helpless and indefinably desperate. The misdirected flight becomes an irresistible metaphor for his directionless existence, whose insufficiency is suddenly strikingly apparent. Too long a drone within massive corporate systems, he has come to accept inconsequentiality as sufficient—until strapped into an assigned seat of an airplane he never intended to fly, he glimpses the magnitude of his intimidation, the dimensions of his helplessness. He tells Delfina how he had then headed for the plane's lavatory with a razor and the plastic bag containing the airline's complimentary blanket; and how, once in the lavatory, he had sliced open the bag and calmly wrapped it around his head, securing it with dental floss, to await death, choosing nothingness over grief, while all the time assessing the harrowing implications of an existence as pointless in its ending as it had been in its duration. "Out there in the hard and fast, I devised a kind of glancing man. Picnicked with the sales managers in the sheep meadows. For my wife, I built a husband, contractually bound. Loved and touched. Tossed the salad. But who was I? *Ga ga ga ga ga.* In the seams of being, nobody. In the final spiral strand, nobody, soul-lonely, smoke" (101–2). It is a moment of profound possibility, an inauthentic self scalped and exposed, gifted with the difficult promise of awareness—save that Majeski lacks the requisite courage to accept the implications of his awareness and seeks the convenient dodge of suicide. As it turns out, he lacks the courage even for that. When the plane suddenly pitches, Majeski, terrified over the rolling turbulence, aborts the suicide and docilely heads back to his seat and to the comfort and security of his seat belt.

It is a strategy of retreat that also defines Majeski's subsequent rush to celebrity, where, in the endless rounds of Q&A, he can talk his life into conviction, purpose, and form, where he can be the grid-dots of television, an unfleshed life, an unreal self. The promise of his airborne epiphany is cashiered; he is too content with superficial changes: he is learning Spanish and growing a beard. His touted "new life" is sadly inauthentic (on Delfina's show, he admits a new passion in his marriage but oddly qualifies that by acknowledging the sex is impersonal; indeed, during the taping, his wife admits she is pregnant by the documentary filmmaker sent to scope out Majeski as a possible project). With honed predatory instincts, Delfina Treadwell stalks Majeski's "naked shitmost self" (91), a commodity that television can exploit, probe, expose—and then ultimately discard. Of course she has no interest in what actually stirs in the skies over Chile: Majeski's soul. "We're not running a redemption racket," she sniffs disdainfully (82). Her vision stubbornly horizontal, in her exuberance over the unexpected exposé of the interview, Delfina crudely silences Majeski (literally—she shoves her stage microphone into his mouth) signaling the end of his fifteen minutes even as a creepy chorus of flight attendants chants the familiar in-flight safety instructions, a taunting reminder of the attraction of security and Majeski's return to the banality of his nonlife. The turbulence Majeski encounters over Chile—that is, the emotional turbulence of his sudden moment of introspection—marked an opportunity to break through into his soul, into authenticity, an opportunity Majeski rejects. He is thus left at play's close an erased self. As the play opens, the stage-set of the Majeski living room is dominated, without explanation, by a backdrop of a crude videotape image of a man's blurred and obscured face. That same projected image returns at the close of the play—save that now we recognize it as footage from the airplane security camera that had filmed Majeski, plastic bag over his face, in the lavatory awaiting death. At the close of the play, however, the image of the wrapped head is gradually enlarged until it consumes the stage space: it is emptiness multiplied, obscurity magnified, metaphorically underscoring Majeski's elective two-dimensionality even as the stage blacks out, leaving the unsettling sense that the self is disposable and the soul irrelevant.

The Body Artist (2001)

Lauren Hartke will also have a turbulent moment of self-assessment, her own opportunity to accept the difficult gift of awareness—but she will manifestly not refuse its implications. We watch as Lauren, an artist, is abruptly dislocated from the aesthetic sensibility and dropped into the hard and fast, a rude reminder that the artist (like the rest of us) must reside within the imperfect casing of flesh and bone and thus be prone to the brusque intrusion and harsh accidents of contingency. In her mid-thirties, Lauren is a successful performance artist (or body artist) whose consummate confidence in her craft is badly shaken by the intrusive trauma of grief: specifically, the gunshot suicide of her husband, Rey Robles, a one-time critically hailed avant-garde film director who, as his career did a slow-motion crash and burn, slid into alcoholism and depression. Stunned by the sudden awareness of vulnerability that inevitably accompanies the graceless thunderclap of mortality, Lauren the artist is compelled into time, the heavy horizontal plane of experience, the bruising world that unfolds with roiling unpredictability just off the computer screen in the closing pages of *Underworld* and that Majeski contemplates in his chilly descent, the inelegant real world so elegantly mediated by Lauren's onstage aesthetic structures.

After her husband's funeral, Lauren opts for a safe (and, for DeLillo readers, familiar) strategy of retreat, withdrawing to the cavernous shelter of the spacious New England coastal cottage that she had been renting with her husband; determined to be alone, she closes herself off from friends, from newspapers and radio, parses her days in the distracting busyness of trivial errands, spends long nights monitoring an Internet Web site that broadcasts an unedited live feed from a nondescript stretch of two-lane road in, of all places, rural Finland. It is at this point that Lauren encounters a mysterious presence in a small third-floor bedroom, a man (?) of indeterminate age and vague physical definition (a smallish stick figure, chinless, with a cartoon head). He speaks in an unstructured, syntactically fractured babble that suggests more than it says: "Coming and going I am leaving. I will go and come. Leaving has come to me. We all, shall all, will all be left. Because I am here and where. And I will go or not or never. And I have seen what I will see. If I am where I will be. Because nothing comes between me."[2] In time, Lauren notices that he is actually mimicking fragments of conversations she had had with her husband, parroting their voices like some eerie tape recorder (how long, she wonders, had he been living in the house unnoticed, listening to them); but even as she begins to suspect he may have been a boarder, he starts to forecast bits of conversation days before he and Lauren will actually have them. Despite such a nonstop barrage of talk, however, he never identifies himself or justifies why he is in the house. Lauren, however, never panics, never notifies the police, never weighs leaving the secluded cottage. Although she considers numerous explanations to account for the enigmatic presence (some reasonable—he is a mentally challenged ex-boarder, an autistic drifter, a schizophrenic patient gifted with memory retention released by or escaped from some nearby facility; some not so—a benevolent alien, a protective angel, a private muse, a grief hallucination, the residue of her husband's psychic energy left from his premature death), she is never certain, nor are we, exactly who (what?) Mr. Tuttle is (she names him after a long-ago science teacher he apparently resembles). One thing is certain, however, even as the conversations she conducts with Mr. Tuttle grow more cryptic: with his presence, Lauren need not face the reality of her grief or the implications of her isolation; indeed, she can defer acknowledging her husband's absolute absence, his violent self-destruction and its entailing mystery. Thus free to claim a bogus recovery, she begins to rigorously attend to her body for a return to the protective aesthetic shelter of her stage-world—stretching, exercising, exfoliating her skin, cutting and dying her hair, losing weight.

Shortly after Mr. Tuttle inexplicably disappears, Lauren does in fact return to the stage. We read a glowing review of her new piece, an intriguing work in which, we are told, Lauren effortlessly sheds her self to inhabit others, channels their voices, and alters her body to create an evening of convincing characters, beginning as an ancient Japanese woman and ending, some seventy-five minutes later, as an emaciated man who writhes on the stage struggling but unable to say anything. The piece continues a career in which she has submerged her self into roles as various as a Pentecostal preacher, a 120-year-old woman, and even a pregnant man. This new work is an "obscure, slow, difficult and sometimes agonizing" piece intended to compel a receptive audience to retard, even stop time itself, to master, in effect, the very element that has so terrorized Lauren's real-life existence (109). The piece is an artistic triumph, a reclamation of a wounded artist, an apparently unironic affirmation of the aesthetic process as tonic to trauma and psychic distress, the privileging of the artist figure—all themes squarely within the agenda of this slender novel's massive predecessor, *Underworld*.[3]

Still, something disturbs. Consider, for instance, the cover of the first edition. We are given a corner detail from an early Caravaggio masterpiece, *The Musicians* (1595), which, taken as a whole, is a rather straightforward allegory of music, a traditional confirmation of the aesthetic enterprise, which Caravaggio centers on a lute player tuning his instrument presumably preparing to play, surrounded by two supportive figures (one, Caravaggio himself; the other, Cupid, a god traditionally pictured in the company of music, who is here bearing a cluster of ripe grapes, which promises the happy gift of wine). What disrupts the composition, however, is a fourth figure at the right whose face is actually turned away and whose back, muscled and shockingly undraped, is thus turned to us. His instrument, a violin, has been inexplicably set aside; he appears distracted by music sheets he cradles in his lap, unable, unwilling, or perhaps simply uninterested in the ongoing celebration of the artistic process all around him. The cover of *The Body Artist*, in fact, is a detail of that figure's exposed shoulder, the detail so greatly magnified that it is in turn exposed to us as an artifice, specifically as applied pigment: we see not a smooth back but rather a scored surface, spiderwebbed with lines, thus destroying any illusion of realism and cautioning us that the aesthetic artifact, inspected too closely, will inevitably, necessarily crack, will reveal its artificiality. Thus, even before engaging Lauren Hartke's narrative, we are distanced from the aesthetic experience, encouraged to step back from its enthralling lure.

It is not entirely surprising, then, that DeLillo does not close the narrative by affirming Lauren's reclamation as artist, her triumphant return to the aesthetic process that so generously allows her to slip away from flesh and blood, from the responsibility of being a specific body locked within a steady time-motion that cannot be coaxed into slowing down—in short, to slip away from the complex responsibility of being Lauren Hartke. In the closing section, Lauren will finally be restored, yes, but not as an artist—by itself a narrow sort of reclamation that is for public consumption (as the reviewer of the performance piece notes), more for Lauren's audience than for Lauren (indeed, the account of Lauren's stage piece is given to us secondhand, through the review). DeLillo will complete Lauren's reclamation as a human being, a wounded, woundable, intensely fallible flesh-and-blood construction subject to vulnerability and exposure, subject to the steady, draining pull of time, left to navigate without explanation within a splendid and terrifying now.

The obituary of Lauren's husband quotes the film director as observing with Godardesque glibness, "The answer to life is the movies" (28)—clearly, DeLillo cautions, it is not. Rey himself had spent his life within aesthetic refuges: after a painful childhood torn from his family by political unrest in Spain, he would seek the comforting escape of cinema, even changing his name to a character he played in a film. His only successful directorial work, two films whose synopses we are given in his obituary, indicates his preference for exotic escapism in his art: one was an elaborate kidnapping tale involving a wealthy woman, the other a surreal crime drama. Unable to handle the difficult negotiation within the real world, drawn by the comforting narcotics of alcohol and promiscuity, Rey eventually played out his need for control through the ultimate director's cut: suicide. But DeLillo distances himself from such strategy. It is only fitting that after the intricate temptations of *Underworld*'s formidable aesthetic playground, after the inelegant dodge of Michael Majeski's strategic retreat from its implications, DeLillo would return with subdued and elegant grace to the stubborn immediate, the grief-world. *The Body Artist* is, in fact, an elegant affirmation of the failure of art, an admission of what art cannot finally fix or dodge (Lauren's parents indicate this tension: her father, an archaeologist, was steeped in the real; her mother, an accomplished harpist, engaged within the precious aesthetic). *The Body Artist* is something of a therapeutic return after *Underworld,* a sort of necessary corrective to *Valparaiso,* an austere parable that affirms the unmediated now, reclaims the unrestored moment too easily diminished even as we linger within the luxurious, enthralling enclosure of *Underworld* and wander amid the garish distractions of *Valparaiso.*

The novel's opening section—the last breakfast, as it turns out, shared between Lauren and her husband—introduces this critical estrangement between the artist and the immediate.[4] Nothing much happens—the couple takes turns switching on and off the radio, Rey smokes a cigarette with his coffee and newspaper, he spreads a fig on his toast, Lauren momentarily speculates why she uses a dented kettle despite having bought a new one, she studies the birds that gather at the feeder,

Rey loses his keys. We share an ordinary breakfast on an ordinary Sunday morning, but one in which the two characters, both artists—one failed and inching toward suicide, the other at the top of her craft—struggle awkwardly against the heavy press of an unprocessed world that is so stubbornly ordinary. It is the morning after a heavy storm, the natural world rinsed clean and apparently primed to reveal itself. As artist, Lauren feels the oppressive urgency that the world around her must needs disclose some shattering epiphany; unable to settle into its readily available grace, she is intent on force-igniting her aesthetic imagination, on adorning its accidental distribution of shape, line, color, and shadow with some shattering meaning. Yet Lauren struggles (and fails) to describe satisfactorily even the slenderest elements of that world: the sound of the birds at the feeder, the smell of the soya granules she sprinkles on her cereal, the implications of the jay that appears to stare at her momentarily from the feeder. Ironically, of course, even as she struggles to "understand" what the jay means or exactly what her soya flakes taste like, Lauren misses entirely her husband's lonely struggle against the pressing logic of suicide. Even as a forbidding murder of raucous (and emphatically symbolic) crows settles into the trees outside, Rey remarks cryptically that he has shaved that morning to ensure that God will see his face, then comments darkly about how Lauren would have to wait until later to understand the real terror of confronting "another ordinary day" (15), and even acknowledges wistfully how, despite their long marriage, he never really knew her. Unavailable to such disturbing signals, Lauren dismisses dailiness as inconsequential—they reveal themselves only to us and then only after invoking the special privilege of the reader: the act of rereading. Like the cottage tap water that runs within seconds from clear to murky, the world refuses to confirm the aesthetic urge to ignite with epiphanic clarity. Like the jay at the feeder outside the window that stares through the window into the cottage, Lauren, an artist estranged from her surroundings, is alienated from the fullest implications of this domestic world and in the process absent from its fullest experience.

Given this unsettling discomfort within the unrecovered immediate, the two artists are themselves distant from each other, not surprisingly, their shared domestic sphere riven into territories, things that are "his" and "hers." Their conversation is disjointed, they near-sleepwalk through breakfast as they are both slow to wake up. What conversation they have is regularly punctuated by "What?"; the radio is turned off and on and off and on, first as background noise, then as distraction (its droning voice sounds like Hindi to Lauren); both hide behind a forced interest in sections of the massive Sunday paper; struggling with conversation, Rey compares chitchat to pushing a boulder. Rey pours orange juice for Lauren, who in turn tells him testily that she has never liked orange juice. Each detail of the breakfast yields unsettling suggestions about the artists' strained relationship to their world, a sense of anxiety, absence, dislocation, even repulsion: Rey has heard a strange, unsettling noise in the walls; Lauren has no honey for her tea; she decides the soya flakes actually smell like feet; she pulls a human hair that is neither hers nor her husband's from her cereal; the radio blandly announces that a missile has exploded mysteriously underground in Montana. And as Rey departs for the city (to his first wife's Manhattan apartment, there to blow his head off), we are left with two innocuous remarks that suggest, on the one hand, Rey's anxious depression, his sense of lostness, and his miasmic regrets (he has lost his keys and rues putting all his keys on a single ring) and, on the other, Lauren's presumptive sense that as artist she is to ease rather than engage the oppressive pain of the world (she tells Rey of a wonderful muscle balm she has purchased and promises him a therapeutic rubdown later—ironic given his plans for the day, that irony confirmed by the brief newspaper account of Rey's suicide that DeLillo positions immediately after without narrative explanation or reaction).

The lengthy section that follows the obituary becomes exactly what the reeling artist Lauren seeks: an elaborate aesthetic shelter lost to any reliable commitment to a clear and definable present. With no reliable form or defined presence, Mr. Tuttle exists purely as a convenience within Lauren's strategic retreat; we never know who he is, and what he says never makes sense. We thus lose grounding in realistic narrative. We know only that Mr. Tuttle exists in the two time frames within which the grieving Lauren now feels comfortable: the past (he recounts conversations Lauren had with her husband, he reminds her physically of her former science teacher) and the future (his conversations become ultimately predictive). His cryptic first words—"It is not able" (43)—indicate his full-force negation of the present tense.[5] His presence permits Lauren a comforting distance from the difficult present, a release into her own conjurings. Indeed, she treats the mysterious Tuttle in relational roles she has never actually experienced: at one point, she stretches atop him like a cheating lover; later she bathes him gently like a new mother; and she even takes him on errands to the local mall like a harried Yuppie. Because he never presses upon her the present tense, he embodies the aesthetic impulse: he is time without a narrative, a fluid construction without a fixed identity, a presence without a clear definition, time without a measured present. The present becomes irrelevant. Lauren will conduct a disturbing phone conversation with Rey's first wife in which the woman will detail the film director's life-long depression, his artistic frustrations, his keen self-loathing, his penchant for violence—all stunning revelations to Lauren, which in turn serve only to distance her from an immediate that continues to baffle. Of course, she is far too certain, far too comfortable in retreat, and DeLillo undercuts such surety. Driving through town, for instance, Lauren glimpses a man seated on his porch and in an intuitive flash understands his life in toto; she creates his life: he is an unsuccessful real-estate agent, divorced, alcoholic, and emotionally distant from his own family, hungover and marooned on his porch. Only then does she notice that the "man" is actually a paint can poised on a board between two chairs.

Revived, nevertheless, by her separation from the problematic now, Lauren undergoes an all too predictable restoration as artist: in addition to her physical regimen (itself an exercise in control), she finds herself engaging in ventriloquist's dialogues in which she actually speaks in Tuttle's voice; she creates a story of an encounter with the cottage's previous owners who tell her of a brain-damaged boarder who considered the cottage his home—a tidy explanation that is, of course, only a satisfying exercise in invention. Like Michael Majeski and his celebrity performance, Lauren, dodging the dark implications of her husband's suicide, cultivates her imagination, her aesthetic muscle, the artist's enduring privilege to rescue events from their confusion—and enjoys, in turn, the safety of her own edifices, the triumphant affirmation of her skills as artist. Recall her moment under the chilling open sprawl of the night sky and her acknowledgment that, given the "awe and shame" of our puniness (101), we conjure the comforting idiocy of measurements such as light-years to domesticate such unnerving vastness. Distanced from the present, uncomplicated by grief, her stage triumph disturbs us even as we read the glowing review.

When Lauren decides to extend her lease and return to the coastal cottage after her three-night performance run in Boston, we are immediately reminded of how she has managed to estrange herself from the actual experience of death: as she drives up, she mistakes a strip of curled burlap in her driveway for a dead squirrel. As she reclaims her place in the cottage, she still relishes her isolation, monitors that country road in Finland as a world real-enough, avoids the newspaper and the phone, works diligently to keep her husband's physical features vivid even as such details commence their inevitable slide into the chill fog of memory. Lauren is determined to tidy the unnerving mess of the present (her first task is disinfecting the cottage bathroom) and determined thus to prolong her cozy sense of (sanitized) presentlessness. But we recognize that Lauren has in fact too casually destroyed her identity, her authenticity—as she cleans the bathroom, she pauses to hold the spray-gun disinfectant up to her head and pulls the trigger in a creepy gesture that fuses self-destruction with self-tidying. She confesses, "I am Lauren. But less and less" (117)—a hissing away that is a harrowing parallel to her husband's own suicide.

The reclamation of Lauren Hartke begins appropriately with an intrusion into her sanctuary—specifically, the owner of the cottage arrives to tell Lauren not (as she hopes) about the mysterious Mr. Tuttle (the owner, obviously, is unfamiliar with her private constructions) but rather to tell her that he and his wife have decided to restore a damaged and neglected dresser they had left long ago on the upper floor of the cottage and that movers would be coming to reclaim the forgotten piece. That project suggests a robust energy distinctly missing in Lauren's strategic withdrawal: damaged, neglected, the valuable dresser can nevertheless be restored, an affirmation of unsuspected resilience but only if the damaged and forgotten object is liberated from its protective recesses (the dresser is not only tucked away in the upper floors but wrapped with insulating quilts).

Like a Zen satori in which a character undergoes a rapid and ultimately inexplicable influx of awareness, Lauren will move within pages to embrace the very immediate she had so pointedly abandoned. As a first gesture, she will note (entirely out of character) the exact time: it is 7:30. Thus positioning herself squarely in the present, she heads to the upper floors, to the very room where she had initially "met" Mr. Tuttle, searching for his presence to relieve the panicky press she feels from the owner's visit, feeling suddenly "exposed, open, something you could call unlayered maybe . . . aware of the world in every step" (121). Nearing the room, however, she indulges an erotic reverie about her dead husband—his limp member "rising in her slack pink fist" even as their tongues, nipples, fingers touch in "whispers of is and was" (122, 123).

Swept forcefully into the awkward fantasy of such projections (the violent juxtaposition of present and past tense), Lauren finally confronts what she has studiously avoided: her devastating guilt, the responsibility she feels for her husband's death, how insulated she had been from her husband's quiet agony that Sunday morning: she replays the morning breakfast, except this time she *does* intuit Rey's signals of deep pain, and this time she takes his car keys and "hides them, hammers them, beats them, eats them, buries them in the bone soil on a strong bright day in late summer, after a roaring storm" (123). The sheer fantasy of such conjuring, however, finally shatters her protective insulation: she cannot turn back time, she cannot reimagine events, she cannot save her husband. Suddenly, she feels "emptiness around her" (123). It is her moment of turbulence: she collapses in the hallway, groaning and rocking back and forth slowly. In a single breathless instant, she refuses to step into the room ("It was pathetic to look" [123]) and thus shatters the grip of Mr. Tuttle. "Then she worked herself up along the doorpost, slowly, breathing completely, her back to the fluted wood, squat-rising, drawing out the act over an extended length of time. Her mother died when she nine. It wasn't her fault. It had nothing to do with her" (124)—an entirely unexpected gesture of absolution, a wrenching liberation from some unspecified, long-buried guilt, apparently, over her mother's too early death, a guilt surely exacerbated by the suicide of her husband.

She then enters the room, and it is empty (no Tuttle). The room is bathed in a vibrant morning light. Lauren can see the "true colors of the walls and the floor. She had never seen the walls before" (124). It is a striking moment of restoration not to the artistic imperative to restructure the chaotic immediate but rather to the difficult human imperative to see the world as it is. Boldly, she goes to the window and throws it open, feeling "the sea tang on her face and the flow of time in her body, to tell her who she was" (124). With dramatic flourish, Lauren Hartke re-claims the now, not the "live" computer feed from obscure Finland but rather the bright and brittle data of the enlivened senses alerted and enthralled by their sur-roundings; the relentless motion of time that cannot be slowed except within the exaggerated artifice of aesthetic artifacts, which she feels now in the only way each of us ever registers its processes, in the vulnerability of the fragile body; and, as a consequence, she finally reclaims her identity, a self undiverted into other per-sonae. Lauren is finally alone and at last alive—to borrow from her earlier diagno-sis, she is Lauren, but now more and more. She is necessarily helpless, vulnerable (recall the Japanese woman Lauren had seen watering a garden who becomes in her performance piece an image of quiet strength and control; since her return, Lauren had seen the same woman coming out of a store, this time with her hands concealed in her sweater, an image that now suggests helplessness). Stripped of the imagination, Lauren is liberated into the immediate, itself now bathed in redo-lent showers of morning light. Like the mysterious fourth figure in the Caravaggio canvas, Lauren resolutely distances herself from the aesthetic process, sets aside her instrument, so to speak, accepts exposure and vulnerability; alone, she turns her back on her audience and accepts the sad/beautiful reality of her own human skin, the fallible, imperfect thing that ticks away in the now, the thing called Lau-ren Hartke—an epiphany that promises engagement not with what the imperfect immediate means or suggests but simply, splendidly, terrifyingly what it is.

Cosmopolis (2003)

Eric Packer is a creature of that same horizontal plane, a young, smart, thoroughly unlikable Manhattan asset manager and cyber-capitalist whose billion-dollar finan-cial empire will collapse in the tight spiral of a single ruinous day in April 2000. *Cosmopolis* is a defiantly apocalyptic narrative that, despite its slender storyline and sleek conciseness, confirms the possibility of nothing less than the transcendence and authenticity for which DeLillo's characters have searched since David Bell headed west out of Manhattan (indeed Packer, like Bell, is a corporate wunderkind at twenty-eight and, like Bell, makes a spiritual journey westward—Packer will take a day-long limo ride west along 47th Street). Like all apocalyptics since John of Patmos, DeLillo does not exploit fear by indulging lurid accounts of an amoral secular landscape blasted righteously into ruin; rather, he extends a fragile gesture of hope in a dark time that, within the apocalyptic tradition, always appears to be carnival high times, in this case the heady bull-market era of the 1990s. *Cosmopo-lis* introduces into the twenty-first century, itself stubbornly secular, the complex assumption that the complicated circuitry of the human animal—that mysterious matrix of hungers and drives—is made infinitely more complicated by a soul, an essence unreachable through the senses, undetectable by the sciences, and indescribable via language (particularly problematic for a precision stylist such as DeLillo). Despite the persistent evidence of the culture that he has anatomized for forty years—the pain and waste of violence, the ugly complacency of materialism, the erotic fascination with the simulacra of the media age, the unrestricted indulgence of carnal itches, the curious embrace of the oppressive depersonalization inevitable in the information glut of the computer age—DeLillo here dares to affirm a larger beauty. We are not merely the data we generate nor the flesh we inhabit; he refuses to concede the material universe to dumb matter and offers in a breathless closing, cast in the defiant viability of the present tense, an energizing confirmation of a vast something beyond the arrogant presumption of the twentieth century's defining manias: measurement and definition. Whereas *The Body Artist* affirms the sweeping sufficiency of the immediate, DeLillo follows with a companion parable-narrative that gloriously reveals its insufficiency.

It is difficult to define *Cosmopolis* if not as a parable. It flirts with but finally frustrates three obvious genres. It does not quite succeed as a high-tech financial thriller. Although a high-stakes gamble by a Trump-like financial guru does go terribly awry, the details of Packer's actual cyber-market maneuverings and his consequential financial fall are only vaguely sketched in fragmentary conversations he has with associates. Nor does *Cosmopolis* succeed as a *Bonfire of the Vanities / Less Than Zero*–styled social satire. Although the narrative centers on a stubbornly materialistic, obviously overdrawn super-rich cartoon, this Master of the Universe's precipitous fall and ultimate destruction (Packer will be shot dead by a disgruntled ex-employee) linger as more than merely a predictable caution against the glittery lure of easy money and the shallowness of the Internet's first-generation rich and famous. And the book certainly does not succeed as a psychological case study— we are not given sufficient interior coloring for Eric Packer to appreciate the logic behind his market gamble or the depth of its consequences. As an uncompromising parable-narrative of unearned redemption, however, *Cosmopolis* confirms that beneath and beyond the pressing chaos, the irredeemable banality, and gross materialism of our cultural moment lurks, nevertheless, a sustaining essence, a conviction offered here without the pull and drag of any specific institutional faith. Like some Dostoyevskian hero, ruthless billionaire Eric Packer, penniless at the moment of his death, shot in cold blood in an abandoned tenement in (appropriately) Hell's Kitchen by a derelict vagrant who once worked for Packard Capital, taps into an unsubtle illumination that, far from Lauren Hartke's modest epiphany (which serves only to clarify the condition of a single self), here transforms all selves by confirming the viability of a larger dimension beyond the "sheer and reeling need to be" whose complex integrity would be violated by description (209).[6]

Urged by the stifling press of imminent death, Packer is gifted by the compelling illumination that the body finally cannot tolerate its own absurdity, an intuitive conviction in which he is lifted out and apart from the predatory banality of the material world (as he comes to understand the dimension of his financial fall, he rejects outright the idea of rebuilding his empire by rejoining the carnivores in the fast track). Blasted by insight, now "alive in original space" (209), Packer understands in the slender now left him—the moment before he registers the report of the gunshot that will kill him—that the self he has so long valued is merely a vulnerable part of a mightier frame of reference. As with all visionary literature, *Cosmopolis* can only testify to this spiritual confirmation—it is neither facile invitation nor a crude self-help, how-to book. Resolution here is mystery, not solution. Not surprisingly, in an interview coinciding with the book's release, DeLillo defined the novel genre itself as "the deepest route into the landscape of our motives and soul." Of course, the redemptive ending of *Cosmopolis* may frustrate, even put off readers uneasy with the suggestion of the spiritual dimension in the human creature, which may help account in part for the particular virulence of the critical reaction to the book.[7] The reward for the participatory reader sharing this parable-narrative is the difficult gift of living henceforth on the edge of expectation, sustained by possibility, compelled by a compassionate love of living, despite the culture's glaring ugliness, inexplicable perversions, and casual cruelties.

Fabulously wealthy as only characters in parables can be, Eric Packer yearns, nevertheless, to brush against the spiritual dimension, to confirm the soul in a distressingly shallow materialistic culture (as Packer watches television news, the president of the United States appears to be eerily motionless, a contentless zombie), a culture that accepts as sufficient the Darwinian imperatives of acquisitive capitalism and relishes the accessible comforts of affluence and social position. Like all centering parable characters, Eric Packer from the beginning is difficult to like—he is morally thin, grandly flawed, stubbornly narcissistic, redundantly vicious, indifferent, and aloof (his limousine has been lined in cork, "prousted," to insulate him from distracting city noise). Flattened into near caricature by accepting as sufficient the oppressive horizontal plane of experience, he nevertheless evidences the promise of responding to the rich pull of a spiritual sensibility. His every action reveals the typical makeup of a parable character: a yearning for transcendence constantly undercut by an inordinate need to control and by a stubborn delight/addiction in the stimulations of the horizontal plane of experience, its pleasures and its pains. Early in the morning, for instance, he pauses at his penthouse window to note poetically the grace and lift of a single gull's flight, marveling at the "ripple in a furl of air" and feeling the "sturdy earnest beat of its scavenger's ravenous heart" (7); at breakfast he will inhale pancakes and sausage and can literally feel the metabolic surge from the sucrose and fat; later, he relishes the stabbing pain from his weekly prostate exam; in a single day, he indulges sexual release with four women without the bothersome complication of a conscience; he feels an involuntary erotic charge from watching again and again the television newsfeed of the fatal knifing of a prominent monetary executive, the "pulpy face blowing outward in spasms of shock and pain" (33); he opens the sunroof to relish the sweet sensuality of a spring rain; he begs a lover to administer a shock from her stun gun simply to feel the jolt; he will feel suddenly old in a rave club as he watches the gyrating frenzy of teens high on a trendy new street painkiller; when he impulsively joins a midtown movie set, strips naked, and plays dead with hundreds of extras lying in the streets as part of a postapocalyptic sci-fi film, he will relish the "textual variation" of the chewing gum stuck on the pavement and the clingy odor of oil leaks (174).

Unlike with Lauren Hartke at the cottage window, however, the horizontal plane here cannot satisfy. DeLillo is prepared to move beyond. But initially Packer is caught, suspended between options, between grief and nothing. Entowered eighty-nine stories above Manhattan in an opulent penthouse, Packer cannot sleep. Even as he pores over the pulsating symbols and flowing numbers that track international money markets, he relishes dense, fragmentary postmodern poetry that makes him "conscious of his breathing" (5); he is haunted by a line in "Report from a Besieged City," the harrowing account of a city in ruins that preaches the worth of a single moral conscience in such a blasted landscape, a lyric meditation by Polish dissident poet and moralist Zbigniew Herbert (like DeLillo, a winner of the Jerusalem Prize). A predatory capitalist, Packer nevertheless studies both natural sciences and foreign languages. He installs two private elevators to his penthouse, each piping in a different soundtrack. In one, he plays the dry eccentric minimalist piano experiments of ever-ironic avant-garde shock artist Erik Satie. In the other, he listens to the mystical throb of Sufi music as interpreted by a Harlem rapper and street mystic known only as Brutha Fez, urgent and exploratory music that seeks the purification of the self beyond the prison of the body—when the elaborate street procession that marks the funeral of Brutha Fez passes Packer's limo, he will feel the urgent grief of the devoted mourners and will yield completely to "enormous body sobs" (139). The elevators are, of course, a variation on the dead-end choices of grief and nothing. A collector of the sort of experimental contemporary art that his friends do not even know how to look at, Packer wants to secure a stunning Mark Rothko—but, clumsy in his expression of such appreciation, he crudely schemes to buy the entire Rothko Chapel, an internationally renowned nondenominational meditation chapel on the campus of Houston's Rice University, and to relocate its artworks in his own penthouse ("I want everything that's there. Walls and all" [30]). He has studied Taoism and understands the vital reward of meditation and even compares himself to a monk. During an echocardiogram that is part of his weekly physical, he will watch his heart's palpitating image on a monitor screen, mesmerized by its "distance and immensity," the "poetry and chemistry" he senses decidedly beyond the crude scan of medical surveillance (44). On a long-ago otherwise forgettable wild boar hunt in the snowy wastes of the former Soviet Union, Packer glimpsed in the bleached distance a Siberian tiger—it registered as a "sting of pure transcendence" (81), and, even as his world crashes and burns in the narrative present, Packer still recalls that moment, "outside all previous experience," how that tiger, "aflame in high snow," bound him momentarily, inexplicably, to a "brotherhood of beauty and loss" (81). Clearly, Packer's considerable binding to the horizontal gives him no comfort. Too egoist to accept grief, too wounded to accept nothing, Packer begins what shall prove his epiphanic journey beyond.

The narrative plot, such as it is, patterns itself after the familiar spiritual metaphor of the journey, specifically the descent into hell that marks the authentic ascent of a soul. Packer will begin his odyssey in his spacious penthouse high above Manhattan and will end the day in the squalor of Hell's Kitchen. On Packer's calendar is listed a single errand: get a haircut in the working-class neighborhood where he was raised. It is a simple crosstown drive—entirely along 47th Street. It is early morning when Packer departs his Xanadu, a $104 million, forty-eight-room penthouse triplex overlooking the East River that features among its ostentatious appointments a lap pool, a fully equipped gym, even a shark tank lined with coral. Packer will summon his lavishly customized white limo, outfitted with blinking computer consoles, some monitoring the financial markets while others (so-called spycams) provide his limo with its surveillance security feeds. There is particular urgency today. Packer is in an extraordinary financial dilemma: he has borrowed yen heavily to back his risky market speculations and he must carefully track the Japanese financial markets—if the yen continues to rise, so will his catastrophic debt. As a Master of the Universe, he is confident the yen will fall. Although only twenty-eight, Packer has made a fortune from his uncanny ability to peer into financial data and to predict from such welter reliable patterns of rise and fall. He has thus always found the world "knowable and whole" and data "soulful and glowing," revealing ultimately in "electronic form, in the zero-oneness of the world, the digital imperative that defined every breath of the planet's living billions" (24). He relishes that command and control, that invulnerability and strength—a physical-fitness fanatic, he is bothered when his doctor tells him during his weekly physical (a creepy indication of his need to control) that his prostate is "asymmetrical," a nagging imperfection that, although not indicative of anything fatal, nevertheless haunts Packer.

Today, however, his confidence will be more profoundly shaken, doubts will begin to spiderweb as he tracks the steady, irrational rise of the yen he bet so heavily would drop—but rather than take the counsel of his own corporate strategists who will make cameo appearances during the long limo ride, Packer will simply fuel the disaster by tapping secretly into his new wife's considerable private accounts (she is heir to a fabulous banking fortune) to continue what turns out to be his suicidal enterprise. Typical of parable characters, Packer is bent on precipitating his own downfall, on spiraling to the point of absolute nothingness, where, in such literature, authentic recovery can commence. As one of his financial consultants tells him, "You're beginning to think it's more interesting to doubt than to act. It takes more courage to doubt" (32).

As Packer's limo inches across town, the ride will be hampered by unexpected snarls (each an indirect admonishment to the monomaniacal Packer of his inability to control events)—a winding presidential motorcade, the massive street funeral for Brutha Fez, a burst water main, even violent demonstrators angrily agitating against the globalization of capitalism. Despite the tedious progress of his limo ride and despite the accelerating urgency of his portfolio meltdown, Packer (typical of reprobate parable types) will find time to indulge his insatiable appetite, specifically here for food and sex. After glimpsing his wife of twenty days pass his limo in a cab, the two share an impromptu breakfast in which Packer, as he inhales the stack of pancakes, presses her about having sex; a self-styled experimental poet, she has apparently been abstaining, since it would divert precious energy she requires for her writing. Thus frustrated, Packer will depart his limo-bunker for two assignations in between other meals, one with an art dealer who is trying to broker the Rothko purchase, the other with one of his bodyguards (as part of his fetishistic demands, she will wear her body armor in bed), an exotic Egyptian who will lick vodka off his genitals and then administer, at his request, that savage jolt from her stun gun. But the sexual excess does not end there. While undergoing his weekly prostate exam in the limo (specifically, an anal probing), he discusses his impending financial peril with his chief of finance, who is on her day off and has interrupted her jog to meet with him, her body aglow in a hot sweat. Packer will engage her in a progressively more erotically charged conversation until he shatters her resistance by growling how he would like to pleasure her with her own water bottle, an idea sufficiently appealing that they apparently are both talked into orgasm.

How then to redeem Eric Packer, what is to be done with him? The simplest solution, DeLillo acknowledges, would be to eradicate him. A narrative subplot seethes with a death-to-the-conspicuously-rich activism. Antiglobalization agitators disrupt the financial district: they co-opt the market ticker readout to display their slogans; they pitch live rats into the district's restaurants; they snarl traffic, all compelled by their conviction that economic redistribution is best addressed by attack and protest, part of the centuries-old economic strife inevitable in a consumer society so irredeemably divided between Haves and Have-Nots. Within a larger narrative that will ultimately divide humanity into Ares and Are-Nots, however, poverty and wealth are different angles of the same stubborn fixation with the immediate, the distracting gutter-versus-penthouses drama. As DeLillo's focus here moves toward the transcendent dimension, poverty will bear no more significance than wealth—protest here is frustratingly ineffective and stubbornly horizontal. When Packer and his wife have lunch, two activists dressed as rats and spouting indecipherable slogans enter the luncheonette and toss live rats as part of a protest-qua–performance piece—but no one in the diner understands the exact nature of the protest (the owners, in fact, only speak Spanish). Even after returning to his limo, the streets all around him boiling with protestors and police firing rubber bullets, Packer himself is indifferent—when the protestors attack his limo (they pelt it with rocks, spray paint it, empty trash cans on it, and even urinate on it), Packer finds the riot appealingly theatrical as he watches it on his limo's television. The staggering self-consuming waste of such protest is perhaps best summarized as Packer witnesses the self-immolation of one of the rioters, an action dismissed by Packer's associate in the limo as trite, a cliché plagiarized from Vietnam-era Buddhists; it is nearly ignored by the other rioters who step around the burning man; and Packer, who is fascinated more by the ribbons of flame melting the man's glasses than the gesture's theoretical basis, wonders absently whether the fellow woke up that morning and actually went out to shop for matches.

If street protests then are dead-end exercises in cultural cannibalism, there is a far more specific (and ironically promising) threat to Packer—his bodyguard warns him early on that the corporation had received a credible threat against his life from some crackpot. DeLillo thus establishes the precariousness of Packer's horizontal positioning by providing as a counternarrative the meandering "confessions" of one Benno Levin, a self-styled economic terrorist whose actual name is Richard Sheets, an ex-employee of Packer Capital who had abandoned a modest career as an academic to pursue his fortune in the market (ironically, he believed in Packer, specifically that the wealth he thought inevitable in such an association could save his soul). From Sheets's two slender interchapters (part, he claims, of a projected thousand-page explication of his life), we learn that when his eccentric personality, shabby demeanor, and lax hygiene quickly became professional liabilities unwelcome in the corporate world, he was summarily terminated and then further demoralized when his crippled wife and child left him. As his fortunes tumble, he grows more convinced that his dilemma has a spiritual dimension, that the Internet he surfs has somehow infected his soul. Although the exact reasoning is of course left murky, he comes to obsess over Packer—from his squatter's apartment in an abandoned tenement in Hell's Kitchen, he plots the murder even as his bank account dwindles. Yet it is Sheets's clumsy assassination plot that will provide Packer the moment necessary for spiritual confirmation: Sheets will destroy

Packer's stubborn sense of invulnerability and control, compel him to examine his own thin life; it is Packer's moment of turbulence.

Packer's route to redemption, however, is as tortuous as the traffic-snarled limo ride. After the difficult, humbling moment of emotional sobbing watching the funeral cortege for Brutha Fez and contemplating the empty ritual that his own funeral would most certainly be, Packer makes a complete about-face: he takes a cream pie in the face, apparently the latest victim of André Petrescu, the notorious Pastry Assassin, a harmless gag attack, a guerrilla statement against acquisitive capitalism and the glitzy worship of celebrities. Unamused, however, Packer has his bodyguard apprehend the hapless "assassin," a nerdy little guy wearing a Disney World T-shirt, and then coldly kicks him hard in the crotch (he even attacks the paparazzi who record the cheap shot). He feels the dark reward of empowerment that we recognize as unearned and unattractive. Emboldened, "brass-balled" (144), he then directs his bodyguard to stop the limo at a playground and, in casual conversation with the unsuspecting bodyguard, borrows his gun and then coldly shoots him in a gesture Packer sees as clearing the way now for "deeper confrontation" (148)—the bodyguard was merely shielding him from the experience of authenticity. The moral consequences of the chilling execution do not register with Packer—indeed, he simply leaves the body. Packer is too fiercely bound by the horizontal, too literal, too locked within the logic of hubris of parable proportions.

With this misdirected salvation underway, hungry to experience authenticity, Packer returns (literally, of course) to his own childhood: the haircut in the barbershop in his old neighborhood where he becomes once again Mike Packer's kid. "He wanted to feel it, every rueful nuance of longing" (159). The shop is closed, but the barber opens up for Packer. As he shares a dinner of eggplant stuffed with rice and nuts with the barber and his remaining bodyguard (a victim of political torture whose mashed eye testifies to the harsh realities of the horizontal world of realpolitik), Packer recalls his father's death from cancer when he was only five. The lesson, the barber tells Packer, is how fleeting time is, how ephemeral is the horizontal plane, and how misplaced is any faith in its reliability. Moved by this poignant confrontation with his own emotional past and specifically the evidence of his vulnerability, Packer confides about the threats made to his life and feels in that intimacy a rewarding sense of trust and security. Gratefully, the insomniac Packer drifts off into a momentary rest. Unable to accept such security, however, like a parable character whose mission is not completed, restless even as he settles in the chair for his haircut, he bolts—"I need to leave. I don't know how come" (169)—his haircut only half done.

Bound now to protect himself, he steals a gun from the cash-register drawer and, stepping out into the nightworld, senses its vitality, its strange beauty. He embraces the immediate: he joins the extras on the sci-fi movie set, the hundreds sprawled naked on the streets. As he settles into the stunning spread of bodies, he becomes part, finally, of a whole, his stubborn isolation and aloofness literally violated as he nestles in among the strewn bodies. But what he accepts is the horizontal plane writ large: he is part of a single huge body, a vast flesh-unit. Jazzed by the crudely sensual feel of belonging, when he rises from the heap of bodies after the shoot wraps (in a gesture of mock-resurrection) he meets his wife and is first moved to make crude love-against-the-wall and then to confess to her that he has tapped into her financial reserves to bankroll his financial catastrophe—she only laughs, licks his face, and tells him "love the world" before she gathers her clothes and disappears into the night (178). Any purported spiritual sensibility is clearly cashiered into the flesh, bound by the carnal, satisfied by the immediate.

Abandoned now in Hell's Kitchen, Packer feels at last drained of urgency—then a shot rings out. His stalker has caught up with him and howls out his name. Immediately, with Godardesque sangfroid, Packer is swept into the only frame of reference from which he can draw to understand vulnerability: movies, specifically the cinematic cliché of the manhunt. He follows the shadowy figure of his unknown assailant to an abandoned apartment complex where he waits, breathing hard. Before kicking in the door, Hollywood-style, he delivers a tedious three-page monologue that reviews his long fascination with such cinematic violence, a suggestion, DeLillo broadly hints, that Packer is still far from authenticity.

When Packer finally enters and confronts his would-be assassin (coming out of the bathroom, his head wrapped in a towel), Packer quickly determines he is a harmless sort who pursues the murder because he wants to count for something. Unexpectedly, Packer considers all those disenfranchised by the capitalist system, and he is moved to a complicating sense of unsettling guilt. Typically, however, Packer literalizes the agony of this nascent conscience by impulsively shooting himself in the hand and relishing the hot pain. With the careless insight of the deranged, Sheets understands the enormous hubris of Packer: "You want to fail more, lose more, die more than others, stink more than others" (193). As he generously applies a tourniquet, Sheets, the would-be killer, lectures Packer that after a career of assuming that control, pattern, and precision are the way of the universe, Packer must accept imbalance as a condition of living—the "importance of the lopsided" (200). As Sheets talks, Packer feels the inexplicable "sweep of well-being" (199). But even as Packer protests that his "thoughts have evolved," Sheets insists that he must still go through with the shooting—"I wanted you to heal me, to save me" (203, 204).

Ironically, of course, Sheets *will* save Packer. The narrative here begins its turn to the spiritual: sensing his death imminent, Packer looks at his watch and discovers its micro security cam has apparently been activated by the jolts from running. Its camera has locked onto an ordinary beetle on an exposed wire overhead.

Mesmerized by the arresting beauty of the tiny insect ("so detailed and gleam-ing" [205]), Packer tests an epiphany that recalls Lauren Hartke's at the casement window: specifically, the unsuspected beauty of the immediate. But here such a moment is decidedly insufficient. As only spiritual literature can, the narrative now moves effortlessly into the inexplicable: as Packer studies the watch face, its image changes to a shocking image of a body facedown on the floor. We suspect who it is—a projection of the soon-to-be-shot Packer. Packer covers the watch and then peers again into it like some crystal ball and now sees the interior of an ambulance, the same body now snaked by medical tubes amid the confusion of emergency treatment. Then the image quickly changes to the marble quiet of the sliding vaults in a hospital morgue and finally the grim shadow of an identification tag on an unknown corpse tagged as Male Z: here, Packer finally sees, is the inevitable pay-off for any investment in the immediate. He is struck by a far more jolting epiphany than he felt with the beetle: "O shit I'm dead" (206). For a moment he believes he has finally transcended the limits of his physical frame by being translated into a pure stream of data (recall Sister Edgar), which his watch in turn has shown him—until, of course, the interfering pain from his wounded hand returns him to the imperfect casing of the flesh.

Stubbornly horizontal, unswervingly ego-intensive, he inventories his physical frame, his body's familiar imperfections, its defining smells, "the hang of his cock . . . his strangely achy knee, the click in his knee when it bends" (208). He imag-ines the people at his funeral, particularly his wife and one of his lovers who, he assumes, will be desolated by his death (his lover will masturbate in the back row of the funeral chapel). He reviews his own funeral wishes, typically grandiose: his body is to be placed in a decommissioned Soviet nuclear bomber he purchased that would be crashed by remote control in the desert, his body engulfed in flames, the black-scorched crater to be designated a work of performance art. But even as he reviews this, Packer relinquishes his interest in the "predatory" immediate and feels uninvolved in his own approaching execution (Sheets's presence does not concern him). As he awaits the report of the killing shot, he feels in a stunning moment of spiritual exhilaration a catapulting projection into "original space" (209)—that unexpected and welcome moment of visionary confirmation. He feels (to borrow from his poetic moment that morning with the sailing gull) the "sturdy earnest beat" of a "scavenger's heart." We recall the Sufi lyrics of Brutha Fez played by speakers on a sound truck as the funeral swirled past Packer's limo earlier in the day: "Let me be who I was / Unrhymed fool / That's lost but living" (138).

Eric Packer thus becomes the fourth DeLillo main character to die—each dies violently and each strives for a level of transcendence, but none quite this pure, this unironic. There is Glen Selvy, after his vicious decapitation by the Vietnamese hit squad, who achieves only a gruesome literal transcendence in the bellies of the predatory birds that ravage his unburied corpse; there is Lee Oswald, even as he is led away by the Dallas police to his rendezvous with Jack Ruby, who conceives of his eventual transcendence as an image fed into the media machinery and looped for generations in a ghastly parody of immortality; there is Willard Skansey, succumbing to the injuries of the hit-and-run, who slides away into anonymous death on the deck of the steamer bound for Beirut, assured the narrow transcendence of a published writer, the aesthetic artifacts left behind, which DeLillo here parodies with Packer's plans for his burial site-qua-art piece. Packer's shattering confirmation of a soul has none of the limitations of these other three and rests as a spare and splendid reassurance of a writer who has long wrestled with the implications of a spiritual sensibility.

Cosmopolis is positioned appropriately against the backdrop of the 1990s, that intoxicating cultural moment poised between two monumental ages of anxiety (the long fears of the cold war and the chilling realities of post–September 11), the Clinton decade that has since become synonymous with bull-market materialism, the promise of limitless wealth through speculation, the impressive reach of revolutionary new computer technologies, as well as the casual indifference to social inequalities, simmering class unrest and the manic licensing of the libido. DeLillo's narrative reminds the lost souls of such a graceless era that the soul itself is still a possibility. Even the prose here resists that decade's casual sense of decadent inflation—DeLillo dispenses with the attractive embellishment of figurative language: the sentences are spare, disciplined, clean, and lean. But transcendence is a complicated offer in the twenty-first century. Raised within the fetching aura and rich mysteries of pre–Vatican II ritual Roman Catholicism, educated by the relentlessly inquisitorial spirit of the Jesuits, nurtured by the Eastern sensibilities of the high 1960s urban counterculture, fascinated by the implicit spiritual intensities of jazz, DeLillo, a self-described failed ascetic, here acknowledges that spiritual yearning, entangled in flesh, loses its depth, too content with immediate satisfactions—it is the danger implicit in Lauren Hartke's tender embrace of the immediate. Lauren Hartke's epiphanic acceptance of vulnerability, mortality, the energetic Geiger-counter register of the senses, and the grand drama of time and flesh does not, as it turns out, stand as DeLillo's closing word. Grief and nothing—neither finally sustains.

Cosmopolis is a parable not of one man, one flawed character, but rather of the remarkable resiliency of the human soul itself that exists even in a cultural climate inhospitable to its implications and indifferent to its responsibilities; DeLillo recovers such an essential vitality within an individual so clearly, so consistently, so unapologetically material that its eventual manifestation in Eric Packer testifies finally to its indestructibility and gives to DeLillo's rich oeuvre the urgent notion that the individual is finer than the sorry cultural environment it has collectively fashioned. That essence, which defies translation into words, has in DeLillo's long career been the special privilege of artists and children, poets and shamans, but is here extended to the reader in a breathless closing moment, uncut by irony, that moves, finally, beyond grief and nothing. We are reminded that "cosmopolis" is a community of citizens bound not by nationality but by moral principle. Resistant and at times obtuse, Eric Packer, reprobate billionaire, crass market speculator, serial adulterer, murderer, is neither reformed or saved, thwarted or destroyed, punished or damned; rather, he is reclaimed, what DeLillo characters from David Bell to Lauren Hartke have sought: an unanticipated, unearned spiritual recovery in which weakness becomes strength; submission, triumph; confusion, wisdom; and death, ultimately, a passage.

Love-Lies-Bleeding (2005)

We will actually witness that difficult passage in the harrowing closing scenes of DeLillo's stage piece Love-Lies-Bleeding, which premiered at Washington's Kennedy Center in the summer of 2006. Although DeLillo, a robust seventy, undoubtedly has more to write, Love-Lies-Bleeding could serve as a fitting, even heroic capstone, a sort of resolution text as DeLillo accepts the particular responsibility of visionary writers whose sensibility extends beyond the reach of the immediate: to trace without sentimentality the translation from "is" to "was," always thorny given the peculiar burden of our awareness of time, and ultimately to deny death's apparent privilege. Environmental artist Alex Macklin (like DeLillo himself, an artist at seventy) has suffered two debilitating strokes and is now seven months into what his doctors have defined as a persistent vegetative state. On stage, he is marooned, isolated in cloaking shadows, bound to a wheelchair strung with feeding tubes. An unnerving Beckettesque figure, Alex is unable to speak (literally a lex, without words), unable to gesture, his eyes wide open, a shattering reminder of the body's proneness to catastrophic failure, now imprisoned within the claustrophobic grip of unendurable time—his doctors have diagnosed that the condition could stretch for years.

With the humane confidence of a writer convinced that both time and the body are hobgoblins of the timid, DeLillo freely upends the omnipotence of both. He disrupts the iron lockstep of linear time: the play's action freely shuffles, scene to scene, between past, present, and future. In the past, we watch a vigorous Alex some six years earlier beginning an ambitious landscape project in the desert Southwest, the construction of a meditation chamber, a cubical room with six congruent sides, painted entirely in earth tones, cut into the hard rock of a precipitous mountain; in the present, we watch as Alex's son, Sean, his second wife, Toinette, and his current wife, Lia, struggle with the decision whether to administer sublingual morphine to end Alex's suffering; and in the future, we attend the memorial service conducted after Alex's death. Time thus denied its authority, DeLillo under-cuts as well the compelling grip of mortality. How are we to confront the terrifying evidence of our vulnerability as flesh and blood creatures given the grim immobil-ity of the wheelchair-bound artist, more an it than a he? Do not concede its appar-ent pull. DeLillo begins the play with Alex in conversation with Lia shortly before his second, devastating stroke. Suddenly compelled to confront the reality of his own dying, he recalls a subway ride with his father when he was a child. He had noticed a man in the seat across the aisle, a man very much dead. But the corpse, the child's first, had generated no excitement among the few dull-eyed commuters, even the boy's father had been more interested in the racing handicaps in the sports section. Unable to command the expected anxiety, unable to generate even modest interest, death is thus rendered stingless, the body quietly, unobtrusively riding through the tunnels of the urban underworld, another unremarkable com-muter.

But, as we have seen in DeLillo's tetralogy, it is difficult to pull free of the gravi-tational pull of the temporal. Lia, only in her thirties, emerges in the play as DeLillo's passionate (and ultimately ironic) defender of the horizontal plane. Inter-estingly, "li," within the doctrines of Confucianism, is the virtue of appropriate out-ward behavior, the expression of propriety. Lia clings to the body of Alex Macklin and the sufficiency of the biological, the premise that Alex persists in the ghastly, unresponsive thing that sits rigidly in the wheelchair, the form that Lia diligently washes, shaves, dresses, and puts to bed each night. Let him die in his own time, she repeatedly argues. She clings to the barest evidence of response; some weeks earlier, she is certain that Alex had reacted to a stunning bolt of lightning, although she is cautioned that the body reflexively reacts to such massive atmospheric changes. She clings to memories of his vitality. She is certain that Alex moans— not out of pain (she is told the feeding tubes cause discomfort) but rather out of frustration as he struggles to communicate. Not surprisingly, once she agrees to Sean's proposed morphine treatment, Lia leaves the house to take a long walk, unable to watch Alex die. Lia feeds on the clean energy of the immediate and clings to its conventional virtues: the confirmation of community, the rich pull of family, the enduring strength of love, the sheer power of positive thinking, the gen-erous consolation of memories, the healing power of sympathy. Appropriately, Lia will be given Alex's ashes (at his memorial service, she will speak of her decision to scatter them in the desert hills), a fitting gift for one so compelled by the physical world. It is a measure of how DeLillo has evolved since the emphatic, open-throated affirmations of the jazzy urban nightworld of his earliest fictions that Lia's steady confirmation of the immediate and its conventional virtues here represents an untenable vision, the narrowest assessment of the human predicament; a joy-less, even gutless concession to unthinking earth-hugging; a timid and limited insight that never approaches clear sight, its thinness vividly underscored by the physical ruin of Alex himself.

Is Alex Macklin then more than the ruin left in the wheelchair? Certainly Alex himself long indulged the distracting persuasion of the immediate, that is until (as with other DeLillo characters) its insufficiency became clear: the scattered evidence of his multiple marriages, each savaged by the destructive cut of his own betrayals; the emptiness of his career success in the Manhattan art world; his brooding struggle with cocaine; his disquieting urges toward violence, including a hapless self-inflicted gunshot wound; his routine discontent; the dreary, persistent itch of the carnal; the cool distance he maintains from Sean, his only child. Long fattened on the horizontal plane, Alex's soul languished, never approached such scale, never neared sublimity. Then, as with DeLillo pilgrims since David Bell and his impromptu decision to head west, Alex feels inexplicably beckoned to a holy place. With Lia in tow, Alex some six years earlier had journeyed to the remote reaches of western India to walk among the ancient caves of Ajanta, thirty magnificent artificial caves that date back to the second century cut into the forbidding sides of a natural rock gorge, their walls decorated by religious frescos and statues, caves that have long served as meditation sites for Buddhist monks.

Like Packer in Hell's Kitchen, Alex in those ancient caves touches a vastness at last appropriate to his neglected soul. Alex abandons studio painting, forsakes the tight grid-world of New York, and heads west to realize his desert project. His soul, too-long caught up in the fetching play of the immediate, too-long diminished by the thin sustenance of the media age, too-long enervated by its voluntary restraint, is permitted at last access to sublimity, that need for scale evidenced not only in Alex's ambitious landscape project but also in Alex's luminous awareness of the effortless scale of nature itself: he begins to catalog the limitless abundance of desert wildflowers. DeLillo underscores that reanimation by the use of bold, unambiguous stage lighting: unlike the dim, claustrophobic shadows of act 1, the second act, which takes place in Alex's desert studio, is aglow in a blazing, clarifying light. Indeed, Alex quotes a gnomic couplet from the early-twentieth-century Catholic mystic Giuseppe Ungaretti: "M'illumino / d'immenso." Written out of the anguish Ungaretti experienced amid the brutalities of the bloody trench warfare of World War I, the couplet, loosely translated (its subtlety defies easy conversion into English), testifies to that epiphanic moment, uncut by irony, when "I flood myself in the light of the immense," suggesting the soul's magnitude when permitted to merge with the physical universe itself, that sense of expansion that leaves the soul both exhilarated and luminous. Shattering in its implications, the Ungaretti couplet could serve as fitting summary of the uncompromising visionary urgency of DeLillo himself, another twentieth-century Catholic mystic as it turns out.

The ghastly hulk of Alex Macklin and its grim there-ness thus terrifies only those unable to see that long ago, bathed in the endless illumination of the open desert, Alex Macklin's soul had soared free of its clumsy casing, such liberation suggested by the running shoes that Alex wears even as he sits immobile in the wheelchair throughout act 1. Of course, DeLillo sorely tests our ability to accept the implications of that epiphany; as victims of the age of fetching surfaces, we struggle to relinquish our own clingy fondness for the immediate. It is difficult not to flinch as we must watch Toinette and Sean repeatedly administer the morphine doses; watch them clumsily maneuver Alex's jaw to get the syringe under his tongue; watch as nearly a half-hour of stage time passes as the morphine does its work with excruciating deliberateness (Sean suspects he has acquired a dated batch); listen as Sean and Toinette grimly discuss the back-up plan (Sean has brought along a turkey-sized freezer bag to asphyxiate his father, recalling Michael Majeski and the blanket bag in the airplane restroom); and finally listen to the last, labored breaths of the dying artist.

But with expiration Alex Macklin is freed finally, catapulted into the welcoming embrace of mystery itself. Consider the play's title. Amaranthus is a slender, spiky wildflower that with its bright scarlet flowers has a shocking resemblance to a dripping wound, thus it is popularly (and poetically) known as love-lies-bleeding. Alex had noted the plant growing in rich abundance around the caves at Ajanta. Within the field of alternative medicine, however, the plant is widely held to contain healing power to relieve melancholia. DeLillo's *Love-Lives-Bleeding* is a similar act of generous consolation, the ghastly body of Alex Macklin as much an illusion as the "bleeding" of the wildflowers, his soul has already been freed from that imperfect casing. If Lauren Hartke struggles against the intrusive cut of mortality to make her peace with the accessible plenty of the sensual world and Eric Packer is taught with stunning swiftness that world's insufficiency, Alex Macklin discovers long before he is incapacitated the very affirmation that Packer glimpses only in the half-second that the gunshot flash leaves him. That affirmation animates Alex's closing years, his soul reclaimed, its ancient privilege consecrating what is otherwise the interminable grind of the sort of contemporary life that has haunted DeLillo characters since a spiritually enervated David Bell first heard the Salvation Army bells amid the soulless busyness of a midtown Christmas: the life confined by measurement, distracted by surfaces, reduced to cliché blandness, frustrated by the implications of its own pointlessness, and terrified of its equally pointless, ever-approaching end.

Across forty years, from the shadow perils of the cold war through the noontime nightmare of Dealey Plaza to the anxious awakening of September 11, Don DeLillo has tracked the American experience with an unblinking eye, a grasping intelligence, a pitch-perfect ear, and, as it turns out, a generous soul. He understands the loneliness at the heart of the American century. He offered initially the splendid complexities of an accessible world denied value by insidious entertainment media that have bound us to sophisticated simulations and depthless substitutions. He then coaxed us to return to the vivid, audacious reach of language and the compelling engine of the imagination and narrative's traditional privilege to restore experience to nuance and enticing ambiguities and to reward our ongoing struggles within that complex moral universe by endowing those uncertainties with the dignity of being recorded in words and in the process creating fragile communities of readers and writers that can un-isolate the lonely self. Ultimately, DeLillo salvaged our deepest hope, that the world through which we so clumsily maneuver cannot conceivably define the limits of the cosmos and that contemporary narrative can resume its ancient responsibility to return a reader to that difficult immediate spiritually heavier, fuller, richer, a most difficult transcendence, a bold move finally beyond—a last provocative gift of this era's defining novelist.

Notes

Introduction

1. Both quotes come from Vince Passaro, "Dangerous Don DeLillo," *New York Times Magazine,* May 19, 1991, 38.

2. From the Emma Brockes interview "View from the Bridge," *Guardian* (Manchester) May 24, 2003, http://books.guardian.co.uk (accessed January 24, 2006)

3. Jonathan Bing, "The Ascendance of Don DeLillo," *Publishers Weekly,* August 11, 1997, 261–63.

4. Quote from Brockes's "View from the Bridge."

5. Tom LeClair, "An Interview with Don DeLillo," in *Anything Can Happen: Interviews with Contemporary American Novelists,* ed. LeClair and Larry McCaffery, 79–90 (Urbana: University of Illinois Press, 1983), quote on 87. Further references in the text to this seminal interview are noted parenthetically.

1. Narratives of Retreat

1. Don DeLillo, *Americana* (1971; repr., New York: Penguin, 1989), 9. Further references to this novel are noted parenthetically.

2. When asked by Tom LeClair about the novel's obvious use of Eastern religion, DeLillo disingenuously indicated a passing interest ("An Interview," 85).

3. Stuart Hutchinson analyzes David Bell's hunger to touch the real ("'What Happened to Normal? Where Is Normal?' DeLillo's *Americana* and *Running Dog,*" *Cambridge Quarterly* 29, no. 2 [2000]: 117–32). Hutchinson connects this hunger to David Bell's investigation of his father's war experiences. On how the media created David Bell, see Keesey's reading of the novel in *Don DeLillo,* Twayne's United States Authors Series (New York: Twayne, 1993), 14–17.

4. Tom LeClair makes this scene pivotal, arguing the Oedipal guilt that Bell carries with him, coupled with his inability to help her during her cancer treatment, ultimately translates into the intimacy issues he faces with Sullivan (*In the Loop: Don DeLillo and the Systems Novel* [Urbana: University of Illinois Press, 1987], 44–46, 50–51). Douglas Keesey's *Don DeLillo* also develops a Freudian reading of this awkward moment (18–19).

5. Bell is crushed later when he learns that Beasley, finding the vulnerability of live radio too demanding, now tapes his "improvisational" monologues.

6. For readings that accept Bell's exile, see both LeClair, *In the Loop,* 53–57, and Keesey, *Don DeLillo,* 130–33.

7. LeClair (*In the Loop*, 80–92) argues that retreat here is beneficial, a chance for Harkness to find himself. Mark Osteen cites the appeal of the desert as a traditional site for purification (*American Magic and Dread: Don DeLillo's Dialogue with Culture* [Philadelphia: University of Pennsylvania Press, 2000], 40–44), and Neil Berman sees language as an ordering agent that ultimately fails (see *Playful Fictions and Fictional Players: Game, Sport, and Survival in Contemporary American Fiction* [Port Washington, N.Y.: Kennikat, 1981], 67–71).

8. Don DeLillo, *End Zone* (Boston: Houghton Mifflin, 1972), 188. Further references to this text are made parenthetically.

9. In 1982 DeLillo told LeClair: "It may be the case that with *End Zone* I began to suspect that language was a subject as well as an instrument in my work" ("An Interview," 81). LeClair reviews the language strategies that DeLillo deploys (In *In the Loop*, 68–77). Berman, who reads the novel as a sports novel, sees language as a joyless ordering system set against the primitive joy of the game itself (*Playful Fictions*, 64–65).

10. Critical opinions on Robinson vary. LeClair, in *In the Loop*, sees Robinson as a presence that haunts the book and is instrumental in encouraging Harkness's own adaptation of the meditative lifestyle (68–69). Berman, in *Playful Fictions*, sees Robinson as an *Invisible Man*–type figure in the tradition of Ralph Ellison's allegorical character who, denied his essence by racism, turns finally to monklike retreat as a way to define the self in such a world (54–55).

11. Keesey, in *Don DeLillo*, makes an intriguing case for Myna's reclamation (40–42). See Berman for a differing slant: he sees Myna's post-Christmas reclamation as banal and her attempt to be ordinary as a cop-out, and he uses the mynah bird's stupid attempt to repeat what it hears as a metaphor (*Playful Fictions*, 56–59).

12. Osteen is particularly helpful in assessing how DeLillo shatters the form with the closing (*American Magic and Dread*, 44–45). Berman is unhappy with the end as a suicide attempt that is never adequately motivated (*Playful Fictions*, 69–71).

13. Motives for this departure are varied: Keesey sees it as a defensive retreat, a self-purifying rejection of corrupt society (*Don DeLillo*, 50–53). Osteen sees it more as self-annihilating, akin to Thoreau's ultimate movement toward immobility and silence (*American Magic and Dread*, 46–48). LeClair sees the withdrawal as a struggle by Bucky to touch some private self and that *Great Jones Street* works best as a Beckett-like theater piece, a claustrophobic narrative that investigates the troubling implications of fame and power on the self (*In the Loop*, 91–92, 104–9).

14. For discussions of the novel as a *künstlerroman*, see LeClair, who sees the artist ultimately reclaimed from the product-commodity (*In the Loop*, 88–92, 94–96); Osteen ties Bucky to DeLillo himself and sees the novel as DeLillo's assessment of a reclusive lifestyle in which the artist loses management of his own fame (*American Magic and Dread*, 58–59); Cowart, however, sees Bucky as a shallow man trying hard to have a spiritual crisis and whose music reveals hysteria, not genuine passion, and whose celebrity status indicates DeLillo's conviction that the artist in the media age has lost moral

authority (David Cowart, *Don DeLillo: The Physics of Language* (Athens: University of Georgia Press, 2002), 33–38.

15. Because of these mountain tapes, Bucky is most often compared to Bob Dylan and his Basement Tapes, although Keesey, in *Don DeLillo*, 49, uses Johnny Rotten of the Sex Pistols and LeClair, in *In the Loop*, invokes Jim Morrison (89–90). Elvis to Michael Jackson, Elton John to Madonna, Kurt Cobain to Tupac, virtually any musician in the rock era—an artistic movement tied to media and promotion, the casual construction of the self as a moment's style, and the fame industry itself—could be used.

16. Don DeLillo, *Great Jones Street* (Boston: Houghton Mifflin, 1973), 68. Further references to this text are made parenthetically.

17. See LeClair's analysis, in which he argues that the drugs and tapes are agencies of control, lessons in "pragmatic paranoia" (*In the Loop*, 87). Keesey sees the drugs and the tapes as part of an intrigue designed to destroy Bucky's fragile individuality (*Don DeLillo*, 51–55).

18. Opel is often regarded as a redemptive figure—see Keesey (*Don DeLillo*, 56–58) and Osteen (*American Magic and Dread*). LeClair sees her death as an object lesson in the danger of thinging the self that in turn exposes Bucky's unwillingness to help her in her obvious distress (*In the Loop*, 103–5).

19. For analyses of the walk as redemptive, see both Keesey's *Don DeLillo* (62–64) and Osteen's *American Magic and Dread* (56–60), although Osteen finds the redemption short-lived and hence indicating Bucky's passivity. LeClair sees *Great Jones Street* as the closing work of a trilogy in which a DeLillo first-person narrator at last recovers the real world (*In the Loop*, 107–9).

20. In the LeClair interview, DeLillo described the book as "almost all structure. The structure of the book *is* the book. . . . I was trying to build a novel which was not only about mathematics to some extent but which itself would become a piece of mathematics" ("An Interview," 86).

21. Don DeLillo, *Ratner's Star* (New York: Knopf, 1976), 22. Further references to this text are made parenthetically.

22. Although the boomerang configuration is readily apparent, see Osteen's *American Magic and Dread* (particularly 71–76) for a helpful analysis.

23. See LeClair (*In the Loop*, 125) for a detailed chart; see Keesey (*Don DeLillo*, 76–78) for a compact overview.

24. See Osteen, *American Magic and Dread*, 84–94. In "Ironic Mysticism in Don DeLillo's *Ratner's Star*," *Papers on Language and Literature* 35, no. 3 [Summer 1999]: 301–32, Jonathan Little offers a fascinating slant: part 2 signals a turn inward for Billy, and the Logicon team is actually instrumental in this evolution toward the metaphysical.

2. Narratives of Failed Engagement

1. Don DeLillo, *Players* (New York: Knopf, 1977), 8. Further references to this text are made parenthetically.

2. DeLillo himself described the prologue as a "kind of model-building," the "novel in miniature" (LeClair, "An Interview," 82). LeClair (*In the Loop,* 52–55) is particularly helpful in defining how the prologue manipulates distance by creating expectations for violence, only to expose them as exploitations.

3. See, for example, Keesey's reading of Lyle (*Don DeLillo,* 86–95) and John A. McClure, who sees Lyle as drawn to the terrorist organization out of a need to lose the self in something mysterious and vast ("Systems and Secrets: Don DeLillo's Postmodern Thrillers," in *Late Imperial Romance* [London: Verso, 1994]: 118–51).

4. See, for example, Osteen's analysis. He is particularly expansive on the metaphoric use of the World Trade Center towers (*American Magic and Dread,* 145–49).

5. In *Don DeLillo* (92–93), Keesey argues Lyle is left exploited and emptied of meaning; in *In the Loop* (164–66), LeClair usefully compares the closing scene to a cinematic fade-out as Lyle surrenders to, rather than overcomes, his malaise.

6. Keesey is not quite so harsh: he argues DeLillo leaves open the possibility that Pammy (unlike Lyle) has accepted her place in an unmediated world (*Don DeLillo,* 97–99).

7. Don DeLillo, *Running Dog* (New York: Knopf, 1978), 135. Further references to this text are made parenthetically.

8. See Osteen, *American Magic and Dread,* 100–103.

9. For analyses of Selvy as automaton, see LeClair, (*In the Loop,* particularly 166–70) and Stuart Johnson ("Extraphilosophical Instigations in Don DeLillo's *Running Dog,*" *Contemporary Literature* 26 [1985]: 74–90, particularly 76–79).

10. A radial matrix itself is a tidy geometric figure that describes sets of numbers in tight rows which branch out from a common source in an elegant, entirely arbitrary design.

11. Interestingly, in the closing sequence of the 1939 Chaplin classic that Selvy watches, *The Great Dictator,* Chaplin steps entirely out of character to address the film audience in a stirring call for hope and tolerance in a world growing steadily darker. His words provide an apt description of Selvy himself: "Soldiers, do not give yourself to brutes who despise you, enslave you, who regiment your lives, tell you what to do, what to think, how to feel . . . who treat you like cattle. . . . Unnatural men, machine men with machine hands and machine hearts. You are not machines. You are not cattle. You are men. You have the love of humanity in your hearts."

12. Johnson argues that the character in the bunker film is never actually verified as Hitler but may be an extraordinary act of doubling, a nameless Nazi impersonator, an intriguing idea that layers the black-market film with shifting uncertainties. Indeed, the gallery owner, an expert in Nazi lore, dismisses the film's premise—Hitler, he says, had no affection for the Chaplin film or for Chaplin's Little Tramp and would never have given such a generous performance of the celebrated impersonation ("Extraphilosophical Instigations," 88–89).

13. Don DeLillo, *The Engineer of Moonlight, Cornell Review* 5 (Winter 1979): 44. Further references to this text are made parenthetically.

3. Narratives of Recovery

1. Adam Begley, "Don DeLillo: The Art of Fiction CXXXV," *Paris Review* 35, no. 128 (Fall 1993): 274–306, quote on 284.

2. Robert Harris, "A Talk with Don DeLillo," *New York Times Book Review,* October 10, 1982, 26.

3. Although universally conceded as the centering theme of the novel (largely due to DeLillo's own assessment of his interest), language is helpfully illuminated in Paula Bryant, "Discussing the Untellable: Don DeLillo's *The Names,*" *Critique* 29 (Fall 1987): 16–29.

4. Osteen draws on the importance of secrecy to the cult's suspect ordering system and how Axton's own book—the one we are reading—destroys that system by revealing the secret of the killings (*American Magic and Dread,* 135–41). See also LeClair, who concedes the premise of the cult is improbable but affirms the cult as a symbol of the "powerful sway of language" (*In the Loop,* 194).

5. Don DeLillo, *The Names* (New York: Knopf, 1982), 210. Further references to this work are made parenthetically.

6. Keesey is helpful in assessing Owen Brademas's evolution and his intellectual apartness (*Don DeLillo,* 124–28). In "A 'Christian Dispersion' in Don DeLillo's *The Names,*" *Christianity and Literature* 47, no. 4 (Summer 1998): 403–25, Clement Valletta presents an extensive reading of the novel's Christian influences and explores the implications of Brademas's religious crisis.

7. For a more positive take on Tap's manuscript, see Osteen, *American Magic and Dread,* 138–41. Keesey assesses the manuscript generously as it attempts to create community, specifically between Tap and his mentor Owen Brademas (*Don DeLillo,* 128–30). See Bryant's "Discussing the Untellable" for a thorough discussion of the manuscript's Joycean puns and wordplay.

8. Don DeLillo, *White Noise* (New York: Viking, 1985). Further references to this work are made parenthetically.

9. See Frank Lentricchia, "Tales of the Electronic Tribe," in *New Essays on "White Noise"* (New York: Cambridge University Press, 1991: 87–113), which explores the strategy of first-person narration and specifically the differences between what Gladney thinks and what DeLillo knows. He then positions Gladney with Huck Finn, Ishmael, and Nick Carraway as undercut narrators.

10. See John N. Duvall, "The (Super)Marketplace of Images: Television as Unmediated Mediation in DeLillo's *White Noise,*" *Arizona Quarterly* 50, no. 3 (Autumn 1994): 127–53.

11. For analysis of how these triads indicate the ominous reach of television, see John Frow ("The Last Things before the Last: Notes on *White Noise,*" in *South Atlantic Quarterly* 89 [Spring 1990]: 414–29, reprinted in Lentricchia, *Introducing Don DeLillo*).

12. LeClair describes the narrative as unfolding in a fluid immediate (*In the Loop,* 207–9). Lentricchia finds the first part plotless, its aimlessness shattered by Gladney's exposure to the airborne toxic event ("Tales of the Electronic Tribe," 90–93).

13. Readings have varied on this change of heart. Keesey sees the shooting as a jolt of mortality that triggers (pardon the pun) Gladney's reclamation (*Don DeLillo,* 148–50). Osteen suspects the compassion is more ego-intensive, Gladney still seeking control (*American Magic and Magic,* 86–91). For LeClair (*In the Loop,* 222–26), helping Mink indicates that Gladney has begun to adjust to mortality and that he is now dealing with reality. Arthur M. Saltzman argues that after the shock of being shot, Gladney moves toward intimacy and caring ("The Figure in the Static: *White Noise," Modern Fiction Studies* 40, no. 4 [1994]: 807–26).

4. Narratives of Redemption

1. Passaro, "Dangerous Don DeLillo," 36.

2. Don DeLillo, *Libra* (New York: Viking, 1988), 12. Further references to this work are made parenthetically.

3. John Johnston asserts that constructing Oswald leaves him coherent but ironically less than clear ("Superlinear Fiction or Historical Diagram? Don DeLillo's *Libra," Modern Fiction Studies* 40, no. 2 [1994]: 319–42); Osteen sees *Libra* itself as an exercise in plausible theory with an emphasis on the adjective rather than the noun (*American Magic and Dread,* 153–55).

4. See Glen Thomas, "History, Biography, and Narrative in Don DeLillo's *Libra," Twentieth-Century Literature* 43, no. 1 (Spring 1997): 107–24; and Christopher Mott, "*Libra* and the Subject of History," *Critique* 35 (Spring 1994): 146–56.

5. Joseph Tabbi suggests a less ennobling role for DeLillo, that of a powerless outsider, the composition process stubbornly unable to repair or replace the real (*Postmodern Sublime: Technology and American Writing from Mailer to Cyberpunk* [Ithaca, N.Y.: Cornell University Press, 1995], 169–207). Paul Civello suggests that in a late-century scientific universe governed by chaos theory and the principles of dynamic uncertainty, DeLillo's role parodies the model of knowledge and objectivity defined by the naturalistic novel ("Undoing the Naturalistic Novel: Don DeLillo's *Libra," Arizona Quarterly* 48 [Summer 1992]): 33–56).

6. Keesey defines the novel's tension between the writer/voice and the electronic age of images and celebrities (*Don DeLillo,* 177–82); Cowart places Bill Gray in the generation of writers losing its place within society but ultimately argues that DeLillo counters this apparent irrelevancy with the testimony of narrative (*Don DeLillo,* 126–28); Osteen (*American Magic and Dread,* 193–97) identifies Bill Gray as the persuasive romantic figure of the writer out of place in contemporary culture. DeLillo told interviewer Adam Begley in 1993 that the "novel's not dead, it's not even seriously injured, but I do think [novelists] are working in the margins, working in the shadows of the novel's greatness and influence" ("Don DeLillo: The Art of Fiction CXXXV," 290).

7. Don DeLillo, *Mao II* (New York: Viking, 1991), 39. Further references to this work are made parenthetically.

8. Of course, Salinger and Pynchon have been prominently mentioned as models for Bill Gray. DeLillo often related the impact of seeing an April 21, 1988, *New York Post* photograph of a frightened and angry Salinger "caught" coming out of a supermarket.

9. Although DeLillo admits that as a child he would carve a space for himself by announcing imaginary baseball games as he would walk along the streets of the Bronx with his cousins, he does not treat Bill Gray's reclusiveness sympathetically: indeed, DeLillo himself emerged with generous availability during the 1980s, including reading tours and publicity interviews and participating in conscience-raising events surrounding the fatwa against Salman Rushdie.

10. For differing critical discussions on Brita and the camera, compare Osteen in *American Magic and Dread,* 212–13, who analyzes this scene as crucial to understanding how Brita emerges as the best hope in the media age, to Laura Barrett, who argues that the camera is predatory, replacing Gray's complex and living self with a disposable image ("'Here, But Also There': Subjectivity and Postmodern Space in *Mao II,*" *Modern Fiction Studies* 45, no. 3 [1999]: 788–810).

11. In *Late Imperial Romance* (London: Verso, 1994), John A. McClure investigates DeLillo's terrorists but argues that DeLillo simplifies the Eastern mindset as a threat to the individual and too easily finds Western culture as the best hope for its preservation and dignity (118–51). Steffen Hantke helpfully analyzes the DeLillo terrorist as orderer ("'God Save Us from Bourgeois Adventure': The Figure of the Terrorist in Contemporary American Conspiracy Fiction," *Studies in the Novel* 28, no. 2 [Summer 1996]: 219–43).

12. See Cowart, *Don DeLillo,* 116, for a persuasive reading of this creepy scene.

13. There is critical disagreement over this closing. To cite representative positions: Cowart (*Don DeLillo,* 111–28) dismisses Bill Gray's reclamation and finds affirmation only in DeLillo's larger authority; Keesey (*Don DeLillo,* 190–93) and Hantke ("God Save Us," 239–42) see Bill Gray's mission as a gesture that ends in his defeat and that he closes his life erasing his self into perfect anonymity; Margaret Scanlan sees Bill Gray's struggle to bring the held poet to life imaginatively as desperate but heroic ("Writers among Terrorists: Don DeLillo's *Mao II* and the Rushdie Affair," *Modern Fiction Studies* 40, no. 2 [1994]: 229–52).

14. As part of a cogent analysis of the book, Philip Nel labels this as both a modernist text that endorses form and a postmodern text that subverts it ("'A Small Incisive Shock': Modern Forms, Postmodern Politics, and the Role of the Avant-Garde in *Underworld,*" *Modern Fiction Studies* 45, no. 3 [1999]: 724–52).

15. Don DeLillo, *Underworld* (New York: Scribner, 1997), 66. Further references to this text are made parenthetically.

5. Parables of Resurrection

1. Don DeLillo, *Valparaiso* (New York: Scribner, 1999), 51. Further references to this text are made parenthetically.

2. Don DeLillo, *The Body Artist* (New York: Scribner, 2001), 74. Further references to this text are made parenthetically.

3. Oddly, some critical opinions cite Lauren's recovery, although clearly positioned midtext, as unironic: Cowart sees Tuttle as enabling Lauren's recovery as artist—indeed, he sees the Tuttle figure as a sort of soul of the artist (*Don DeLillo,* 202–5). Cornel Bonca sees the narrative as a Virginia Woolfe-esque revelation of the artist's need to transcend time and sees the performance piece as a turning point that allows Lauren to experience life again ("Being, Time, and Death in DeLillo's *The Body Artist,*" *Pacific Coast Philology* 37 [2002]: 58–68). Philip Nel sees the novel as affirming not only Lauren's performance piece but DeLillo's own prose as a triumph of language and stylistic precision ("Don DeLillo's Return to Form: The Modernist Poetics of *The Body Artist,*" *Contemporary Literature* 43, no. 4 [Winter 2002]: 736–59).

4. See Bonca, "Being, Time, and Death," 60–63 for a different take—that the breakfast table infuses the ordinary with the artist's vision, alive within Lauren's perceptions, although more often than not such energy is clearly frustrated. Nel ("Return to Form") sees the breakfast chapter as DeLillo's celebration of the ordinary in a sensory-laden rich prose line that reveals to the reader the power of words, a sort of performance piece akin to Lauren's stage triumph. Ultimately, the narrative will shatter such aesthetic refuge.

5. Cowart accepts Tuttle as a retarded man living unnoticed in the rambling cottage, one of nature's mysteries in touch with what the rest of us cannot detect (*Don DeLillo*); Bonca ("Being, Time, and Death," 65–67) sees Tuttle as an angel, a benevolent projection that ultimately restores Lauren to accepting her body; Nel ("Return to Form") sees Tuttle primarily as a language exercise: the breakdown of words into sounds, cryptic, even divine fragments that ultimately restore Lauren.

6. Don DeLillo, *Cosmopolis* (New York: Scribner, 2003), 209. Further references to this work are made parenthetically.

7. Critical reactions dismissed the novel's retro sensibility; its unsympathetic, robotic central character; its cool and depthless language; its lack of compelling suspense; and its obvious "lesson" that money kills the spirit.

Bibliography

Works by Don DeLillo
Books
Americana. Boston: Houghton Mifflin, 1971.
End Zone. Boston: Houghton Mifflin, 1972.
Great Jones Street. Boston: Houghton Mifflin, 1973.
Ratner's Star. New York: Knopf, 1976.
Players. New York: Knopf, 1977.
Running Dog. New York: Knopf, 1978.
Amazons:An Intimate Memoir by the First Woman Ever to Play in the National Hockey League. New York: Holt, Rinehart and Winston, 1980 (published under the pseudonym Cleo Birdwell).
The Names. New York: Knopf, 1982.
White Noise. New York: Viking, 1985 (Viking Critical Edition, ed. Mark Osteen, 1998).
Libra. New York: Viking, 1988.
Mao II. New York: Viking, 1991.
Underworld. New York: Scribner, 1997.
The Body Artist. New York: Scribner, 2001.
Cosmopolis. New York: Scribner, 2003.

Plays
The Engineer of Moonlight. Cornell Review 5 (Winter 1979): 21–47.
The Day Room. New York: Knopf, 1987. Reprint, New York: Viking/Penguin, 1989.
The Rapture of the Athlete Assumed into Heaven. Quarterly 15 (Fall 1990). Reprinted in *Harper's,* December 1990, 44 and in *After Yesterday's Crash: The Avant-Pop Anthology,* ed. Larry McCaffery, 88–89. New York: Penguin, 1995.
Valparaiso: A Play in Two Acts. New York: Scribner, 1999.
The Mystery at the Middle of Ordinary Life. Zoetrope: All-Story 4, no. 4 (Winter 2000): 70–71. Reprinted in *South Atlantic Quarterly* 99, no. 2/3 (Spring/Summer 2000): 601-3, and in *Harper's,* January 2001, 37.
Game Six. Screenplay by DeLillo. Directed by Michael Hoffman. Santa Monica, Calif.: Serenade Films, filmed 2004, released 2006.
Love-Lies-Bleeding: A Play. New York: Scribner, 2005.

Uncollected Short Stories
"The River Jordan." *Epoch* 10, no. 2 (Winter 1960): 105–20.
"Take the 'A' Train." *Epoch* 12, no. 1 (Spring 1962): 9–25.

"Spaghetti and Meatballs." *Epoch* 14, no. 3 (Spring 1965): 244–50.

"Coming Sun. Mon. Tues." *Kenyon Review* 28, no. 3 (1966): 391–94.

"Baghdad Towers West." *Epoch* 17 (1968): 195–217.

"The Uniforms." *Carolina Quarterly* 22, no. 1 (Winter 1970): 4–11.

"In the Men's Room of the Sixteenth Century." *Esquire,* December 1971, 174–77, 243–44.

"Creation." *Antaeus* 33 (Spring 1979): 32–46.

"Human Moments in World War III." *Esquire,* July 1983, 118–26.

"The Runner." *Harper's,* September 1988, 61–63.

"The Ivory Acrobat." *Granta* 25 (Autumn 1988): 199–212.

"Baader-Meinhof." *New Yorker,* April 1, 2002, 78–82.

Selected Essays

"American Blood: A Journey through the Labyrinth of Dallas and JFK." *Rolling Stone,* December 8, 1983, 21–28, 74. Seminal and eloquent investigation into the cultural impact of the Kennedy assassination.

"Silhouette City: Hitler, Manson, and the Millennium." *Dimensions: A Journal of Holocaust Studies* 4, no. 3 (1989): 29–34. A provocative speculation on violence, language, and propaganda, specifically the difficulty the historic record faces in transcribing atrocity.

"The Artist Naked in a Cage." *New Yorker,* May 26, 1997, 6–7. Transcript of DeLillo's remarks at the New York Public Library concerning the pressures facing controversial writers within oppressive political regimes.

"The Power of History." *New York Times Magazine,* September 7, 1997, 60–63. Seminal speculation on the relationship between memory and media and the relationship between fact and historic record and the fictional appropriation of history. Essential to any approach to *Underworld.*

"A History of the Writer Alone in a Room." Address in connection with the Jerusalem Prize for the Freedom of the Individual in Society. Published by the Jerusalem International Book Fair, June 1999, Caspit Press. DeLillo's acceptance speech, a passionate defense of novel-writing and of novelists in the contemporary era.

"In the Ruins of the Future." *Harper's,* December 2001, 33–40. Emotional speculation from a native New Yorker on the impact of the September 11 terrorist attacks and the traumatic sense of entering a new and uncertain era.

"That Day in Rome: Movies and Memory." *New Yorker,* October 20, 2003, 76–78. A fascinating if brief piece on celebrity and the impact of cinema on our memory.

Selected Works about Don DeLillo

Web Sites

Don DeLillo's America. Ed. Curt Gardner. http://www.percival.com

The Don DeLillo Society. Ed. Philip Nel. http://www.ksu.edu/English/nelp

Selected Interviews

Begley, Adam. "Don DeLillo: The Art of Fiction CXXXV." *Paris Review* 35, no. 128 (Fall 1993): 274–306. Wide-ranging, thorough discussion of the place of the writer in a media culture, the role of language, and the achievement of creating prose. Extensive responses to the Kennedy assassination. Includes helpful discussions of the major novels and biographical insights. Essential reading.

Brockes, Emma. "View from the Bridge." *Guardian* (Manchester), May 24, 2003. Available at http://books.guardian.co.uk. Particularly thorough, wide-ranging, and recent interview that includes fascinating insights by friends of DeLillo. Very readable.

DeCurtis, Anthony. "Matters of Fact and Fiction." *Rolling Stone,* November 17, 1988, 113–22. Fuller version reprinted as "An Outsider in This Society," *South Atlantic Quarterly* 89, no. 2 (1990): 281–301, and in Lentricchia, *Introducing Don DeLillo,* 43–66. Although largely concerning the evolution and thematic concerns of *Libra,* a cogent and lively discussion of DeLillo's characters and themes, particularly his interest in film.

Howard, Gerald. "The American Strangeness: An Interview with Don DeLillo." *Hungry Mind Review* 43 (Fall 1997): 13–16. Insightful background to *Underworld,* recounts the novel's inception and its themes. Includes revealing anecdotes of DeLillo's Bronx childhood.

LeClair, Tom. "An Interview with Don DeLillo." *Contemporary Literature* 23, no. 1 (1982): 19–31. Reprinted in *Anything Can Happen: Interviews with Contemporary American Novelists,* edited by LeClair and Larry McCaffery, 79–90. Urbana: University of Illinois Press, 1983. An early and seminal interview. Engrossing revelations about DeLillo's early works, his definition of character in fiction, his sense of language, the importance of writing, his fascination with sports, and his interest in the media. Particularly helpful on *Ratner's Star.* Intelligent questions and fascinating responses.

Passaro, Vince. "Dangerous Don DeLillo." *New York Times Magazine,* May 19, 1991, 34–36, 38, 76–77. Engaging overview of DeLillo's themes, largely centering on *Mao II,* specifically the impact of critical success and his emergence as a force in contemporary literature and the role of the writer as celebrity.

Selected Critical Analyses

Bilton, Alan. "Don DeLillo." In *An Introduction to Contemporary American Fiction,* 17–50. New York: New York University Press, 2002. Among scores of "introductions" to DeLillo, this stands out as readable, on-point, informed, helpful. Cogent presentation of the themes that have dominated DeLillo's works, specifically centers on the tension between the world and the word in the media age, sees the early works as attacks on language, the later works as endorsements of its power.

Burton, Marilee Robin, ed. *Don DeLillo.* Major Novelists Series. New York: Chelsea House, 2003. Compendium of plot overviews and character lists from *The Names,*

Mao II, Libra, White Noise, and *Underworld.* Includes excerpts from significant critical essays on each work.

Cowart, David. *Don DeLillo: The Physics of Language.* Athens: University of Georgia Press, 2002. Thorough and sensitive analysis of DeLillo's signature prose line and specifically DeLillo's revelatory sense of language's luminous complexity. Illuminating readings of the novels up to *The Body Artist.* Particularly good on *The Names.* Listens carefully to the sound of DeLillo's prose and to the seldom-appreciated achievement of DeLillo's dialogue. Investigates DeLillo's career-long speculation on the impact and effect of contemporary jargon, including journalism, science, technology, politics, and advertising.

Dewey, Joseph, Steven G. Kellman, and Irving Malin, eds. *UnderWords: Perspectives on Don DeLillo's "Underworld."* Newark: University of Delaware Press, 2003. Gathers thirteen probing essays that collectively address the novel that has come to define DeLillo. Essays place the novel first within the DeLillo canon, then within the larger argument of post-postmodern fin-de-millennium fiction, and ultimately within larger currents of American literature.

Duvall, John. *Don DeLillo's "Underworld": A Reader's Guide.* New York: Continuum, 2002. Handy and compact overview of the massive novel's intricate plotlines, with sharp analysis of major themes and concise summary of the relevant initial critical reception.

———, ed. *Modern Fiction Studies: Special Issue* 45, no. 3 (1999). Issue devoted to DeLillo and to his emerging prominence. Selections focus particularly (although not exclusively) on the major later works. Particularly strong on *Underworld* and *Mao II.* Includes helpful bibliography.

Hantke, Steffen. *Conspiracy and Paranoia in Contemporary American Fiction: The Works of Don DeLillo and Joseph McElroy.* New York: Peter Lang, 1994. Perhaps the clearest summary of paranoia and conspiracy theory in DeLillo, particularly *Libra.* Places DeLillo within a wider postmodern genre (defined most prominently by Thomas Pynchon) that both endorses and parodies the contemporary need to ascribe order and direction in the universe.

Kavadlo, Jesse. *Don DeLillo: Balance at the Edge of Belief.* New York: Peter Lang, 2004. Approaches DeLillo through his characters' quests for a spiritual dimension. Sees religious and spiritual issues as central to DeLillo's oeuvre and ties his work to Nathanael West's. Deals particularly with how the later works center on spiritual crises and moral dilemmas, specifically the search to affirm hope against the press of despair.

Keesey, Douglas. *Don DeLillo.* Twayne's United States Authors Series. New York: Twayne, 1993. Consistently helpful overview of the defining themes of DeLillo's work. Includes biographical overview. Responds to criticism that DeLillo novels are about ideas, not characters, and more about style than substance. Sees *Libra* as DeLillo's best work.

LeClair, Tom. *In the Loop: Don DeLillo and the Systems Novel*. Urbana: University of Illinois Press, 1987. First book-length study of DeLillo's work and still a seminal work by one of the earliest and most insightful proponents of DeLillo. Sophisticated and intricate appreciation of DeLillo's use of the metaphors and implications of contemporary information-systems theory. Examines the complex structure of the early narratives and the role of DeLillo's reader within such postmodern constructs. Particularly effective on *Ratner's Star*. Coverage through *White Noise*.

Lentricchia, Frank, ed. *Introducing Don DeLillo*. Durham, N.C.: Duke University Press, 1991. Reprint of a special issue of *South Atlantic Quarterly* (1990) devoted to DeLillo. Essential reading. Although it includes essays on individual novels, the book is most helpful in providing several solid introductory (and very readable) overviews of DeLillo's consistent thematic interests. Excellent and instructive.

————, ed. *New Essays on "White Noise."* New York: Cambridge University Press, 1991. Four dense, provocative readings of a novel often seen as DeLillo's breakthrough achievement. Includes essays on consumerism, the figure of Hitler, the relationship between technology and nature, and DeLillo's manipulation of a first-person narrative.

Orr, Leonard. *Don DeLillo's "White Noise": A Reader's Guide*. New York: Continuum, 2003. Introductory approach, includes significant themes, relevant critical reception, and structural analysis. Centers on the novel's treatment of death anxiety and contemporary culture's relationship with its own massive technology.

Osteen, Mark. *American Magic and Dread: Don DeLillo's Dialogue with Culture*. Philadelphia: University of Pennsylvania Press, 2000. Indispensable. Articulate and thoughtful analysis that sees DeLillo as a cultural anatomist whose characters are suspended between the depersonalizing pressures of consumer/technological capitalism and their deep hunger for transcendence and mystical purification. Art, specifically the novel itself, is ultimately endorsed as redemptive.

Ruppersburg, Hugh, and Tim Engles, eds. *Critical Essays on Don DeLillo*. New York: G. K. Hall, 2000. Helpful compilation of reviews and previously published essays. Particularly good in covering the controversy surrounding the publication of *Libra*. Coverage up through *Underworld*.

Index

Eliot, T. S. See *Love Song of J. Alfred Prufrock, The*
End Zone, 26–33, 66; the character of Myna Corbett in, 32, 33, 156n11; the character of Taft Robinson in, 31–32, 156n10; language in, 28–29, 30; the need for order in, 27, 28, 30, 31, 33; nuclear war in, 28, 30; strategy of retreat in, 27–28, 29, 30–32; structure of, 32–33. See also Harkness, Gary
Engineer of Moonlight, The, 66–68
Eugenides, Jeffrey, 3

Farrell, James. See *Studs Lonigan* trilogy
Faulkner, William, 2, 10, 12–13, 21, 35, 51, 79, 107
football. *See* sports
Fordham University, 2
Franzen, Jonathan, 3

Gaddis, William. See *Recognitions, The*
Gladney, Jack, 92. See also *White Noise*
Godard, Jean-Luc, 4, 12–13, 24, 53, 56, 59, 63, 64, 133, 146
Gravity's Rainbow. See Pynchon, Thomas
Great Jones Street, 33–41, 47, 66; artist in, 34–35, 36, 37, 39, 40–41; celebrity in, 34, 36; the character of Opel Hampson in, 36, 38, 157n18; language in, 39–40; love in, 38; the need to engage the world in, 38–39, 40; as satire, 36–37; self in, 36–37, 40–41; the strategy of retreat in, 34–35, 36, 37–39, 40–41. *See also* Wunderlick, Bucky
Gulliver's Travels (Swift), 25, 42, 43

Harkness, Gary, 34, 36, 37, 38, 39, 40, 41, 48, 57, 58, 127. See also *End Zone*
Hartke, Lauren, 128, 139, 141, 147, 148, 149, 152. See also *Body Artist, The*
Hawthorne, Nathaniel. See "Custom-House, The"

Herbert, Zbigniew. *See* "Report from a Besieged City"
Hillsborough Soccer Catastrophe, 107, 110
Hitler, Adolf, 59, 60, 61, 63–64, 83–84, 85, 87, 158n12
Hopper, Edward, 52
"Human Moments in World War III," 10, 71–72

Ikiru (Kurosawa), 19, 26
"In the Men's Room of the Sixteenth Century," 11
"Ivory Acrobat, The," 91

jazz, 9, 18, 40, 56, 118, 119, 148
Jerusalem Prize, 3, 141
John of Patmos, 138
John Paul II, 8
Johnson, Samuel. See *Rasselas*
Joyce, James, 2, 10, 24, 78, 101, 159n7

Keesey, Douglas, 4
Kennedy assassination, 3, 6, 7, 25, 53, 85, 92–95, 100–102, 152
Kerouac, Jack, 18
Kertész, André, 117
Kesey, Ken, 18
Khomeini, Ayatollah, 107, 110
King, Rodney, 8
Kurosawa, Akira. See *Ikiru*

LeClair, Tom, 1, 4, 57, 61
Libra, 3, 92, 102, 117; the definition of the imagination in, 93–94, 96, 101–2; DeLillo's role in, 101–2; history in, 94–95, 96, 98–99, 100–101; structure of, 95–98; title of, 101–2
Love-Lies-Bleeding, 12, 149–52. *See also* Macklin, Alex
Love Song of J. Alfred Prufrock, The (Eliot), 17, 25, 57, 119

Salinger, J. D., 104, 160n8

Satie, Erik, 141

satire, 3, 6, 23–24, 36, 37, 41–44, 114

Selvy, Glen, 147. See also *Running Dog*

Skansey, Willard, 148. See also *Mao II*

"Spaghetti and Meatballs," 9

spirituality, 2, 6, 8, 11–13, 18, 38, 61–66, 74, 81, 90, 103, 110–14, 122, 127–28, 130, 137–38, 138–39, 140–53

sports, 2, 4, 6, 10, 19, 27, 28, 30–33, 43–44, 48, 65–66, 88, 102–3, 105, 111, 114–15, 161n9

Stevenson, Robert Louis. See *Treasure Island*

Studs Lonigan trilogy (Farrell), 9

Swift, Jonathan. See *Gulliver's Travels*

"Take the 'A' Train," 9

terrorism, 4, 7, 41, 49, 52–56, 58–59, 72, 75, 94, 95–96, 102, 104–7, 111–12, 144–45

Thomson, Bobby, 115, 120, 122, 123

Tiananmen Square, 107, 111, 113

Treasure Island (Stevenson), 23, 25

Twain, Mark. See *Adventures of Huckleberry Finn, The*

Twillig, Billy, 57. See also *Ratner's Star*

Ulysses. See Joyce, James

Underworld, 3, 4, 92, 113–124, 127, 128, 131, 132, 133; the character of Nick Shay in, 114, 118–20; the character of Sister Alma Edgar in, 117, 118, 121–22, 147; genre of, 114–16; narrative structure of, 120, 124; as reader's text,

115–16, 117, 118, 122–24; as subversive text, 116–18, 123–24

Ungaretti, Giuseppe, 151

"Uniforms, The," 49

Valparaiso, 11, 128–30, 133. *See also* Majeski, Michael

Vietnam War, 8, 17, 20, 37, 58, 61, 93, 114

Vollmann, William, 3

Voltaire. See *Candide*

Wallace, David Foster, 3

Warhol, Andy, 36, 109, 128

West, Nathanael, 13

White Noise, 3, 4, 79–80, 81–91, 102; crowds in, 79–80, 82, 83, 85, 90; fear of death in, 80, 81–82, 83–85, 86–87, 90–91; Hitler in, 83–84, 85, 87; isolation in, 82, 83, 90–91; and *Moby-Dick*, 83; science in, 83, 85–86, 90; television in, 83, 84–85, 88; violence in, 88–89. *See also* Gladney, Jack

Whitman, Charles, 6

Whitman, Walt, 9, 39, 99

Wild Palms, The. See Faulkner, William

William Dean Howells Medal, 3

World Trade Center, 8, 50, 52, 85, 115–16, 112, 152, 158n4

writing, the act of, 4, 8, 9–10, 13, 21–22, 24, 33, 37, 40, 67–68, 72–73, 76–78, 79, 92, 101–2, 102–13, 115, 121–24, 152

Wunderlick, Bucky, 41, 47, 48, 57. See also *Great Jones Street*

About the Author

An associate professor of American literature at the University of Pittsburgh at Johnstown, JOSEPH DEWEY is the author of *Understanding Richard Powers, Novels from Reagan's America: A New Realism,* and *In a Dark Time: The Apocalyptic Temper in the American Novel of the Nuclear Age* and coeditor of *UnderWords: Perspectives on Don DeLillo's "Underworld."*